Book of Akathists

II

To Our Saviour, the Holy Spirit, the Mother of God, and Various Saints

HOLY TRINITY PUBLICATIONS
The Printshop of St Job of Pochaev
Holy Trinity Monastery
Jordanville, New York

Printed with the blessing
of Metropolitan Laurus of Eastern America and New York
First Hierarch of the Russian Orthodox Church Outside of Russia

Anthology: Book of Akathists II © 2008 Holy Trinity Monastery

Text © 2020 Reader Isaac E. Lambertson
All akathists translated from the Church Slavonic
by the Reader Isaac E. Lambertson

PRINTSHOP OF
SAINT JOB OF POCHAEV

An imprint of

HOLY TRINITY PUBLICATIONS
Holy Trinity Monastery
Jordanville, New York 13361-0036
www.holytrinitypublications.com

First printing 2008
Second printing 2021

ISBN: 978-0-88465-141-3 (hardback)

All rights reserved.
Printed in the United States of America

Contents

Akathists to the Saviour

Akathist Hymn to the All-glorious Ascension of
Our Lord Jesus Christ 9

Akathist Hymn to the Nativity of Christ 25

Akathist to the Holy Spirit

Akathist Hymn to the All-Holy and Life-Creating Spirit 43

Akathists to the Most Holy Theotokos

Akathist Hymn to the All-holy Theotokos, Chanted before
Her Icon, "The Abbess of Mount Athos" 59

Akathist Hymn to the All-holy Theotokos in Honor of
Her Wonder-working Icon "Assuage My Griefs" 77

Akathist Hymn Chanted before the Icon of the Theotokos
"The Deliverance of Those Who Suffer from Misfortunes" 95

Akathist to the Most Holy Theotokos in Honor of Her
Wonderworking Icon, "The Inexhaustible Cup" 105

Akathist Hymn to the Protection of the All-Holy Theotokos 121

Akathist Hymn to the All-holy Theotokos, in Honor of
Her Miraculous Icon, "She Who Healeth" 137

Akathist Hymn to the All-Holy Theotokos in Honor of
Her Wonder-working Icon, "Unexpected Joy" 155

Akathists to Various Saints

Akathist Hymn to Our Venerable Father Ambrose of Optina 175

Akathist Hymn to Our Venerable and God-bearing Fathers
Anthony and Theodosius of the Caves of Kiev 191

Akathist Hymn to All the Venerable Fathers of Athos,
the Holy Mountain 213

Akathist Hymn to Our Father Among the Saints
Basil the Great, Archbishop of Cæsaria of Cappadocia 229

Akathist Hymn to the Holy Hieromartyr Cyprian 249

Akathist Hymn to the Holy and Venerable New-martyr
Elizabeth, Grand Duchess of Russia 261

Akathist Hymn to the Holy Martyrs Faith, Hope and Love,
and their mother, Sophia 279

Akathist Hymn to the Holy Hierarch John, Archbishop
of Shanghai and San Francisco, the Wonderworker 299

Akathist Hymn to the Holy and Righteous Juliana the
Merciful, of the Village of Lazarevo, near Murom 313

Akathist Hymn to the Holy Apostle and Evangelist Luke 331

Akathist Hymn to the Venerable Mary of Egypt 345

Akathist Hymn to the Holy Apostle and Evangelist Matthew 363

Akathist Hymn to the Holy New-hieromartyr
Maximus Sandovich, Protomartyr of the Lemko People 381

Akathist Hymn to Our Venerable Father Moses of the
Carpathians 397

Akathist Hymn to the Venerable Fathers and Elders
Who Shone forth in the Optina Hermitage 411

Akathist Hymn to the Holy Photius, Patriarch of
Constantinople, the Confessor, Great among
Hierarchs and Equal of the Apostles 425

Akathist Hymn to the Holy Hierarch Theophan,
Recluse of Vyshensk 439

Akathist Hymn to the Holy Great-martyr Zlata
(Chrysa) of Mglen 453

Akathists to Our Lord Jesus Christ

Akathist Hymn to the All-glorious Ascension of Our Lord Jesus Christ

Ascension of Christ

Akathist Hymn to the All-Glorious Ascension of Our Lord Jesus Christ

Kontakion I

O Jesus most sweet, Thou champion leader, Who by Thy death hast destroyed the kingdom of death, and by Thine ascension into the heavens hast opened the doors of paradise to those who believe on Thee: For Thy great benefactions toward the human race we offer this hymn of praise and earnest supplication:

> Jesus Who ascended, bear our souls up to the heavenly kingdom!

Ikos I

When Thou hadst accomplished our redemption on earth, O Christ God, didst Thou ascend in glory from the Mount of Olives in the presence of a multitude of the faithful, and didst seat our nature on the right hand of the Father. Wherefore, in thanksgiving we cry unto Thee:

> Jesus, our Creator and Redeemer;
> Jesus Who breathed life into our inanimate clay!
> Jesus, Renewer of our race, which had fallen through sin;
> Jesus Who in Thy mercy hast brought about our reconciliation with the Father!
> Jesus Who by becoming man through the Ever-virgin Mary hast accepted us as Thy kin;

Jesus Who hast taught us to call God Thy Father our father!

Jesus Who hast enriched with heavenly blessings us who had become paupers!

Jesus Who hast promised a heavenly reward to Thy good and faithful servants;

Jesus Who ascended, bear our souls up to the heavenly kingdom!

Kontakion II

Beholding the divine ascension of Christ into the heavens, the apostles worshiped Him as their Creator and God; and with them we sinners also ever worship Him, crying out in gladness: Alleluia!

Ikos II

The noetic armies of the incorporeal hosts reverently greeted Thee at the gates of heaven, O Christ God, crying out and saying: "Lift up your gates, O ye princes, for, lo! the King of glory cometh!" And, emulating the incorporeal ones, we cry out thus:

Jesus, our all-glorious King;

Jesus, our all-merciful Master!

Jesus Who hast not disdained us who languish in our fall;

Jesus Who camest down to earth for our salvation!

Jesus Who didst live as a man among men;

Jesus Who in Thyself hast provided a model of the virtues!

Jesus Who hast all-wisely accomplished the whole of our salvation;

Jesus Who didst free us from slavery to the enemy by Thy sufferings and death upon the Cross!

Jesus Who ascended, bear our souls up to the heavenly kingdom!

Kontakion III

Heeding the angels who appeared to them, announcing the second, glorious Coming of Christ, the apostles returned to Jerusalem from the Mount of Olives, joyfully chanting: Alleluia!

Ikos III

The holy apostles, accepting the admonition of Christ not to depart from Jerusalem until they were invested with power from on high, abode together in prayer and fasting, awaiting the fulfillment of this promise, which after ten days they received in tongues of fire; and all were filled with the Holy Spirit, Which we also earnestly beg to receive through the grace of the ascended Christ, crying out thus:

Jesus Who commanded Thine apostles not to depart from Jerusalem, cut us not off from Thy gracious aid in defeating the invisible foe;

Jesus Who didst teach Thy disciples the mysteries of the kingdom of heaven, teach us also to understand that this kingdom doth not consist of food and drink, but righteousness, peace and joy in the Holy Spirit!

Jesus, grant that we may ardently sense the unity of grace which existeth between Thee, Thy Father and the Holy Spirit;

Jesus Who didst send Thine apostles throughout the whole world to preach the Gospel to all creation, grant us faith unfeigned!

Jesus, help us to preserve the Faith unadulterated to the end of our life;

Jesus, impart unto us the grace to justify our faith by good works!

Jesus, teach us to be well-pleasing unto Thee in our understanding;

Jesus, grant that we may finish our life in peace and repentance!

Jesus Who ascended, bear our souls up to the heavenly kingdom!

Kontakion IV

Stilling the tempest of unbelief, and softening the stony hearts of the people, Thou didst soften hard stone, O Saviour, impressing thereon the prints of Thy feet as a true witness to Thine ascent into heaven. Wherefore, the faithful of all times reverently worship Thee in that place, crying out: Alleluia!

Ikos IV

Christ God, Who in Thine ascension didst fill with ineffable joy the apostles and the Mother of God, who gave Thee birth, grant unto us joy and gladness of spirit which annul all the grief of sin, that we may continually cry out to Thee from the depths of our souls:

> Jesus most sweet, Who pourest spiritual sweetness into the hearts of the faithful;
> Jesus, true joy of those who love Thee, Who doest away with all grief that harmeth men's souls!
> Jesus, Light of the world, Who dispellest the gloom of our sins;
> Jesus Who dost cleanse our conscience of vile deeds!
> Jesus Who by Thine ascension didst gladden Thine all-pure Mother;
> Jesus Who didst carry her in body and spirit to the heavens!
> Jesus Who at the supplications of Thine all-pure Mother hast sent down upon us Thy mercies;
> Jesus Who because of her mediation hast not deprived us of the inheritance of eternal good things!
> Jesus Who ascended, bear our souls up to the heavenly kingdom!

Kontakion V

The wondrous Elijah, the traverser of the heavens, prefiguring Thine ascension, O Christ God, was upborne to the heights of heaven on a chariot of fire by the hand of God; but Thou, O Saviour, as almighty

God, the Master of all things, didst ascend into heaven with glory through Thine own will, as the ranks of the angels, which preceded and followed Thee, chanted together: Alleluia!

Ikos V

Beholding the Preëternal One hidden by a luminous cloud, the apostles marveled; and the angels present declared unto them: "Ye men of Galilee, why stand ye gazing up at the sky? This Jesus, Who hath ascended from you into heaven, shall come again in the same way." Wherefore, with unwavering faith in the glorious Second Coming of Christ, we humbly cry:

Jesus Who camest into the world to save us;
Jesus, Who hast ascended into the heavens, where Thou preparest for us a place of eternal rest!
Jesus Who shalt come again in glory, vouchsafe that we may greet Thee with joy;
Jesus, condemn us not at that time according to our deeds!
Jesus, have mercy upon us according to Thy great mercy;
Jesus, wash away our iniquities according to the multitude of Thy compassions!
Jesus, grant that at that time we may hear Thy longed-for voice, calling the elect to the kingdom of heaven;
Jesus, make us worthy of a place at Thy right hand!
Jesus Who ascended, bear our souls up to the heavenly kingdom!

Kontakion VI

Thine apostles, the divine heralds, O Christ God, fulfilling Thy commission—"Go ye, and teach all the nations!"—preached the Gospel to the nations of the earth, baptizing those who believed in the name of the Father, the Son and the Holy Spirit. Wherefore, we, rightly following their preaching, cry out: Alleluia!

Ikos VI

After the glorious ascension of Christ, the light of the preaching of the Gospel was divinely poured out upon the whole world, and erring nations were enlightened thereby; wherefore, all the faithful cried aloud:

Jesus, true Light Who hast shone forth preëternally from the essence of the Father;
Jesus Who on Mount Tabor didst reveal the glory of Thy divinity to Thy disciples!
Jesus, Sun of righteousness, Who by Thy coming hast driven away the deep night of unbelief;
Jesus Who hast illumined the whole world with the light of the knowledge of God!
Jesus Who out of the race of Israel didst assemble the choir of the apostles;
Jesus Who hast called to Thy Church all tribes and nations!
Jesus Who hast raised up children to the faithful Abraham out of the barren race of the heathen;
Jesus Who didst bring the nations, which were formerly rejected, into the fullness of Thy Church!
Jesus Who ascended, bear our souls up to the heavenly kingdom!

Kontakion VII

Although Saul was a blasphemer and persecutor, O Saviour, Thou didst appear to Him on the road to Damascus, to call him to the knowledge of Thee; and Thou didst say: "Saul! Saul! Why persecutest thou Me?", and didst turn him to the knowledge of the Truth. And, straightway moved to believe, he cried aloud: Alleluia!

Ikos VII

In wondrous and incomprehensible manner did our Saviour, Who is true God, receive human nature from the Ever-virgin Mary and ascend with glory into heaven, uniting those on earth with those in heaven, and providing free access to the mansions of heaven for those who cry out to Him:

Jesus Who in Thine essence art God;
Jesus Who didst dwell on earth as a man with true flesh!
Jesus Who hast left us Thine image not made by the hands of man;
Jesus Who in the Holy Eucharist art ever present in Thy divine essence!
Jesus, Who in the heavens art now seen in Thine all-pure flesh, by the holy angels and the souls of the righteous;
Jesus, the sight of Whose deified flesh filleth with joy and gladness the inhabitants of heaven!
Jesus, Who hast promised to glorify our bodies with incorrupt glory after the resurrection;
Jesus, Who hast not deprived even our unworthiness of this glory!
Jesus Who ascended, bear our souls up to the heavenly kingdom!

Kontakion VIII

A strange wonder is it that human nature, which before was rejected and far removed from divine glory, now, in the ascension of Christ, mounteth higher than the heavens and is crowned with glory and honor surpassing the ranks of the angels. Wherefore, all of us born of earth rejoice and sing with gladness to the ascended Christ: Alleluia!

Ikos VIII

Thou didst fulfill all the mysteries of our salvation, O Christ God, when Thou didst ascend from the Mount of Olives to the heavenly mountain, and having sat on the throne at the right hand of the Father, didst send to Thy disciples the promised Comforter Who proceedeth from the Father. And now, with the voice of the Gospel, Thou callest unto all: "Come unto Me, all ye who labor and are heavy laden, and I will give you rest!" And, desiring to obtain this longed-for rest, we cry out with compunction:

Jesus Who sent Thine all-holy Spirit upon Thy beloved
 disciples, send down the Spirit Comforter upon us
 from the Father;
Jesus, create in us a pure heart and renew an upright
 spirit within us!
Jesus, enlighten us with the light of Thy grace, that we
 may ever meditate upon heavenly things;
Jesus, grant that we may be ever mindful of Thy great
 benefactions, which have been revealed to us in the
 creation and redemption!
Jesus Who callest to everlasting rest those who labor for
 Thy name, summon us also, who are weighed down
 by many sins;
Jesus, avert our eyes from the vanity of the world, and
 grant that we may ever direct our gaze on high and
 desire the good things of heaven!
Jesus Who dost receive divine worship from all the hosts
 of heaven, vouchsafe that we sinners may ever offer
 Thee worship and glorification;
Jesus, grant that with humblemindedness we may serve
 Thee all the days of our life!
Jesus Who ascended, bear our souls up to the heavenly
 kingdom!

Kontakion IX

All angelic nature doth unceasingly glorify Christ our God, Who hath ascended into the heavens and sitteth at the right hand of the Father; wherefore, redeemed by His precious blood from slavery to the enemy, we cry out to Him in thanksgiving: Alleluia!

Ikos IX

The words of rhetors and philosophers are not adequate to say how, after Thine ascension, O Saviour, Thou dwellest in heaven in Thine all-pure flesh, yet ever abidest on earth with the faithful as Thou didst promise; and marveling at this mystery, we cry out in humility of mind:

Akathist to the Ascension of Our Lord Jesus Christ

Jesus divine, Who art seated with the Father in heaven;

Jesus, perfect Man, Who abidest with the faithful on earth!

Jesus Who preparest a habitation for Thyself in the hearts of those who love Thee;

Jesus Who with the Father and the Spirit comest to Thine elect and mystically dwellest within them!

Jesus Who dost not reject even our impure hearts;

Jesus, for as Thou camest and spake unto Zacchæus, so do Thou say unto us: "Today hath salvation come to this house!"

Jesus Who unitest the divided, unite us all with Thyself and Thy Father;

Jesus Who reconcilest all, grant that we may all be of one mind in the Faith and in love for Thee!

Jesus Who ascended, bear our souls up to the heavenly kingdom!

Kontakion X

O Saviour, send Thy speedy aid down upon us who desire to be saved, but are overcome by the weakness of the flesh, and are ever prompted by an evil will, that unto Thee, Who hast ascended into the heavens to prepare a place of everlasting rest for those who love Thee, we may fittingly and rightly chant: Alleluia!

Ikos X

O Christ our Saviour, Thou preëternal King Who ascended with glory into the heavens and dost cause Thine elect to ascend with Thee, deprive us not of their portion in the bridal chamber of heaven, that we may cry out to Thee with faith and hope:

Jesus, Who didst say: "Where I am, there also will My servant be";

Jesus, Who didst say: "In My Father's house there are many mansions!"

Jesus Who hast prepared ineffable good things for those who love Thee, deprive us not of the inheritance of these heavenly good things;

Jesus, grant that we may behold Thy glory and be illumined with the light of Thy countenance!

Jesus, vouchsafe unto us everlasting rest in the bosom of Abraham;

Jesus, grant that we may abide eternally in Thy light!

Jesus, grant that even now we may have a foretaste of the blessedness of paradise in our hearts;

Jesus, send down help from on high, that we may enjoy this blessedness of heart!

Jesus Who ascended, bear our souls up to the heavenly kingdom!

Kontakion XI

Hymns of praise do we offer Thee, O Saviour, for Thine all-glorious ascension; and mindful of Thy glorious Second Coming and righteous Judgment, we humbly entreat Thee not to send us then, as ones condemned, into the everlasting fire, but to grant that with Thine elect we may sit at Thy right hand and cry out in thanksgiving: Alleluia!

Ikos XI

O Christ God, Bestower of light, Who hast called even us, the unworthy, to the wondrous light of the teaching of the Gospel, we humbly entreat Thee: O Saviour, reveal Thy name to the nations, who to this day languish in the darkness of error, that they may acknowledge Thee to be the true God, Who becamest incarnate for our sake, suffered, arose, and ascended with glory into the heavens; and teach them to cry out to Thee with us, thus:

Jesus, preëternal God, Who art of the same essence as the Father and the Spirit;

Jesus Who didst receive our nature from the pure Virgin and becamest man!

Jesus Who in the beginning didst create man in Thine image;

Jesus Who by Thyself didst renew the image of man, which had waxed old through sin!

Jesus Who didst call many publicans and harlots to the knowledge of Thee;

Jesus Who didst show many penitent sinners to be heirs of the kingdom of heaven!

Jesus Who didst turn to the Faith the heart of the Emperor Constantine, the peer of the apostles, and thus didst bring an end to the cruel persecutions of Thy Church;

Jesus, turn us away from our evils, and grant that we may ever serve Thee in newness of life and love unfeigned!

Jesus Who ascended, bear our souls up to the heavenly kingdom!

Kontakion XII

Send Thy grace down upon us from heaven, O Christ God, that, enkindled with love for Thee thereby, we may put away all thoughts which drag us down to earth, and may thus be able, in mind and heart, to ascend unto Thee in the mansions beyond the heavens, ever crying out: Alleluia!

Ikos XII

Hymning Thy most glorious ascension into the heavens, we glorify Thy wondrous sending of the Spirit Comforter, Who is of the same essence as Thee, from the Father unto Thy holy disciples and apostles, who, invested with power from on high, catechized the whole world with the preaching of the Gospel, and illumined a great multitude of souls with the light of the Faith, teaching them to baptize in the name of the Father, and the Son, and the Holy Spirit. Wherefore, together we all cry out to Thee:

Jesus Who on the Mount of Olives gavest a final blessing to the faithful, bless us also who praise Thee;

Jesus, Who by Thine ascension didst hallow the air, sanctify our thoughts and senses!

Jesus Who by Thine ascent on high didst ease for us the path to the heavens;

Jesus, Who for the souls of the Orthodox didst remove all obstacles on that path!

Jesus Who hast given us the holy angels as companions and guides for our ascent into heaven;

Jesus Who with aid and succor dost defend us all against the trials of the toll-houses!

Jesus, Who openest unto us the shut gates of paradise;

Jesus, Who dost not forbid entry into the blessed habitations of the righteous, but hast bestowed them upon us!

Jesus Who ascended, bear our souls up to the heavenly kingdom!

Kontakion XIII

O all-sweet and most compassionate Jesus, Who hast wrought our redemption on earth, Who didst arise from the dead and ascend with glory into the heavens with the all-pure flesh Thou hadst assumed: Accept these thanks, which are offered unto Thee with all our soul, and as Thou shalt come again in glory, vouchsafe that at that time we may stand at Thy right hand and cry out with the choirs of the righteous: Alleluia! Alleluia! Alleluia!

This kontakion is recited thrice, whereupon Ikos I and Kontakion I are repeated.

Prayers to Our Ascended Lord

I

O Christ our Saviour, Who hast ascended into the heavens, we humbly beseech Thee: Let our mind ascend from transitory things and vain desires to the eternal blessedness which is in heaven, which Thou didst promise to those who love Thy holy commandments and keep them; that, strengthened by the expectation of those ineffable good things and the power of Thy grace, we may be able to flee passionate attachment to worldly lusts, and may live in this world in repentance and the doing of good works, unto the glory of Thine all-holy name. And at Thy glorious Second Coming vouchsafe that with joy we may greet Thee, our Saviour and Judge, and hear Thy most sweet voice calling the righteous to inherit the kingdom of heaven, that with all who have been well-pleasing unto Thee in times past we also may enter Thine all-radiant bridal chamber, and there glorify Thee, and the Father and the Holy Spirit, for endless ages. Amen.

II

We thank Thee, O Christ God our Saviour, that Thou hast not left us, who are fallen, to perish utterly, but in Thine ineffable love for mankind didst come and save us, and lead us back to Thy Father, lost as we were, granting us the freedom to be children of God and heirs of eternal blessedness in the kingdom of heaven. Help us now, O Lord, that through grace we may overcome the temptations of the enemy, lest we fall again into grievous slavery to the sin which before held sway within us: that, strengthened thus by Thy grace, we may all obtain salvation, and glorify Thee, and the Father and the Holy Spirit, in Thy eternal kingdom, unto the ages of ages. Amen.

Akathist Hymn to the Nativity of Christ

Nativity of Christ

Akathist Hymn
to the Nativity of Christ
Which the Holy Church Doth Celebrate On the 25th of December

Kontakion I

O Christ our God, Who didst choose the most pure Virgin from among all generations and wast born of her in the flesh, we Thy servants offer hymns of thanksgiving unto Thee. As Thou art possessed of ineffable lovingkindness, O Master, from all manner of misfortunes free us who cry: O Jesus, Son of God, Who becamest incarnate for our sake, glory be to Thee!

Ikos I

A multitude of angels assembled in Bethlehem to behold the unapproachable Nativity; and seeing their Creator lying in the manger as a babe, they were filled with awe. And offering homage with fear, they honored the godliness of Him Who was born and of her who bore Him, chanting such things as these:

> Glory to Thee, O Son of God, Who wast begotten of the Father before time began!
> Glory to Thee Who with the Father and the Spirit didst create all things!
> Glory to Thee Who camest to save the perishing!
> Glory to Thee Who didst condescend even to assume the form of a servant!
> Glory to Thee Who wast ineffably born of the Virgin!
> Glory to Thee Who searchest for the lost!

Glory to Thee, O Saviour of the perishing!
Glory to Thee Who hast demolished the wall of separation!
Glory to Thee Who again hast opened paradise, which was shut by disobedience!
Glory to Thee Who ineffably lovest the human race!
Glory to Thee Who didst show the cave to be heaven on earth!
Glory to Thee Who hast shown the Virgin, who gave Thee birth, to be the throne of the cherubim!
O Jesus, Son of God, Who becamest incarnate for our sake, glory be to Thee!

Kontakion II

Seeing that their Master had received flesh from the pure Virgin, the incorporeal angels were filled with awe and said one to another: "This is an all-glorious mystery past understanding!" And marveling at His ineffable condescension, they chanted with fear: Alleluia!

Ikos II

All of noetic creation is filled with awe and with thanksgiving hymneth the mystery of Thy nativity, O Master. The hosts of heaven rejoice, chanting: "Glory to God in the highest!", earth and men are filled with gladness, and we unceasingly cry out:
Glory to Thee, O God, Who art glorified in the highest!
Glory to Thee Who didst reveal Thyself to us on earth!
Glory to Thee Who hast reconciled Thyself with us!
Glory to Thee Who didst appear to us on earth!
Glory to Thee Who wast ineffably incarnate of the Virgin!
Glory to Thee Who didst cause the star to shine forth!
Glory to Thee Who by it summoned the Magi to worship Thee!
Glory to Thee Who didst mercifully accept their gifts!
Glory to Thee Who hast taught all creation to minister unto Thee!

Glory to Thee Who hast given us the understanding to hymn Thee!
Glory to Thee Who hast united Thyself with us!
Glory to Thee Who Thyself hast saved us!
O Jesus, Son of God, Who becamest incarnate for our sake, glory be to Thee!

Kontakion III

The God of peace and Father of compassions, Who is mighty in strength, came to earth to save the world which is perishing; and in Bethlehem He is now born as a babe of the Virgin, whom He hath shown to be a Mother and Mediatress of salvation for all who glorify His incarnation and chant: Alleluia!

Ikos III

Having her who gave Thee birth in an all-pure manner praying unceasingly for us, rejoicing, we hymn the mystery of Thy becoming man, O Master; and glorifying Thy nativity from the God-pleasing Virgin, we cry:

Glory to Thee, O Son of God!
Glory to Thee, O Son of the Virgin!
Glory to Thee Who upon us hast shown forth the abyss of Thy love for mankind!
Glory to Thee Who hast ineffably loved us!
Glory to Thee Who hast sought out the lost sheep!
Glory to Thee Who hast told the angels to rejoice in its finding!
Glory to Thee Who hast taken it upon Thy shoulders!
Glory to Thee Who hast led it to the Father!
Glory to Thee Who hast united men and angels in a single flock!
Glory to Thee Who hast delivered the world from delusion!
Glory to Thee Who hast shown us great and ineffable mercy!

Glory to Thee Who lovest us more than all other creatures!

O Jesus, Son of God, Who becamest incarnate for our sake, glory be to Thee!

Kontakion IV

The chaste-minded Joseph, who before had within him a storm of doubting thoughts, now beholdeth all-glorious things within the divine cave; for even though he beheld as a man Him Who was born of the Virgin, yet did he understand from things revealed to him that He is the true God. Wherefore, doing homage to His divinity, He chanted with joy: Alleluia!

Ikos IV

The shepherds heard the angel proclaiming to them that the Saviour of the world was born in the city of David, and running swiftly, they beheld Him lying in the manger, like an unblemished lamb which had been tended in the womb of the Virgin, and her who had given birth to Him reverently ministering unto Him, and Joseph standing by with fear. And they spake of what they had been told, and, bowing down before Newborn, they said:

Glory to Thee, O Lamb of God, Saviour of the world!

Glory to Thee, O Son of God, Who hast revealed to us an ineffable miracle!

Glory to Thee Who hast caused us to hear the song of angels!

Glory to Thee Who hast taught us to glorify Thee with them!

Glory to Thee Who hast moved angels and men to hymn Thee!

Glory to Thee Who hast brought joy to earth and heaven!

Glory to Thee in Whom those in heaven rejoice with those on earth!

Glory to Thee, for by Thee are those on earth united with those in heaven!

Glory to Thee Who hast shown the power of the devil to be impotent!
Glory to Thee Who hast delivered us from His tyranny!
Glory to Thee, O ineffable joy of those who believe in Thee!
Glory to Thee, O unspeakable delight of those who love Thee!
O Jesus, Son of God, Who becamest incarnate for our sake, glory be to Thee!

Kontakion V

Beholding the divinely guided star which pointed beforehand to the nativity of Christ, the Magi observed it; and by its guidance they reached the Unapproachable One and beheld Him Who is invisible. And they rejoice, crying out to Him: Alleluia!

Ikos V

The Persian kings, seeing the King of kings sitting on the arm of the Virgin as upon the throne of the cherubim, and understanding Him to be the Master, even though He had assumed the form of a servant, hastened to offer Him gifts—gold, as to the King of all; frankincense, as to God; and myrrh, as to One immortal;—and making obeisance, they chanted:

Glory to Thee Who hast shone forth light upon all!
Glory to Thee Who by a star hast summoned us to do Thee homage!
Glory to Thee Who didst reprove the malice of cruel Herod!
Glory to Thee Who didst show his plotting to be in vain!
Glory to Thee Who hast delivered us from his deception!
Glory to Thee Who hast taught us to worship Thee, the Sun of righteousness!
Glory to Thee Who hast enlightened all with the light of understanding!
Glory to Thee Who by Thy nativity hast abolished the delusion of polytheism!

Glory to Thee Who hast utterly laid low the dominion of the enemy!

Glory to Thee Who hast taught us to worship Thee with the Father and the Spirit!

Glory to Thee Who hast crushed the head of the serpent who beguiled us!

Glory to Thee Who hast delivered us from everlasting death!

O Jesus, Son of God, Who becamest incarnate for our sake, glory be to Thee!

Kontakion VI

Fulfilling the prophecies concerning Thee, which were uttered by the God-bearing heralds, Thou hast revealed Thyself on earth, O Saviour, being born now of the pure Virgin in a wretched cave; and though rich, Thou didst willingly impoverish Thyself for our sake, that Thou mightest enrich men, who chant to Thee with faith: Alleluia!

Ikos VI

Thou didst shine forth from the Virgin, Thy Mother who knew not man, O Jesus, shining like the sun and driving away the darkness of falsehood; for all the demons trembled, unable to withstand Thy might, and hades, beholding the miracle, was filled with terror. And we cry out to Thee in thanksgiving:

Glory to Thee, O Saviour of men!

Glory to Thee, O Destroyer of the demons!

Glory to Thee Who by Thy birth didst fill the prince of lies with dread!

Glory to Thee Who hast abolished the delusion of the idols!

Glory to Thee Who hast illumined all with the light of the knowledge of God!

Glory to Thee Who hast driven away the darkness of ignorance!

Glory to Thee, O Rock Who hast poured forth the water of salvation upon all!

Glory to Thee Who hast quenched the thirst of Adam and David!

Glory to Thee Who like the sun hast enlightened all by Thy nativity!

Glory to Thee Who hast made the whole world radiant with beams of grace!

Glory to Thee Who hast shown us the promised land!

Glory to Thee Who hast delivered us from the curse of our whole race!

O Jesus, Son of God, Who becamest incarnate for our sake, glory be to Thee!

Kontakion VII

Desiring to reveal to us the mystery hidden from before time began, Thou didst show the mystery to servants from all creation, O Saviour: to Gabriel from among the angels, to the Virgin from among men, to the star from among the heavens, and from an earth to the cave wherein it was Thy good pleasure to be born. Wherefore, marveling at Thine ineffable wisdom, we cry out: Alleluia!

Ikos VII

The Creator of all showed forth a new creation, revealing Himself in flesh, springing forth from a seedless womb, which He preserved incorrupt; and He showed it to be the mediation of salvation for those who chant:

Glory to Thee, O Son of God, Who hast shown her who bore Thee to be a Mother of lovingkindness!

Glory to Thee Who didst preserve her a virgin even after she gave birth!

Glory to Thee Who camest to save Adam!

Glory to Thee Who hast comforted the tears of Eve!

Glory to Thee Who camest to save all men!

Glory to Thee Who hast shone forth an image of the resurrection!
Glory to Thee Who hast rent asunder the record of our sins!
Glory to Thee Who has given us a model of humility!
Glory to Thee Who didst impoverish Thyself for our sake!
Glory to Thee Who hast enriched us with Thy poverty!
Glory to Thee Who hast clothed us in the raiment of salvation!
Glory to Thee Who hast delighted us by Thy love!
O Jesus, Son of God, Who becamest incarnate for our sake, glory be to Thee!

Kontakion VIII

Seeing Thy strange and all-glorious nativity which took place in the cave, let us all the more spurn the vanities of the world, for the divine Mind appeared on earth as a humble man, that He might lead up to the heavens those who cry out to Him: Alleluia!

Ikos VIII

Thou art all desire, all delight for those who love Thee and glorify Thy divine condescension, O Christ God; for, having been born of the pure Virgin on earth, Thou leadest up into the heavens those who chant:

Glory to Thee, O Son of God, Who wast born on earth!
Glory to Thee Who wast ineffably incarnate of the Virgin!
Glory to Thee Who hast shown Thyself to us!
Glory to Thee Who summoned to Thee those afar off!
Glory to Thee, our ineffable Joy!
Glory to Thee, O delight of our hearts!
Glory to Thee Who in Thy nativity hast shone forth the light of salvation!
Glory to Thee Who didst shed tears for our salvation!
Glory to Thee Who hast thereby quenched the flame of our passions!

Glory to Thee Who hast cleansed us of the defilement of
    sin!
Glory to Thee Who hast set at nought our transgression!
Glory to Thee Who hast delivered us from corruption!
O Jesus, Son of God, Who becamest incarnate for our
    sake, glory be to Thee!

Kontakion IX

No mind or understanding of angels or men is able to comprehend the mystery of Thine unapproachable nativity, O Master; yet do Thou accept our love and faith, O good Master, and save us who chant unto Thee: Alleluia!

Ikos IX

We see the most eloquent of orators mute as fish when confronted by Thine incarnation, O Master; for they are at a loss how, being perfect God, thou didst appear as a perfect man, and how Thou wast born of the Virgin who knew not wedlock. But we, refusing to delve into these mysteries, glorify Thee with faith alone, crying:

    Glory to Thee, O hypostatic Wisdom of God!
    Glory to Thee, O ineffable Joy of all!
    Glory to Thee Who didst show those lacking in wisdom
        to be lovers of wisdom!
    Glory to Thee Who hast given understanding even to the
        simple!
    Glory to Thee Who didst put to shame those who tested
        Thee!
    Glory to Thee Who didst break the webs of all who devise
        myths!
    Glory to Thee Who hast shone forth the light of divine
        knowledge upon all!
    Glory to Thee Who didst pour forth wisdom in Thy
        works!
    Glory to Thee Who hast enlightened the minds of many!
    Glory to Thee Who hast shown us the path to salvation!

Glory to Thee, O unfathomable abyss of lovingkindness!
Glory to Thee, O depth of compassions and love for mankind!
O Jesus, Son of God, Who becamest incarnate for our sake, glory be to Thee!

Kontakion X

Desiring to save the world which is perishing, the Adorner of all is born of the Virgin as a babe; He Who looseth the intricate bonds of transgressions is wrapped in swaddling clothes and laid in a manger; and being the Son of God, He becometh the Son of the Virgin, and wisely arrangeth all things, that He might save those who chant unto Him: Alleluia!

Ikos X

Herod, the enemy of God, showed himself to be a pillar and wall of God-opposing malice and a spawn of great iniquity, who tried to slay Him Who giveth life unto all, and at his command innocent babes were reaped by the sword, like unripe grain; wherefore, having driven all malice from our hearts, let us glorify Him Who came to save us, crying:

Glory to Thee Who didst show Herod's intention to be in vain!
Glory to Thee Who hast numbered with the angels the babes he slew!
Glory to Thee, O Destroyer of malice!
Glory to Thee, O Instructor in humility and Lover of mortals!
Glory to Thee Who hast broken the horn of pride!
Glory to Thee Who hast shone the light of righteousness upon all!
Glory to Thee Who Thyself hast taught meekness and humility to all!
Glory to Thee Who hast brought all to acknowledge Thee!
Glory to Thee Who by Thy nativity didst sanctify the womb of her who bore Thee!

Glory to Thee Who didst accept the shepherds' wonder and the gifts of the Magi!

Glory to Thee Who didst teach even irrational creatures to serve Thee!

Glory to Thee Who hast sanctified all creation!

O Jesus, Son of God, Who becamest incarnate for our sake, glory be to Thee!

Kontakion XI

All laudation of Thine incarnation for our sake falleth short, and for those who wish to offer fitting praise, silence is better. For even were we to offer Thee hymns as numerous as the sands of the sea, O all-holy King, we would accomplish nought that is meet; wherefore, we chant with fear: Alleluia!

Ikos XI

They who sat in darkness and the shadow of death, beholding Thee, the never-waning Light Who shone forth from the Virgin, were illumined by the fire of Thy divinity, and hymned Thee, the Bestower of wisdom and understanding, crying out such things as these:

Glory to Thee, O Son of God, ineffable Light!

Glory to Thee, O Sun of righteousness, Who hast enlightened all by Thy nativity!

Glory to Thee Who hast shone forth most radiant enlightenment!

Glory to Thee Who hast poured forth upon us a most torrential river of grace!

Glory to Thee Who hast richly provided the water of salvation as drink!

Glory to Thee Who hast shown to those who love Thee that Thy yoke is easy and Thy burden is light!

Glory to Thee Who hast lifted from us the weight of sin!

Glory to Thee Who hast delivered us from slavery to the enemy!

Glory to Thee Who hast filled all with gladness by Thine appearance on earth!

Glory to Thee Who hast given us consolation through rebirth!

Glory to Thee Who hast shown Thyself to us as our utmost Desire!

Glory to Thee Who hast reconciled with the Father us who are His enemies!

O Jesus, Son of God, Who becamest incarnate for our sake, glory be to Thee!

Kontakion XII

O our Saviour, Who didst come to give grace unto all and to loose the debts of men by Thine incarnation, loose also our debts and rend asunder the record of our sins, that we may glorify Thine ineffable nativity and chant without ceasing: Alleluia!

Ikos XII

Hymning Thy becoming man, we praise, bless and worship Thee, O our Saviour; and we believe that Thou art the Lord and God Who saveth all who hope on Thee, who glorify Thine ineffable nativity from the Virgin, and chant such things as these:

Glory to Thee, O Son of God, Who art worshiped in the highest with the Father and the Spirit!

Glory to Thee Who art glorified by all the ranks of heaven and earth!

Glory to Thee Who hast disclosed the mystery hidden from before time began!

Glory to Thee Who hast revealed Thine ineffable love for us!

Glory to Thee, O Adorner of all creation!

Glory to Thee, O our most merciful Saviour!

Glory to Thee Who makest firm the scepters of those who reign with piety on the earth!

Glory to Thee Who adornest devout hierarchs and priests with wisdom and majesty!
Glory to Thee, O foundation and confirmation of the Church!
Glory to Thee, O salvation and adornment of all the faithful!
Glory to Thee, O Physician and Healing of our bodies!
Glory to Thee, O Adorner and Saviour of our souls!
O Jesus, Son of God, Who becamest incarnate for our sake, glory be to Thee!

Kontakion XIII

Jesus all-sweet and most compassionate, our Saviour, Creator and Master! Accept this, our meager supplication, thanksgiving and glorification, as Thou didst accept the gifts and worship of the Magi; and preserve us, Thy servants, from all perils. Grant us the forgiveness of sins, and from everlasting torment deliver those who with faith glorify Thy nativity from the pure Virgin, and who cry out to Thee: Alleluia! Alleluia! Alleluia!

This Kontakion is recited thrice, whereupon Ikos I and Kontakion I are repeated.

Prayer to Our Lord, God and Saviour Jesus Christ On the Day of His Holy Nativity

O great and unapproachable God, unoriginate Father, Son Who art equally without beginning, and Spirit Who art equally eternal, Who givest being to things which were not in existence, Who savest the perishing, Who givest life to the dead, Who doest what Thou willest among the hosts of heaven and in Thine earthly habitation, and directest all according to Thy wondrous providence! Incline Thine ear from the heights of Thy holiness, and accept from us, Thy lowly and unworthy servants, to whom Thou hast revealed Thy great salvation from misfortunes and plague, these grateful supplications, confessions and glorifications, which we offer to Thee with heart and mouth. For Thou hast not dealt with us according to our iniquities, O Lord, neither hast Thou rewarded us according to our sins. Thou didst say of old to the children of Israel that if they would not act to keep Thy words and do all Thy commandments, Thou wouldst bring against them a nation of unashamed countenance, which would assail them in their cities until the walls thereof were broken. And we have come to realize that this dread sentence hath been directed against us and our fathers as well. For, failing to fear Thy threat and paying no heed to Thy lovingkindness, we have forsaken the path of Thy righteousness and walked in the will of our own hearts, and have made no attempt to hold Thee, the God of men's understanding and hearts, in our mind. Moreover, treating the traditions of our fathers as of no import, we have abandoned Thee for others. For these reasons, grievous ill fortune overtook us, as it did the children of Israel of old, and because we paid no heed to their lessons, mindless and savage-minded foes have come against us. But do Thou, O compassionate and merciful Lord God, Who art long-suffering, greatly merciful and true, Who maintainest justice and workest mercy among the thousands, Who takest away iniquities, injustices and sins, having abandoned us for a little time, have mercy upon us according to Thy great mercy, and having visited our unrighteousness with the rod, as a compassionate father doth his children, so do Thou spare us. For Thou hast looked down on our tribulation, and upon our entreaties which, trusting not in our own righteousness, but upon Thy many compassions, we cast at Thy feet O Lord; and Thou hast shown us the back of our ungodly adversaries, for, melting away before the face of Thy Christ, Thine enemies have vanished like smoke, and those who love Thee shine forth like the rising of the sun in their power. We have seen, O Lord, we have seen, and in us all nations have seen, that Thou art God, and there is none other besides Thee. Thou slayest and makest to live, Thou smitest and healest, and there is no one who can deliver from Thy hand. Wherefore, our heart hath been established in our Lord, our horn hath been lifted up in our God, and we have been gladdened in Thy salvation. We thank Thee, O Lord, that, chastizing us, Thou hast chastened us but a little, lest Thou give us over utterly unto death. Grant, O Lord, that we may hold the memory of this, Thy glorious visitation, firmly and continually within us, that made steadfast in Thee by filial fear, faith and love, and protected by Thy might, we may ever, as we do today, hymn and glorify Thy holy name. Confirm Thy blessing also upon our civil authorities, that Thy good Spirit may continually rest upon them. In our land grant holiness unto pastors, judgment and justice to those who govern, peace and tranquility to the people, efficacy to the laws and advancement to the Faith. O Lord of all lovingkindness, extend Thy mercy unto those who know Thee; and reveal Thyself even unto those who seek Thee not; turn the hearts even of our enemies unto Thee; and make Thyself known to all nations and peoples in Thy true Christ: that from the rising of the sun, even unto the setting thereof, all nations may with one heart cry out to Thee with a voice of rejoicing: Glory to Thee, the God and Saviour of all, unto the ages of ages! Amen.

Akathist Hymn
to the All-Holy and Life-Creating Spirit

The Descent of the Holy Spirit

Akathist Hymn
to the All-Holy and Life-Creating Spirit
Whom the Holy Church Doth Celebrate on the Day after Pentecost

Kontakion I

Come, O ye faithful, let us glorify the descent of the Holy Spirit, Who poured forth upon the apostles from the bosom of the Father, covered the earth with the knowledge of God as with waters, doth account those who come to Him in purity worthy of the divine adoption of life-bearing grace, and doth sanctify and deify those who cry:

> Come Thou, O Comforter, Holy Spirit, and make Thine abode within us!

Ikos I

In radiant choirs the angels in heaven unceasingly chant glory to the Holy Spirit, as immaterial Light and the Source of life; and with them we also glorify Thee, O unapproachable Spirit, for Thy manifest and hidden mercies; and we humbly entreat Thee to overshadow us with Thy blessing.

> Come, O Light of Truth and spiritual Joy;
> Come, dew-laden Cloud and ineffable Beauty!
> Come and accept our praise like incense of sweet savor;
> Come and grant that we may taste the joy of Thine outpouring!
> Come and gladden us with the abundance of Thy gifts;

Come, O eternal and never-setting Sun, and make Thy
    dwelling-place in us!
Come Thou, O Comforter, Holy Spirit, and make
    Thine abode within us!

Kontakion II

In the form of tongues of fire, amid light and a rushing, stormy wind, the Holy Spirit descended upon the apostles. Wherefore, enveloped in His flames, the fishermen summoned the whole world to the Church of Christ; and, joyfully enduring tribulations on dry land and on the waters, they were undaunted by cruel deaths. And all throughout the world went forth the proclamation of their divinely beauteous hymn: Alleluia!

Ikos II

O Holy Spirit of God, Thou Cup giving rise to dew and emitting fire, poured forth upon the apostles in the upper chamber on Sion: we hymn Thee, we bless Thee, and we give thanks unto Thee.

    Come, Thou Who dost sanctify and preserve the
        Church;
    Come and grant one heart and one soul to Thy
        faithful!
    Come and enflame our cold and barren piety;
    Come and dispel the darkness of ungodliness and im-
        piety which doth thicken over all the earth!
    Come and lead us to the path of correction of life;
    Come and guide us to every truth!
    Come, unapproachable Wisdom, and by the judg-
        ments which Thou knowest save us;
    Come Thou, O Comforter, Holy Spirit, and make
        Thine abode within us!

Kontakion III

O mystery most profound! O unattainable Spirit of God, Who with the Father and the Word art the Creator of all! Thou hast adorned the ranks of angels on high in the temple of unapproachable Light. The choirs of fiery luminaries Thou hast called into being with the majesty of glory. And uniting flesh and spirit in a lowly union, Thou didst create the human race! Wherefore, everything that hath breath doth sing Thy praise: Alleluia!

Ikos III

Thou, O eternal Spirit, the Alpha and the Omega, the Beginning and the End, didst enliven all beings and all things by Thine awesome envelopment and the formless power of mist over the waters. By Thy life-bearing breath, out of the formless abyss Thou didst produce the ineffable beauty of pristine creation. Wherefore, we cry out to Thee:

> Come unto us, O all-wise Fashioner of the world;
> Come, O Great One, Who art present in a little flower
> > and a star of heaven!
> Come, O ineffable Variety and eternal Beauty;
> Come and bring light to the dark chaos of my soul!
> Come and reveal us to be a new creation in Christ;
> Come Thou, O Comforter, Holy Spirit, and make
> > Thine abode within us!

Kontakion IV

O unattainable and all-good Spirit, Thou Source of sanctity! Thou didst clothe the all-pure Virgin Mary in the blinding and unapproachable radiance of Thy Divinity, making her the Mother of God the Word, the Queen of the angels, the salvation of men. With Thy transcendent power Thou didst overshadow the prophets and the apostles, and dost raise them up to the third heaven, and dost wound their hearts with celestial beauty, instilling in their speech a fiery urgency that leadeth people to God. Thou dost seek out the uttermost sinners, and, filled with burning ecstasy, they chant: Alleluia!

Ikos IV

By the Holy Spirit is every soul enlivened; and by His power will all created beings be raised up in the fellowship of the resurrection at the final hour of this age and the first of that which is to come. Then do Thou also raise us up from our graves, O good Comforter, not unto damnation, but to the divinely radiant blessedness of all the saints, our friends and kinsmen!

>Come and deliver us from spiritual death;
>Come and, before our end, satisfy us with the Body
>>and Blood of Christ the Saviour!
>Come and grant that we may fall asleep in peace, our
>>conscience clean;
>Come and make radiant our awakening from the sleep
>>of death!
>Come and vouchsafe that we may gaze with joy upon
>>the morning of eternity'
>Come and make us children of incorruption!
>Come and, like the sun, enlighten our bodies, which
>>will then be immortal;
>Come Thou, O Comforter, Holy Spirit, and make
>>Thine abode within us!

Kontakion V

Hearing Thee say, "If any thirsteth, let him come to Me and drink," we beseech Thee, O Son of God: Quench Thou our thirst for the spiritual life, and grant us the water of life. Pour forth a stream of grace upon us from the Holy Spirit Who is Thy Peer, that we may never again thirst, but may chant with compunction: Alleluia!

Ikos V

O incorrupt and uncreated, eternal and compassionate Spirit, Preserver of the righteous and cleansing of sinners! Free us from all impure deeds, that the radiance of the light of grace may not be extinguished within us who cry out to Thee:

Come, O most Blessed one, and grant us compunction
    and a fountain of tears;
Come and teach us to worship Thee in spirit and in
    truth!
Come, O Thou Who art truly Most High, and make
    clear the doubts of our feeble minds;
Come, O Life Who growest not old, and accept us
    with the brevity of the earthly age!
Come, O eternal Light, and dispel our forebodings
    and fears;
Come, O Power Who art eternally transcendent, and
    refresh Thy children who are weak!
Come, O endless Joy, and passing misfortunes will be
    forgotten;
Come Thou, O Comforter, Holy Spirit, and make
    Thine abode within us!

Kontakion VI

Dance thou, O holy mother Sion, daughter of the light! O universal Church of Christ, thou great bride, adorn thyself like unto the sky, brilliant with radiance! The Holy Spirit resteth on thee, healing the infirm, filling those who lack, giving life to the dead, and leading to eternal life all who rightly cry out as is meet: Alleluia!

Ikos VI

"In the world there will be sorrows," said the Lord. Where shall we find joy, and who will comfort us? Do Thou assuage our griefs! Be Thou a Mediator for us with Thine ineffable inspirations, and lighten the hearts of those who pray to Thee:

Come, sweet Coolness of those who labor and are
    heavy laden;
Come, Converser with the imprisoned and Support of
    the persecuted!
Come and have pity on those worn out by poverty and
    hunger;

Come and cure the sufferings of our souls and bodies!
Come and visit all who thirst for Thine effulgence;
Come and make sense of our sufferings with the hope
  of joy everlasting!
Come Thou, O Comforter, Holy Spirit, and make
  Thine abode within us!

Kontakion VII

"He who blasphemeth against the Holy Spirit will not be forgiven in this age or that which is to come," said the Lord. Hearing this dread pronouncement, we tremble lest we be condemned with those who disobey Thee and contend against God. Grant that our hearts not be inclined toward words of wickedness, O Holy Spirit. All who stray do Thou turn away from schisms, heresies and ungodliness, and grant that with the Church of Thy firstborn all may chant forever: Alleluia!

Ikos VII

When the Holy Spirit departed from Saul, fear and despondency overtook him, and the darkness of despair cast him down into the uttermost depths. Thus do I also, in the hour of my despair and affliction, understand that I have fallen away from Thy light. But grant that I may call upon Thee with urgency, O Joy of my soul, until Thy light will illumine me who am of little faith.

Come, therefore, and reject me not for my complain-
  ing and impatience;
Come and still the cruel tempest of turmoil and
  vexation!
Come and calm those beset by the misfortunes of life;
Come and soften hearts when they have become hard
  and wrathful!
Come and break the snares of tribulation and the ter-
  ror of the spirits of darkness;
Come and breathe into us a contrite spirit, that in
  patience we may save our souls!
Come Thou, O Comforter, Holy Spirit, and make
  Thine abode within us!

Kontakion VIII

Save us, O heavenly Father! Poor and destitute are we, spiritually blind and naked! Grant us Thy gold, which hath been purified by fire; cover our shame with white raiment; heal our eyes with Thine anointing. Let the grace of Thy life-creating Spirit descend upon the unclean vessels of our souls and give rebirth to those who chant: Alleluia!

Ikos VIII

Like the Tower of Babylon is earthly happiness destroyed. Pitiful are all the undertakings of men! It is good that Thou hast humbled me, that amid my sins and falls Thou hast revealed to me that I am utterly weak and of no account. Without Thee we can accomplish nought; but by Thy grace we hope to be saved.

>Come, therefore, O only wise Arranger of our life;
>Come and make clear to us Thine unfathomable ways!
>Come like lightning, and illumine the end of our
>   earthly existence;
>Come and bless our every good undertaking!
>Come and be Thou our Helper in good deeds;
>Come and enlighten our minds in time of doubt!
>Come and grant us the spirit of repentance, that we
>   may thus escape the tribulation which will
>   befall the world;
>Come Thou, O Comforter, Holy Spirit, and make
>   Thine abode within us!

Kontakion IX

God so loved the world that He gave His only-begotten Son, Who became man through the Holy Spirit and the Virgin Mary, stretched out His creative hands upon the Cross, and by His Blood redeemed the whole world from sin and death. Wherefore, all creation, awaiting the freedom of the glory of the children of God, doth chant to the beloved Father, the redeeming Son and the sanctifying Spirit: Alleluia!

Ikos IX

The life-creating Spirit, Who descended like a dove upon Christ in the Jordan, rested also upon me in the font of baptism. But the affect of His goodness hath weakened because of the darkness of my falls into sin. Wherefore, as a traveler lost in the forest at night doth wait for the light, so do I await Thy rays, O Good One, lest I perish utterly.

> Come, therefore, unto me who have been sealed with Thine awesome name;
> Come and lighten my tormented conscience, which is pitilessly scorched!
> Come and renew in me Thy darkened image;
> Come and dispel sinful visions!
> Come and teach me to pity the woes of others;
> Come and move me to love for Thine every creature!
> Come and grant me the joy of Thy salvation;
> Come Thou, O Comforter, Holy Spirit, and make Thine abode within us!

Kontakion X

The Holy Spirit giveth new birth, unto life eternal. The Holy Spirit inspireth martyrs, sanctifieth priests, and crowneth the righteous; He maketh bread and wine the divine Body and Blood. O the depth of the richness and wisdom of God! Grant us the crown of Thy gifts—all-forgiving, everlasting love, which hath compassion for enemies and desireth that all be saved; that, illumined thereby, as children of the light we may chant: Alleluia!

Ikos X

Who can separate us from the love of God? Can tribulation, or imprisonment, or persecution, or starvation, or nakedness, or misfortune, or the sword? Even if we are bereft of everything on earth, we have in heaven an inheritance that will not wither away. But grant, O Lord, that we may love Thee not with word or tongue, but with incorrupt works and the struggles of our whole life.

> Come, O almighty Spirit, and increase for us the Faith
>   that prevaileth over all;
> Come and grant us boldness in prayer!
> Come and warm Thou our hearts, that our love not
>   grow cold within us because of the abundance
>   of our iniquities;
> Come and grant that we not fall away in time of per-
>   secution and the mockery of the Faith!
> Come and preserve us from temptations and trials
>   beyond our strength;
> Come and refresh our hearts with the sprinkling of
>   Thy dew!
> Come, heal, sanctify and raise us up, O Good One, by
>   Thy grace;
> Come Thou, O Comforter, Holy Spirit, and make
>   Thine abode within us!

Kontakion XI

Thus saith the Lord: "I will pour forth My Spirit upon all flesh, and your sons and daughters will prophesy, your young men will see visions, and your old men will dream dreams." O Spirit most desired grant if but a crumb (from the table of the chosen children of Thy consolation,) unto us who cry out in compunction: Alleluia!

Ikos XI

Even if for but a brief instant, like a flash of lightning, Thou shinest forth in the hidden depths of the soul, yet unforgettable is the outpouring of Thine effulgence whereby our nature of clay is transformed by the awesome and deifying change. Wherefore, O good Comforter, vouchsafe that, even in this earthly life, we may look to Thee with a pure heart, and cry out:

> Come, blazing Lightning-flash of eternity;
> Come and illumine us with Thy never-waning
>   radiance!

Come, Treasury of humble-mindedness and gladness
  of the meek;
Come, O living Water, and cool us amid the burning
  heat of the passions!
Come, for apart from Thee there is no joy and rest;
Come, for with Thee the kingdom of heaven is
  everywhere!
Come, and set upon our souls Thy sun-like seal;
Come Thou, O Comforter, Holy Spirit, and make
  Thine abode within us!

Kontakion XII

O Holy Spirit, Thou inexhaustible River of grace, Absolver of sins! Accept our supplications in behalf of the whole world, for those who believe and those who do not, and also for the children of perdition; and lead all to the eternal kingdom of the Holy Trinity, that through Thee death, the ultimate enemy, may be abolished, and the world, reborn through purifying fire, may chant the new hymn of immortality: Alleluia!

Ikos XII

In spirit I behold the city of God, the heavenly Jerusalem, like a bride, all adorned, shining like the sun, triumphant. I hear the celebration of the righteous at the banquet of the Lord, and the voices of the angels and the Lord most splendid in the midst of His elect; and sickness, and grief, and sighing are fled away. O Holy Spirit, Thou King of heaven, grant Thy seven fold gifts, that we also may have a share of the everlasting joy of those who in God cry out to Thee thus:

Come, O Good One, and instill in us a thirst for the
  life beyond the grave;
Come and warm in our souls the expectation of the
  life of the age of Truth!
Come and reveal to us the joys of the kingdom which
  is to come;
Come and invest us with the snow-white garment of
  purity!

Come and fill us with the radiance of God;
Come and escort us to the wedding of the Lamb!
Come and grant that we may reign in Thine everlasting glory;
Come Thou, O Comforter, Holy Spirit, and make Thine abode within us!

Kontakion XIII

O life-creating Spirit, Thou radiant Abyss of saving love! By the breath of Thine indwelling thaw the human race, which is frozen in iniquities; by the power of Thine unapproachable judgments hasten the destruction of evil and reveal the eternal triumph of divine justice. May God be all things in all men, and let every knee bend in heaven, on earth and in the nether regions, chanting: Alleluia! Alleluia! Alleluia!

This Kontakion is recited thrice, whereupon Ikos I and Kontakion I are repeated.

Prayer to the All-holy Spirit

O Holy Spirit, Who fillest the whole universe with Thyself and givest life unto all, and Who withdrawest from defiled men, I humbly entreat Thee: Disdain not the impurity of my soul, but come and make Thine abode within me, and cleanse me of all the defilement of sin; that with Thy help I may live out the remaining time of my life in repentance and the doing of good works, and thus may glorify Thee with the Father and the Son, unto the ages of ages. Amen.

Akathists
to the All-Holy Theotokos

Akathist Hymn to the All-Holy Theotokos Called "The Abbess of Mount Athos"

The Abbess of Mt. Athos

The Icon of the All-Holy Theotokos Called "The Abbess of Mount Athos"
Which the Holy Church Celebrates on the 5th of July

The icon of the Abbess of Mount Athos is enshrined in the Lavra of Saint Athanasius on Mount Athos. It was painted for the following reason. It happened that famine struck the monastery, so that all the monks departed, and Saint Athanasius himself had resolved to leave as well. But along the way, he beheld a woman wearing a mantle, and was amazed, saying to himself: "Whence cometh this woman, all unexpected, when women are forbidden to come hither?" But the woman herself spoke, asking: "Whither goest thou, O elder?" In response, Saint Athanasius asked her: "Who art Thou, and how comest Thou hither?" And he added: "How doth it concern Thee where I am going? Thou seest that I am a monk of this place." "If thou art a monk," continued the unknown woman, "thou shouldst be simple-hearted, trusting and meek. I am aware of thy plight and will help thee. But tell me first, whither goest thou?"

Then did the holy Athanasius relate everything to Her, and the woman said: "Is it for this reason thou hast not endured? Wilt thou cast the monastery away for the sake of a piece of bread? Is this in the spirit of monasticism?"

"Who art Thou?" asked Athanasius. "I am She to whose name thou hast dedicated thy monastery. I am the Mother of Thy Lord," replied the woman. "I am afraid to believe Thee," the elder responded, "for the demons betimes assume radiant guise. What proof canst Thou offer me?"

"Seest thou that rock?" answered the Theotokos. "Strike it with thy staff, and thou wilt know who is still the Abbess of thy Lavra."

Athanasius struck the rock, and water burst forth from it with a sound like thunder. The holy one then returned to the monastery and found that all the storage rooms had been filled from top to bottom with everything needful. To this day the water has continued to flow from the place where that rock is to be found. In the Lavra, by the will of the Queen of heaven, there was for many years no abbot; and so, during that period, the icon itself became known as The Abbess.

Akathist Hymn
to the All-Holy Theotokos, Chanted before Her Icon,
Which Is Known as The Abbess of Mount Athos

Kontakion I

Hymns of praise let us offer to the All-Holy Virgin Mary, the Theotokos, who was chosen from the foundation of the world, and truly gave birth in the flesh unto Jesus Christ, our Saviour and God. She is the Mistress of the universe, Who loved Christ exceedingly, and hath taken these holy monasteries under Her mighty protection. Do Thou, O our most honored Mother Abbess, preserve and save us from all enemies, visible and invisible, that we may cry to Thee:

> Rejoice, O All-Holy Virgin Theotokos, most honored
> Abbess of Athos, the Holy Mountain, and
> Orthodox monasteries throughout the world!

Ikos I

Angels in the flesh were all the venerable fathers and mothers, young men and virgins, who in ages past shone forth among the saints and sojourned in Orthodox manner to the habitations of heaven under the radiance of the precious and life-creating Cross of Christ, during their earthly course, amid the vale of tears and sorrows, under the mighty protection of the Mother of Christ our God, the most honorable Abbess of Orthodox monastic life. And to Her merciful aid let us joyfully cry out thus:

Rejoice, our most honorable Mother Abbess;
Rejoice, our hope of salvation!
Rejoice, preserver of Mount Athos;
Rejoice, Thou who savest the monks who dwell there!
Rejoice, gladness and glory of holy desert-dwellers;
Rejoice, divine bliss of holy hermits!
Rejoice, for through Thee are all the saints saved;
Rejoice, for by Thee is the universe adorned!
Rejoice, Thou who in God art the Mistress of countless worlds;
Rejoice, guide of those who inhabit the paradise of heaven!
Rejoice, good and glorious end of the life of all the saints;
Rejoice, holy stream of joy divine!
Rejoice, O All-Holy Virgin Theotokos, most honored Abbess of Athos, the Holy Mountain, and Orthodox monasteries throughout the world!

Kontakion II

Seeing how full of woe is the path toward salvation for all His saints, our Lord Jesus Christ blessed His Mother, the most honored Virgin Theotokos, to spread the divine mantle of Her abbacy over all the holy monasteries of Holy Mount Athos and of the whole world of Orthodox monastic salvation, that all who are being saved in holiness and sanctity, looking upon this with faith, may cry out unceasingly to God the Saviour: Alleluia!

Ikos II

Possessed of divine reason, all the venerable fathers and mothers have loved the glory of heaven with all their soul; and, hating the world and all its allurements, and trampling them underfoot, they have walked in the struggles of the saints, following Christ in the world of this life; and, gazing with love upon Her countenance in Her holy icons, with compunction they cry out thus:

Rejoice, Thou beginning of our salvation;
Rejoice, O our joy in this life and that which is to come!
Rejoice, wondrous founder of our holy monasteries;
Rejoice, loving Abbess of monastic communities!
Rejoice, blossom sprung forth from a divine shoot;
Rejoice, joy of the universal resurrection!
Rejoice, divine gladness of all the saints;
Rejoice, adornment of monasticism!
Rejoice, true Mother of our Saviour;
Rejoice, for Thou gavest birth in the flesh to the Vanquisher of hades!
Rejoice, for on Athos Thou didst plant a spiritual garden;
Rejoice, for Thou hast guided to salvation those who dwell there in holiness!
Rejoice, O All-Holy Virgin Theotokos, most honored Abbess of Athos, the Holy Mountain, and Orthodox monasteries throughout the world!

Kontakion III

The power of the Most High overshadoweth all who live in holiness, sanctity and righteousness, who have hated the vainglory of this world and fled to the holy monastic communities, and there, in the angelic habit, have taken upon themselves the easy yoke of Christ, struggling in holy manner. And throughout their life they cry out unceasingly to God, the all-holy Trinity: Alleluia!

Ikos III

They who are possessed of an ardent desire for salvation, all the assemblies of the venerable, who shine forth among the saints forever, and now undertake the struggles of salvation in the communities of the monastic life in lavras, monasteries, sketes, cœnobias, cells—and in every place throughout the world, having as a wondrous shield of salvation the divine abbacy of the Mother of God, chant unto Her in praise:

Rejoice, Thou who hast gathered us together in the

midst of this sinful world;
Rejoice, Thou who arrangest the salvation of our souls!
Rejoice, Thou who hast saved the whole generation of fallen Adam;
Rejoice, Thou who didst ineffably give birth to our Saviour and God!
Rejoice, O most honorable Nun, Thou model for all who are working out their salvation;
Rejoice, just Abbess of all of us who are struggling!
Rejoice, invincible champion leader of the Orthodox Faith;
Rejoice, divine and omnipotent might!
Rejoice, Mother of the Lord and of us, O Thou who art full of grace;
Rejoice, Thou who art right pleasing to all the saints!
Rejoice, portal of loving-kindness for the penitent;
Rejoice, hope of those who struggle toward God;
Rejoice, O All-Holy Virgin Theotokos, most honored Abbess of Athos, the Holy Mountain, and Orthodox monasteries throughout the world!

Kontakion IV

Leaving behind the tempest of sin-loving doubts, the venerable fathers and mothers came to love the thorny path of salvation, living amid tribulations and privations for the sake of the kingdom of heaven, adorning with their God-pleasing manner of life many places throughout the world, where, having founded holy communities of monastic salvation, wherein they work out their salvation, they ever chant to Christ our God the angelic hymn: Alleluia!

Ikos IV

The elect of heaven listened to the holy words of the Gospel of Christ, and spurning all the vanities of this world, they proceeded to the holy path, bearing the easy yoke of our Saviour in their life. In the flesh they imitated the holy angels, having an all-wondrous Abbess over all their holy communities, which shine like the stars of heaven throughout the whole world; and to Her they ever cry out:

    Rejoice, all-wise Abbess of Orthodox monasticism;
Rejoice, salvation of the people chosen by God!
Rejoice, tower of virginity and ocean of loving-kindness;
Rejoice, eternal joy of the bliss of paradise!
Rejoice, refuge of repentant sinners;
Rejoice, treasure of poor ascetics!
Rejoice, Thou who coverest the whole world with love;
Rejoice, Thou who with the glory of heaven dost cast Satan down into hell!
Rejoice, divine joy of angels and men;
Rejoice, for Thou hast caused the demons to weep forever!
Rejoice, only hope of the Orthodox Faith;
Rejoice, most glorious Mother of the Lord and of us!
Rejoice, O All-Holy Virgin Theotokos, most honored Abbess of Athos, the Holy Mountain, and Orthodox monasteries throughout the world!

Kontakion V

The righteous lived a godly life, and reached the heavenly homeland with joy, where they rejoice in the Lord with the holy angels for all ages. And we, their brethren, struggle in the holy communities, chanting hymns of praise to God: Alleluia!

Ikos V

The elect of the Lord perceived the quickly fleeting nature of the glory of this world: wealth is impermanent, happiness is transitory, while sorrows, griefs, despair, and all manner of misfortunes are the constant companions of this life, and in the end none can avoid the death of the body. Wherefore, they contemplated the eternal mansions, and loved the narrow and sorrowful path of monastic life, where the all-holy Mother of the Lord Himself is Abbess, guiding Her spiritual children, who are working out their salvation, and who cry out to Her in praise:

    Rejoice, only salvation of our souls;

Rejoice, consolation of paradise for all who sorrow!
Rejoice, enlightener of Athos, the Holy Mountain;
Rejoice, protectress of the whole world;
Rejoice, haven of hope for all who repent!
Rejoice, calm harbor against misfortunes for those working out their salvation;
Rejoice, foundress of the Lavra of the Caves;
Rejoice, defendress of the Lavra of Pochaev!
Rejoice, Abbess of the Lavra of Athanasius of Athos;
Rejoice, Christ's book of the testament of New Sion!
Rejoice, Thou who hast brought all the saints together;
Rejoice, Thou who hast shown the path of salvation to Orthodox Christians!
Rejoice, O All-Holy Virgin Theotokos, most honored Abbess of Athos, the Holy Mountain, and Orthodox monasteries throughout the world!

Kontakion VI

The venerable fathers were shown to be preachers of the rich, angelic way of life in the flesh: Anthony the Great, Pachomius, Macarius, Theodosius, and the other the venerable fathers and mothers, whose life the assemblies of all the venerable followed, becoming heirs to the mansions of paradise with all the saints; and we, now imitating them as we live in the angelic order, chant hymns of praise to the Saviour of the world: Alleluia! Alleluia! Alleluia!

Ikos VI

The model of the angelic life hath shone forth for all who seek salvation far from all the vanities of the world, through the example of Christ our God Himself and of His all-pure Mother, Mary, the Ever-virgin Theotokos, of John, the Forerunner of the Lord, and of the great multitude of the holy favorites of God, whose manner of life all the venerable imitate, and under the mighty guidance of the Mistress of the world, the most honorable Abbess of Orthodox monastic communities, Mary the Theotokos, who is praised thus by all the saints with all-wondrous laudations:

    Rejoice, Mother Abbess of Orthodox monasticism;
    Rejoice, eternal salvation of their angelic life!
    Rejoice, good guide to the path of the life of heaven;
    Rejoice, Superior of the monastic homeland!
    Rejoice, speedy defense of the orphaned;
    Rejoice, for Thou ever preparest crowns for the holy ascetics!
    Rejoice, Thou who lovest all the righteous;
    Rejoice, Thou who hast mercy on penitent sinners!
    Rejoice, for Thy love is like unto the love of God;
    Rejoice, for through Thee is all creation saved in the Lord!
    Rejoice, joy of divine gladness;
    Rejoice, protection and salvation of the whole world!
    Rejoice, O All-Holy Virgin Theotokos, most honored Abbess of Athos, the Holy Mountain, and Orthodox monasteries throughout the world!

Kontakion VII

When our Lord Jesus Christ desired to arrange well the path to heaven, He was well-pleased for His Mother to become Abbess over all the Orthodox monastic communities throughout the whole world, to guide to the heavenly habitation of paradise the assemblies of the elect, who seek salvation and chant unto God our Deliverer: Alleluia!

Ikos VII

The venerable fathers and mothers have shown forth a new life on the model of the life of the angels; for having forsaken the pleasures of the sinful world and loved to tread to heaven the path of Christ God, the King of glory, by the sufferings of the cross, they all became martyrs without shedding blood, enduring all manner of evils for the sake of the kingdom of God, which they have received; and now the companies of the venerable tread such paths, led by the Mother of God, as the most honored Abbess of their venerable life, whom they exalt supremely with praises, chanting:

> Rejoice, Mother of the Lord, the Judge most just;
> Rejoice, Thou who among abbesses art the one chosen before time began!
> Rejoice, Thou who hast surpassed creation in Thy purity of body;
> Rejoice, Thou who hast adorned the heavens with the holiness of Thy soul!
> Rejoice, glad tidings of the heavenly homeland;
> Rejoice, spiritual lily of Orthodox monasticism!
> Rejoice, earnest advocate for all the Orthodox;
> Rejoice, Thou who arrangest all things for the good for the holy elect!
> Rejoice, calm haven for all who are traveling;
> Rejoice, resting place for goodly old age!
> Rejoice, unwedded Bride;
> Rejoice, star of hope rising above the sea of life's misfortunes!
> Rejoice, O All-Holy Virgin Theotokos, most honored Abbess of Athos, the Holy Mountain, and Orthodox monasteries throughout the world!

Kontakion VIII

The chosen ones of God, possessed of a strange life, forsook the passions and pleasures of the body and loved the path of the sufferings of the cross in the wilderness, on islands, in clefts and defiles, in wooded glades, living angelically with wild beasts, where, by the will of God, they built monasteries, wherein they have, like the cherubim, chanted unto the Lord throughout their whole life: Alleluia!

Ikos VIII

Almighty God was wholly in the minds and hearts of His chosen favorites, glorifying His holy ones according to the saying, "Wondrous is God in His saints," gathering them in from the midst of the sinful world, making them to abide in the holy mansions, that His holy name may be praised by them with the holy angels forever; and the Mistress Theotokos, the most good Mother of the Lord, doth act as their Abbess with all wisdom, saving from tribulations and misfortunes those who humbly praise Her mercy, crying:

>Rejoice, Thou who art more honorable than all creation and the whole universe;
>Rejoice, Thou who, as the abode of God, art most sweet!
>Rejoice, holy protection of our life;
>Rejoice, divine source of sweetness most sweet!
>Rejoice, our whole hope of salvation, and our rest;
>Rejoice, our hope, after God, in this earthly life!
>Rejoice, for Thy Son and Lord hath risen;
>Rejoice, for He shall resurrect all flesh!
>Rejoice, Thou whom the armies of heaven do hymn;
>Rejoice, Thou who art praised by all the saints, as is meet!
>Rejoice, great joy of my salvation;
>Rejoice, divine consolation of the whole world!
>Rejoice, O All-Holy Virgin Theotokos, most honored Abbess of Athos, the Holy Mountain, and Orthodox monasteries throughout the world!

Kontakion IX

Disdaining all earthly-mindedness, the holy favorites of God showed themselves to be fools for Christ's sake, fleeing and wandering upon the earth, having nowhere received ought that is bodily. Let us imitate them in manner of life, struggle and love for the Lord, Whom we also praise, chanting like the angels: Alleluia!

Ikos IX

Eloquent speakers of the wisdom of the Lord were the venerable fathers shown to be: Pachomius the Great, Anthony the Great, Macarius of Egypt, and all who were first among Orthodox monks, who have shone forth among the saints; for by their holy and angelic way of life on earth and their words of salvation they have saved great multitudes of disciples, true servants of Christ, at the command of the all-holy Trinity, under the mighty abbacy of the Mistress Theotokos, whom with all their soul they ever praised thus:

> Rejoice, mighty Mistress of the whole world;
> Rejoice, Abbess of our salvation!
> Rejoice, most beloved Daughter of the God of our fathers;
> Rejoice, Thou who, for Thy holiness and humility, wast vouchsafed to become the Mother of the Son of God!
> Rejoice, all-beauteous palace of God the Holy Spirit;
> Rejoice, Thou who in heaven and on earth art most rich in love!
> Rejoice, Nun more honorable than the cherubim;
> Rejoice, Thou who, as Mother of God, art more exalted than the seraphim!
> Rejoice, most wise teaching of the apostles of Christ;
> Rejoice, justification of all the saints!
> Rejoice, our hope amid our earthly sojourns;
> Rejoice, Thou who gavest rise to the Expectation of the nations!
> Rejoice, O All-Holy Virgin Theotokos, most honored Abbess of Athos, the Holy Mountain, and Orthodox monasteries throughout the world!

Kontakion X

Desiring to save the human race, our Lord Jesus Christ came down from heaven to this vale of tears and sorrows, and in the sufferings of His divine life provided an example for all the saints who desire to attain everlasting rest, and who in holiness and righteousness praise Him, chanting with angelic voices: Alleluia!

Ikos X

Thou wast shown to be a rampart of divine might, O our most honorable Mother Abbess, preserving, saving and protecting all the holy communities of monastic life on Holy Mount Athos and throughout the world, from the dawn of the Christian Faith even unto the day of Christ's dread judgment, with divine mercy saving Thy venerable ones, who ever praise Thy compassions with such words as these:

> Rejoice, all-holy Mother Abbess;
> Rejoice, fountain of spiritual resurrection!
> Rejoice, Thou who protectest the whole world;
> Rejoice, Thou who dost gladden the Holy Church of Christ!
> Rejoice, glory and crown of the prophets;
> Rejoice, blessed end even for my life!
> Rejoice, Thou who are more comely than heaven and sweeter than paradise;
> Rejoice, example for the living of a holy life!
> Rejoice, Thou who lovest Athos, Thy portion;
> Rejoice, Thou who adornest Jerusalem and Sion!
> Rejoice, Mother of the kindly Judge;
> Rejoice, Thou who pourest forth streams of tears for the world!
> Rejoice, O All-Holy Virgin Theotokos, most honored Abbess of Athos, the Holy Mountain, and Orthodox monasteries throughout the world!

Kontakion XI

Most compunctionate hymnody do all the saints offer up in the heavenly habitations of paradise; and, giving praise with the holy angels, and supremely exalting the all-holy Trinity, they cry: "Holy, Holy, Holy!" And we Orthodox monastics, seeing this, unceasingly cry out to our God with faith: Alleluia!

Ikos XI

The assemblies of the venerable, who accepted the Light-receiving lamp of the Orthodox way of life with all the saints who have shone forth from ages past, and who in advance of us now tread the path to heaven, having as our omnipotent Mistress in the Lord the Mother of Emmanuel, their Abbess in the venerable life, cry out to Her with joy in praises, thus:

Rejoice, Thou who providest us with a model of humility;
Rejoice, Thou who dost gather us into the community of salvation!
Rejoice, Abbess of Athos, the Holy Mountain;
Rejoice, Superior of all the holy monasteries!
Rejoice, Nun most honorable in Thy way of life;
Rejoice, Thou who art most mighty in battles!
Rejoice, Thou who savest the living and the dead;
Rejoice, gracious Mother of orphans!
Rejoice, pleasing joy of all amid sorrows;
Rejoice, salvation of Orthodox Christians!
Rejoice, divine ocean of holy compassions;
Rejoice, unfathomable deep of loving-kindness!
Rejoice, O All-Holy Virgin Theotokos, most honored Abbess of Athos, the Holy Mountain, and Orthodox monasteries throughout the world!

Kontakion XII

Our all-sweet Saviour ever imparteth grace to all His holy servants who struggle in holiness and sanctity in the arena of this earthly life; for through the Orthodox Church hosts of Orthodox saints in the mansions of paradise already hymn the all-holy Trinity with all the hosts of heaven; and, imitating them, we also cry out to God Who is wondrous in the saints: Alleluia!

Ikos XII

Hymning all the Lord's mercies and compassions which ever rain down upon us, the unworthy monastics, and the most honorable abbacy of our most gracious Mistress Theotokos over all our communities, we are glad and rejoice in godly manner, as ones who have been vouchsafed to work out our salvation in those communities, where great multitudes of venerable ascetics have already reached the kingdom of heaven, by whose holy supplications may we also, by the mercy of God and under the holy protection of our heavenly Mother Abbess, attain unto the mansions of heaven for laudable works of salvation, chanting such words as these:

Rejoice, all-holy Virgin Theotokos;
Rejoice, Thou who dost assist our salvation!
Rejoice, most compassionate Abbess over all;
Rejoice, Thou who art first in holiness!
Rejoice, Thou who coverest the whole world with the protection of Thy mercy;
Rejoice, Thou who feedest orphans and strangers!
Rejoice, guide to chastity for the young;
Rejoice, O good one who grievest for all men!
Rejoice, gladness of the race of Adam our forefather;
Rejoice, calm harbor of salvation!
Rejoice, our most compassionate Mother Abbess;
Rejoice, good beginning and end of our hymnody!
Rejoice, O All-Holy Virgin Theotokos, most honored Abbess of Athos, the Holy Mountain, and Orthodox monasteries throughout the world!

Kontakion XIII

O our most hymned Mother Abbess, All-Glorious Mistress Theotokos! Accept these our entreaties, which are offered now to Thee with all our soul, and vouchsafe that in the angelic ranks we may attain unto the kingdom of heaven, where all saints, angels and men with never-ceasing voices sing in praise of God, the all-holy Trinity: Alleluia! Alleluia! Alleluia!

This Kontakion is recited thrice, whereupon Ikos I and Kontakion I are repeated.

Prayer to the All-Holy Theotokos, Before Her Icon Called "The Abbess of Mount Athos"

O All-Honored Mistress Theotokos, our most honored Mother Abbess of all Orthodox monasteries of monastic life, on Holy Mount Athos and throughout the whole world! Accept and bear to our most compassionate God our humble entreaty, that He save our souls by His grace. Look upon us with the eye of Thy loving-kindness, and in the Lord do Thou thyself effect our salvation, for without the mercy of our

Saviour and Thy holy mediation for us, we the wretched ones would not be able to work out our own salvation, for we have sullied our life in the vanities of the world. The time of Christ's harvest on the day of His dread judgment draweth nigh and is now at hand; but we, the accursed, are perishing in the abyss of sin because of our negligence, according to what hath been said by the holy fathers, the first to live the angelic life in the flesh: "The last monks will, in the negligence of their manner of life, be like worldly men." And this hath been fulfilled today; for in its manner of life our monasticism saileth upon the sea of life amid great tempests and adverse conditions, wherefore our holy communities languish in dust because of our sins. And if our most just Lord Jesus Christ would deem otherwise, we, the unworthy, would have no place to lay our heads. O our most sweet Mother Abbess! Gather us, the scattered flock of Christ, into one fold, and save all Orthodox Christians; vouchsafe the life of paradise with the angels and all the saints in the kingdom of Christ our God, to Whom be honor and glory, with His unoriginate Father and the all-holy, good and life-creating Spirit, unto the ages of ages. Amen.

Troparion Chanted to the All-Holy Theotokos, Before Her Icon Called "The Abbess of Mount Athos"

In Tone IV

O good one, intercession awesome and unashamed, most hymned Theotokos, O merciful Steward of the faithful, disdain not our supplications: make steadfast the Orthodox commonwealth; save our land, and defend all the Orthodox who dwell therein: for Thou gavest birth unto God, O only blessed one.

Akathist Hymn to the All-holy Theotokos in Honor of Her Wonder-working Icon "Assuage My Griefs"

Assuage My Griefs

Akathist Hymn
to the All-holy Theotokos
in Honor of Her Wonder-working Icon
"Assuage My Griefs"
*Which the Holy Church Doth Celebrate
on the 25th of January*

Kontakion I

Thy precious image, O all-blessed Virgin Mistress and Theotokos, hath been given unto us as a victorious and wondrous deliverance; for gazing upon it, we Thy servants, who have been delivered from evils by its appearance, send up to thee hymns of thanksgiving, O Theotokos. As Thou art possessed of invincible might, free us from all misfortunes, that we may cry unto Thee:

>Rejoice, O our joy! Deliver us from every evil and assuage our griefs!

Ikos I

The multitude of angels and all the armies of heaven glorify Thee, the Theotokos and Queen of all, for Thou hast filled our souls with joy by mercifully revealing to us Thy holy image, O divinely chosen Virgin Mistress; and bowing down before it, we send up to thee compunctionate entreaties, crying out to Thy loving aid with fear such things as these:

>Rejoice, Thou who art the blessing of the unoriginate Father;
>Rejoice, Thou who art the dwelling-place of the preternal Son!

Rejoice, abode of the Holy Spirit;
Rejoice, for the many-eyed cherubim glorify Thee!
Rejoice, for the six-winged seraphim offer praises unto Thee;
Rejoice, for all the armies of heaven magnify Thee!
Rejoice, for all the tribes of the earth confess Thee to be the Mother of God;
Rejoice, for through Thee is the whole world filled with gladness!
Rejoice, for by Thee are all our pangs healed;
Rejoice, for through Thy supplications are our griefs assuaged!
Rejoice, for by Thy mediation are our petitions fulfilled;
Rejoice, for before Thee and Thy Son do we bow down in thanks before Thy precious icon!
Rejoice, O our joy! Deliver us from every evil and assuage our griefs!

Kontakion II

All the hosts of heaven behold Thee, O divinely chosen Maiden, standing ever before the throne of the glory of the King of heaven, and praying for Christians to Thy Son and God, O Queen of heaven; and we sinners, beholding Thy holy icon on earth, and falling down before it, worship Thee with joy, crying aloud: Alleluia!

Ikos II

Grant us understanding, O our most ardent intercessor; for how can we hymn Thy name with defiled mouths? Yet Thou art the mediatress of good things for us, and hast the might to aid us in whatsoever we require help, that with compunction we may cry out to Thee thus:

Rejoice, Thou who offerest up for us supplications to Thy Son and God for our consolation;
Rejoice, Thou who by Thy prayers dost deliver our eyes from everlasting lamentation!

Rejoice, Thou who by Thy maternal entreaties dost move Thy Son and God to have mercy on us;
Rejoice, Thou who by Thy pleas dost soften the righteous anger of God which is against us!
Rejoice, Thou who by Thy mediations dost win forgiveness for our sins;
Rejoice, Thou who with Thine aid dost destroy our passions!
Rejoice, Thou who by Thine intercession dost do away with our fleeting sorrows;
Rejoice, Thou who dost help us amid all misfortunes and needs!
Rejoice, Thou who dost ever glorify those who glorify thee;
Rejoice, Thou who by Thy joy dost assuage our griefs!
Rejoice, Thou who givest us unceasing gladness;
Rejoice, Thou who openest unto us the gates of paradise!
Rejoice, O our joy! Deliver us from every evil and assuage our griefs!

Kontakion III

The power of the Most High overshadowed Thee, for the speedy and fervent aid of those who have recourse unto Thee with faith and who bow down before Thy precious image; for unto Thee alone, the incorrupt and all-pure Mother of God, hath been given the gift to fulfill our every good petition, and Thou alone art able to help us as much as Thou desirest. Wherefore, people of every age glorify Thy Son and our God, crying: Alleluia!

Ikos III

Possessing an inexhaustible wealth of loving kindness, Thou extendest a helping hand to all the ends of the world, and impartest healing to the sick, relief to the suffering, and sight to the blind; and for everyone Thou fulfillest all things in accordance with their need. And in thanksgiving we chant unto Thee:

Rejoice, O only Mother, who showest us loving kindness;

Rejoice, priceless treasure of mercy revealed to us!

Rejoice, Thou who grantest countless compassions unto all;

Rejoice, Thou who givest words of wisdom unto those who ask!

Rejoice, Thou who impartest quickness of mind unto the young;

Rejoice, Thou who takest away the wounds of our sins!

Rejoice, Thou who dost establish the righteous in the mansions of paradise;

Rejoice, hope of good things to come and strengthening of the desperate!

Rejoice, Thou who dost quickly restore all the fallen to grace;

Rejoice, Thou who dost help all in everything wherein they require Thine aid!

Rejoice, Thou who with Thy precious omophorion dost shield us from all harm;

Rejoice, Thou who with Thy glorious robe dost shelter us from the storms of life!

Rejoice, O our joy! Deliver us from every evil and assuage our griefs!

Kontakion IV

O Queen of heaven, Thou dost ever help us who are beset by the tempest of many misfortunes, who have recourse unto Thee with faith and bow down before Thy healing icon, concerning the prototype whereof Thou didst once say: "My grace and power is with this image!" And we truly believe that Thou wilt hearken unto the petitions of those who call upon Thy holy name and cry out to Thy Son: Alleluia!

Ikos IV

In heaven the Lord hath hearkened to Thy mediation concerning us, O chosen palace of the Holy Spirit, and fulfilleth Thy petitions; and we sinners on earth, perceiving Thy holy icon to be a radiant sun shining upon us, dare to say unto Thee, as the Mother of God:

Rejoice, Thou who revealest the noetic Sun to us;

Rejoice, Thou who dost illumine us with never-fading light!

Rejoice, Thou who givest life to us who have been slain by our sins;

Rejoice, Thou who looseth the wombs of barren wives!

Rejoice, Thou who dost quickly drive away the wicked enemies who assail us without warning;

Rejoice, Thou who dost ever delight us with the good things we desire!

Rejoice, Thou who dost speedily comfort us amid misfortunes and griefs;

Rejoice, Thou who dost save from sudden death those who with faith call upon Thy name!

Rejoice, Thou who givest never-ending life unto those who trust in Thee;

Rejoice, Thou who liftest up to heaven those who have faith in and love for Thee!

Rejoice, O our mighty intercession;

Rejoice, Thou who dost defend us amid every evil circumstance!

Rejoice, O our joy! Deliver us from every evil and assuage our griefs!

Kontakion V

O Mistress of the world, Thou hast shown us Thy holy icon as a divinely moving star, and gazing upon it and praying to Thee with heartfelt faith, O Theotokos, we say: Thou art an invincible shield and an unassailable rampart for us who cry out to Thee: Alleluia!

Ikos V

The hosts of heaven saw in Thine arms Him Who fashioned men with His own hands, and understand Him to be the Master; and we sinners on earth, gazing upon the depiction of Thee, His Mother, lovingly extending Thy hands to us, say unto Thee with compunction:

> Rejoice, Thou who without being burned dost hold in thine arms the divine Fire whereby our sins are utterly consumed;
> Rejoice, Thou who didst bear in Thine arms the intangible Light whereby our souls are illumined!
> Rejoice, Thou who dost vanquish our enemies, visible and invisible;
> Rejoice, Thou who showest us love and kindness!
> Rejoice, Thou who liftest up Thy hands to God in surety for us;
> Rejoice, Thou who openest unto us the entry into the kingdom of heaven!
> Rejoice, Thou who defendest us with Thine aid;
> Rejoice, Thou who by Thy mediation dost obtain forgiveness of our sins!
> Rejoice, Thou who by Thine entreaty dost assuage our griefs;
> Rejoice, for through Thine intercession we delight in every good thing!
> Rejoice, for through Thee are all our desires for the good fulfilled;
> Rejoice, polar star guiding to safe harbor those who sail the stormy sea of life!
> Rejoice, O our joy! Deliver us from every evil and assuage our griefs!

Kontakion VI

When after the ascension of the Lord the God-bearing preachers and apostles consecrated Thy temple, they found Thine image on the wall, depicted in paints by an invisible hand, O Mistress, and chanted unto God Who was born of Thee: Alleluia!

Ikos VI

Thou didst shine forth in wisdom from the true Sun of righteousness, O divinely chosen Maiden, and emitting rays of the true knowledge of God, Thou dost thereby illumine all who confess Thee to be the true Mother of God, and cry out thus:

> Rejoice, Thou who dost enlighten all in heaven with Thy glory;
> Rejoice, Thou who makest the beginning of the salvation of men!
> Rejoice, ark of our life, preserving us from the deluge of death;
> Rejoice, Thou who grantest us an abode in the mansions of paradise!
> Rejoice, O our intercessor before God, who savest the world;
> Rejoice, Thou who dost quickly help those who find themselves in misfortunes!
> Rejoice, Thou who healest men's sicknesses of body and soul;
> Rejoice, Thou who openest the mouths of the mute and those with impediments of speech!
> Rejoice, giver of every good thing unto those who ask of Thee;
> Rejoice, Thou who pourest forth upon all the teaching of grace!
> Rejoice, Thou who dost thereby greatly delight those of every rank and age;
> Rejoice, Thou who fulfillest the good desires of all!
> Rejoice, O our joy! Deliver us from every evil and assuage our griefs!

Kontakion VII

The long-suffering Lord Who seest all things, desiring to reveal His love for mankind and the abyss of His compassions, chose Thee to be His mother, O inexhaustible wellspring of mercy, that even when someone is deserving of condemnation by the righteous judgment of God, he may be preserved by Thine omnipotent mediation, and may cry aloud to Thy Son and our God: Alleluia!

Ikos VII

In Thine all-pure Mother, O Lord, Thou hast shown forth Thy works as wondrous, and hast given us Her wondrous icon, which more than the rays of the sun enlighteneth the people who gaze upon it as upon the Theotokos Herself, and with heartfelt faith and love cry out from the depths of their souls such things as these:

Rejoice, Thou who for all leavest thine icon on earth like a cloud;

Rejoice, Thou who through it dost reveal to us Thy loving help which is past hope!

Rejoice, Thou who through thine icon dost pour forth springs of miracles everywhere;

Rejoice, Thou who dost enlighten all the people by the appearance of thine icon!

Rejoice, Thou who thereby revealest a new sign of grace in the Church;

Rejoice, for gazing upon Thine icon, we venerate Thee, who art in very truth the Theotokos!

Rejoice, Thou who by thine icon, as by a pillar of fire, dost dispel the gloom of sin;

Rejoice, Thou who dost thereby assuage our griefs!

Rejoice, Thou who dost sanctify the Church by its appearance;

Rejoice, for we sinners are preserved by Thine aid!

Rejoice, Thou who rendest asunder the sackcloth of our sorrow;

Rejoice, Thou who dost clothe us in everlasting joy!

Rejoice, O our joy! Deliver us from every evil and assuage our griefs!

Kontakion VIII

Thy holy icon, strange and all-glorious, which appeared in the church, did the angels hymn, the apostles glorify, and the choir of holy hierarchs venerate; and we sinners, falling down, await Thy great and rich mercy, crying out with gladness: Alleluia!

Ikos VIII

The Lord Who hath dominion over all above and all below, seeing thee, His Mother, ever standing before Him and with compunction offering entreaty unto Him for us sinners, hath promised to fulfil all Thy petitions; and we sinners, trusting in Thy maternal prayers for us, thus offer thee hymns of thanksgiving:

> Rejoice, Thou who reignest eternally with Thy Son and God;
> Rejoice, Thou who ever offerest to Him supplications in our behalf!
> Rejoice, Thou who with Thy mercy dost cover all who have recourse unto thee;
> Rejoice, joy of all, who dost assuage our griefs!
> Rejoice, Thou who hast accomplished our reconciliation with God;
> Rejoice, Thou who hast united God and man!
> Rejoice, Thou who hast arranged the salvation of man;
> Rejoice, Thou who hast annulled the curse of our first parents' sin!
> Rejoice, Thou who hast enlightened our mortal nature with immortality;
> Rejoice, Thou who hast melted the hardness of our hearts!
> Rejoice, Thou who leadest the despairing up to God;
> Rejoice, Thou who hast broken the vessels of death prepared for us!
> Rejoice, O our joy! Deliver us from every evil and assuage our griefs!

Kontakion IX

All of angelic nature offereth hymns of praise unto thee, The Mother of God and helper of all who fall down before Thee and ask Thine aid, for with Thy steadfast and mighty intercession Thou dost gladden the righteous, and Thou dost help sinners, deliver from misfortunes, assuage griefs, and pray for all who cry out with faith: Alleluia!

Ikos IX

Like mute fish the most eloquent of orators are at a loss how to praise the glorious feast of Thine icon, O Mistress; and neither are the praises we offer Thee from defiled lips worthy. Yet seeing the innumerable benefactions revealed to us through Thine icon, rejoicing in soul and heart we say unto Thee:

>Rejoice, Thou who freest us from hunger with the Bread of life;
>Rejoice, Thou who with immortality dost protect us from deadly pestilence!
>Rejoice, Thou who keepest us safe from the earthquake of sin;
>Rejoice, Thou who by Thy mighty hand dost deliver us from the deluge of death!
>Rejoice, Thou who dost rescue us from fire with the dew of Thy prayers;
>Rejoice, Thou who by Thine intercession dost defend us from tribulations!
>Rejoice, Thou who by Thy power dost preserve us from the sword;
>Rejoice, Thou who savest us from the invasion of aliens!
>Rejoice, Thou who with true peace dost keep us safe from civil strife;
>Rejoice, Thou who healest from deadly wounds those who have recourse unto thee!
>Rejoice, Thou who by Thine entreaty dost free us from the righteous threat of God which impendeth over us;

Rejoice, Thou who by thine honored mediation dost remove us from every plague!

Rejoice, O our joy! Deliver us from every evil and assuage our griefs!

Kontakion X

Desiring to save the human race from the deception of the enemy, the Lord Who loveth mankind gave Thee, His Mother, as a help to mortals, saying: "Behold, let My Mother be a protection and refuge for you, consolation for the grieving, joy for the sorrowful, and a helper for the oppressed, that She may raise up all from the depths of sin who cry out: Alleluia!

Ikos X

O heavenly King, the Queen of heaven doth ever pray for us thus: "Accept every man who glorifieth Thee and calleth upon Thy name, and wheresoever the memory of Thy holy name shall be, and where there are those who glorify me for the sake of Thy name, turn them not away from Thy face, but let Thy goodwill abide in them, and accept their every petition, and deliver them all from misfortunes." And we sinners, trusting in Her maternal supplications, say thus:

Rejoice, for Thou art our fervent advocate before God;

Rejoice, for Thy maternal supplication can do much to move the Master to mercy!

Rejoice, hope of the despairing, who dost assuage their griefs;

Rejoice, Thou who by Thy grace dost illumine our unworthiness!

Rejoice, Thou who dost cleanse our defilement by Thy purity;

Rejoice, Thou who by Thy sweet fragrance dost send our entreaties aloft!

Rejoice, Thou who transformest our corruptible clay into incorruption;

Rejoice, Thou who makest our weakness steadfast!

Rejoice, Thou who healest all our ailments of body and soul;

Rejoice, Thou who quickly dispellest the cloud of passions, tribulations and griefs which beset us!

Rejoice, Thou who by Thy mighty entreaty dost grant all things profitable;

Rejoice, Thou who stillest the raging billows which batter the ship of our souls!

Rejoice, O our joy! Deliver us from every evil and assuage our griefs!

Kontakion XI

Accept from us this most compunctionate hymnody, O Queen of heaven, and hearken unto the supplication offered unto Thee, O Virgin Theotokos; for unto Thee do we flee amid perils, tribulations and griefs, and before Thee do we pour forth our tears amid our misfortunes; and we pray: Assuage Thou our griefs, and accept this sacrifice from Thy servants, who cry out: Alleluia!

Ikos XI

Having appeared as the Light-receiving lamp of the true Light of those on earth, Thou dost enlighten those who honor the appearance of thine icon, and guidest to divine knowledge those who hymn Thee thus:

Rejoice, inextinguishable lamp of the immaterial Fire, who enlightenest us;

Rejoice, ray of the never-waning divine Light, who illuminest us!

Rejoice, sun of righteousness who sheddest light upon us;

Rejoice, Thou who pourest forth upon us a wellspring of the life of paradise!

Rejoice, Mother of the true Light, who enlightenest the souls of the pious;

Rejoice, Mother of the God of all, who dost comfort the souls of all the oppressed!

Rejoice, Thou who savest those who call upon Thee and
glorify Thy name;
Rejoice, Thou who grantest an unashamed end of life
unto those who hope on Thee!
Rejoice, Thou who dost unceasingly help those who
honor Thee as the Mother of God and call Thee
the Theotokos;
Rejoice, Thou who by the overshadowing of Thy holy
icon dost drive from us the phantasies of the
evil spirits!
Rejoice, Thou who dost speedily console us amid the
tribulations and griefs which assail us unawares;
Rejoice, Thou who givest joy to all the world!
Rejoice, O our joy! Deliver us from every evil and assuage our griefs!

Kontakion XII

Ask divine grace for us of the heavenly Master, Thy Son and God, and extend unto us a helping hand; and by Thy supplications assuage our griefs. Protect us beneath the shelter of Thy wings, drive away from us every enemy and adversary, and bring peace to our life, lest we perish evilly. And accept us into the everlasting mansions, O our intercessor, that, rejoicing, we may say to Thee: Alleluia!

Ikos XII

Hymning Thee, our mighty helper, we praise Thee; and praying to Thee with compunction, we belief and confess that Thou wilt ask good things, both temporal and everlasting, for those who chant unto Thee:

Rejoice, Thou who by Thy supplications dost save the
whole world;
Rejoice, Thou who helpest the whole world by Thy
mediation!
Rejoice, Thou who hast granted victory over barbarians
to the Orthodox;

Rejoice, Thou who dost vanquish assaults by aliens
  against Christians!
Rejoice, Thou who dost maintain the pious in the Faith;
Rejoice, Thou who blowest away, like dust from the face
  of the earth, those who disdain to venerate Thy
  holy icons!
Rejoice, Thou who dost speedily help those who venerate thine icon, who call upon Thee for help, and
  languish amid griefs;
Rejoice, Thou who guidest us sinners to salvation and
  the acquisition of everlasting good things!
Rejoice, Thou who dost ask that all of us reign with Thy
  Son and our God eternally;
Rejoice, Thou who dost impart never-ending life to the
  faithful!
Rejoice, Thou who grantest unto all everything good
  and profitable amid every necessity;
Rejoice, coffer overflowing with the gifts of God's grace!
Rejoice, O our joy! Deliver us from every evil and assuage our griefs!

Kontakion XIII

O most hymned Mother, Queen and Mistress of heaven, Virgin Theotokos, who gavest birth to the Word Who is holier than all the holy! Accept our present entreaty, assuage our grief, and deliver us from all perils, misfortunes, tribulations and eternal damnation; rescue us from the torment which is to come, and vouchsafe that we, Thy servants, may dwell in the eternal habitations of paradise, who cry: Alleluia! Alleluia! Alleluia!

This Kontakion is recited thrice; whereupon Ikos I and Kontakion I are repeated.

Prayer to the All-holy Theotokos, Recited before Her Precious Icon "Assuage My Griefs"

O all-pure Virgin, Mistress Theotokos, our consolation, Thou hope of all the ends of the earth! Disdain not us sinners, for we trust in Thy mercy. Quench Thou the flame of sin which burneth within us, and bedew our desiccated hearts with repentance. Cleanse our minds of sinful thoughts, and accept our entreaties, which are offered unto thee with sighing from the depths of our hearts and souls. Be Thou a mediator for us before Thy Son and God, and avert His wrath with Thy maternal supplications. Heal Thou our wounds of body and soul, O Lady and Mistress; still Thou the tempest of the evil assaults of the enemy; lift the burden of our sins, and leave us not to perish utterly. Comfort the hearts of us who are crushed by grief, that we may glorify Thee unto our last breath. Amen.

Akathist Hymn
Chanted before the Icon of the Theotokos
"The Deliverance of Those Who Suffer from Misfortunes"

The Deliverance from Misfortunes

Akathist Hymn
Chanted before the Icon of the Theotokos "The Deliverance of Those Who Suffer from Misfortunes"
Which the Holy Church Celebrates on the Sunday of All Saints

Kontakion I

Do battle against our enemies, who seek to do us harm and to separate us from our Lord; and teach us to chant unto Thee with gladness:

> Rejoice, deliverance of us who suffer woes, destruction and misfortunes!

Ikos I

At Thy command, O our Mother, the multitude of angels array themselves awesomely for our deliverance; wherefore, accept this supplication:

> Rejoice, Thou who sendest the angels for our salvation;
> Rejoice, Queen of the hosts on high, who givest us their heavenly aid!
> Rejoice, Thou who commandest the angels to protect us;
> Rejoice, Thou who by the angelic army dost rout our enemies!
> Rejoice, deliverance of us who suffer woes, destruction and misfortunes!

Kontakion II

Beholding the great help Thou grantest unto those who call upon Thee with all their heart, those beset by misfortunes are led to chant unceasingly to Thy Son: Alleluia!

Ikos II

Many understand that Thy Son hath given Thee as the deliverance of those who suffer misfortunes, unto those who call upon Thee thus:

> Rejoice, Mother of the unfortunate;
> Rejoice, comfort of the suffering!
> Rejoice, hope of the hopeless;
> Rejoice, help of the helpless!
> Rejoice, deliverance of us who suffer woes, destruction
>   and misfortunes!

Kontakion III

The power of the Most High hath granted Thee as help and salvation unto the world which is perishing amid misfortunes. And he who hath been delivered by Thee chanteth to Thy Son: Alleluia!

Ikos III

Possessed of unapproachable love for the human race, whose tears Thou hast never rejected, it is not by constraint that Thou hast moved it to call upon Thee, crying:

> Rejoice, Thou who speedily hearkenest to those in
>   tribulation;
> Rejoice, liberation of captives!
> Rejoice, swift salvation of the perishing;
> Rejoice, consolation of the grieving and sorrowful!
> Rejoice, deliverance of us who suffer woes, destruction
>   and misfortunes!

The Deliverance of Those Who Suffer from Misfortunes

Kontakion IV

A tempest of misfortunes descendeth upon us. Save us who are perishing! Save us, O deliverance of those who suffer from misfortunes, crushing the destructive storm down to the earth and accepting our hymn: Alleluia!

Ikos IV

Hearing of all Thy wondrous love for Christians and Thy mighty deliverance from all the griefs which assail us, the generations of men have learned to chant unto Thee:

>Rejoice, deliverance of the human race from misfortunes;
>Rejoice, Thou who drivest despondency away!
>Rejoice, Thou who stillest the tempests of life;
>Rejoice, Thou who givest us joy after sorrow!
>Rejoice, deliverance of us who suffer woes, destruction and misfortunes!

Kontakion V

Like unto a divinely guided star, Thou drivest away the darkness and gloom from sin-loving hearts, that they may behold the Lord in the light of Thy love and cry unto Him: Alleluia!

Ikos V

Seeing in Thee unexpected deliverance from multifarious misfortunes, the people of Russia joyfully chant thus:

>Rejoice, Thou who dost rescue us from amid our misfortunes;
>Rejoice, Thou who dispellest our griefs;
>Rejoice, consolation amid our sorrows;
>Rejoice, restraint amid our joys!
>Rejoice, deliverance of us who suffer woes, destruction and misfortunes!

Kontakion VI

All who have been healed, comforted, justified, and saved by Thee from misfortunes, proclaim Thine aid and love, O Mother, and chant unto Thine exalted and mighty Son: Alleluia!

Ikos VI

Thou hast shone forth upon us the light of salvation amid the darkness of perdition which surroundeth us, and hast led us to chant unto Thee:

> Rejoice, Thou who liftest the pall of sin;
> Rejoice, Thou who hast driven away the darkness of sin!
> Rejoice, Thou who enlightenest the gloom of my soul;
> Rejoice, Thou who dost illumine my soul with the light of joy!
> Rejoice, deliverance of us who suffer woes, destruction and misfortunes!

Kontakion VII

When we were assailed by misfortunes on every side and were about to give ourselves over to utter despair, we thought of Thee, the deliverance of the suffering from misfortunes, and we took heart and were comforted, chanting to Thy Son: Alleluia!

Ikos VII

New and unexpected mercy hast Thou shown us, taking us under Thy mighty arm; wherefore, we cry out to Thee:

> Rejoice, mighty Queen;
> Rejoice, Thou who hast taken us under Thy dominion!
> Rejoice, Thou who hast given us defense;
> Rejoice, repelling of our enemies!
> Rejoice, deliverance of us who suffer woes, destruction and misfortunes!

Kontakion VIII

O strange wonder! Those condemned to destruction, the countless ones who suffer want, suddenly receive salvation and deliverance from Thee, the all-loving Mother, chanting unto God: Alleluia!

Ikos VIII

All ye who find yourselves amid the darkness of tribulations, all ye who are tempest-tossed by storms of woes, come to the good harbor, our help, the protection of the Virgin, Who is the deliverance of those who suffer misfortunes; and let us cry out to Her:

>Rejoice, Thou who deliverest us from starvation;
>Rejoice, Thou who fendest harmful nature off from the corrupt world!
>Rejoice, Thou who savest crops, forests and all plants from destruction;
>Rejoice, comfort and blessed joy of suffering husbandmen!
>Rejoice, deliverance of us who suffer woes, destruction and misfortunes!

Kontakion IX

The whole human race praiseth thee, all hymn Thee, who bringest multifarious deliverance to it, and givest joy instead of griefs unto those who chant: Alleluia!

Ikos IX

Rhetors and great intellects become as fools when they see the speedy and miraculous deliverance Thou givest to those suffering misfortunes; and they fall silent before us, who chant unto Thee:

>Rejoice, Thou who strengthenest us by miracles;
>Rejoice, Thou who dispellest misfortunes by Thy wonders!

Rejoice, Thou who bringest us to our senses by miracles;
Rejoice, Thou who by Thine icon hast brought us
gladness!
Rejoice, deliverance of us who suffer woes, destruction
and misfortunes!

Kontakion X

Desiring to save each human soul, Thou carest for it with love until Thou teachest it to chant unto Thy Son: Alleluia!

Ikos X

Thine image, "The Deliverance of Those Suffering from Misfortunes," hath been found and shown to be a bulwark protecting the Christian world and every soul from enemies, that we may glorify it and bow down and flee to Thy help, O Mother of God, chanting:

Rejoice, our deliverer;
Rejoice, our guide!
Rejoice, our gladness;
Rejoice, our everlasting joy!
Rejoice, deliverance of us who suffer woes, destruction
and misfortunes!

Kontakion XI

Those delivered by Thee, and who through Thee have again found joy, offer Thee unceasing hymnody, and chant with joy to Thy divine Son: Alleluia!

Ikos XI

Thine icon, "The Deliverance of Those Who Suffer from Misfortunes," hath been revealed to us as a radiant beacon shining with light amid the darkness of sin; wherefore, having Thy wondrous icon in our temple as surety of Thy good will toward us and our community, and trusting in Thy maternal supplications and that they will be speedily heard, we sinners rejoice and say with compunction:

Rejoice, fountain of joys;
Rejoice, dispelling of griefs!
Rejoice, lessening of misfortunes;
Rejoice, bestower of all rest!
Rejoice, deliverance of us who suffer woes, destruction
    and misfortunes!

Kontakion XII

The grace which floweth from Thine icon, "The Deliverance of Those Who Suffer from Misfortunes," which emitteth streams of healings in abundance and enliveneth our hearts with gladness, O Mother, moveth all to Thy Son and God of their own will: Alleluia!

Ikos XII

We hymn the wondrous restoration of Thine icon; we hymn Thy merciful care for us sinners; and lifting our voices in song, we chant:

Rejoice, Thou who dost rescue us from death and ever-
    lasting fire;
Rejoice, Thou who dost resurrect the dead!
Rejoice, our hope and defense before death;
Rejoice, our repose after death!
Rejoice, deliverance of us who suffer woes, destruction
    and misfortunes!

Kontakion XIII

O our most hymned, most belovèd Mother, take pity now and have mercy upon us, who find ourselves amid grievous and inescapable misfortunes; and teach us with all our heart to chant unto God, Who alone delivereth and saveth us: Alleluia! Alleluia! Alleluia!

This Kontakion is recited thrice, whereupon Ikos I and Kontakion I are repeated.

Prayer to the All-Holy Theotokos

O Mother of God, our help and defense! When we are in need, be Thou a deliverance for us who are suffering and perishing from grievous misfortunes; for in Thee do we hope, and with all our soul do we ever call upon thee: Take pity and help us, be merciful and deliver us, who are suffering and perishing, from misfortunes; rescue us from the wretched snares of the evil one; incline Thine ear, and accept our tearful and sorrowful entreaties; and as Thou willest, grant rest and joy unto us. Teach us to offer obedience to the Lord God, and with all our heart, all our soul and all our being to love Thy Son and to offer to Him the worthy fruits of our labors. Grant peace to our hearts, that in the one Spirit and with all our works we may glorify the unoriginate Father, His only-begotten Son and His all-holy, good and life-creating Spirit, and Thy merciful maternal intercession, now and ever, and unto the ages of ages. Amen.

Troparion, in Tone IV

Like an all-radiant star hath Thy holy image shone forth with divine miracles, emitting grace and Thy lovingkindness amid the night of tribulations; wherefore, O most good Virgin, deliverance of those who suffer from misfortunes, grant also unto us the healing of infirmities of soul and body, salvation and great mercy.

Kontakion, in Tone VIII

Delivered from evils by Thine aid, those who are afflicted hasten to Thine icon with love, O all-holy Lady. As the Mother of Christ God, free us also from grievous circumstances, transitory and everlasting, that we may cry out unto Thee: Rejoice, deliverance of all who suffer from misfortunes!

Akathist
To The Most Holy Theotokos
In Honor Of Her Wonderworking Icon Known As
"The Inexhaustible Cup"

The Inexhaustible Cup

Akathist
To The Most Holy Theotokos
In Honor Of Her Wonderworking Icon Known As
"The Inexhaustible Cup"
Which the Holy Church Celebrates on May 5th

Kontakion I

A chosen and marvelous deliverance has been given to us: Thine honorable image, O Sovereign Lady Theotokos, for having been delivered from ills of soul and body and from grievous adversities by its appearance, we offer Thee our thankful praise, O all-merciful Protectress. But do Thou, O Sovereign Lady, whom we call "The Inexhaustible Cup," incline Thy compassion to our sighing and heartfelt crying, and grant deliverance to those who suffer from the disease of drunkenness, that with faith we may cry out to Thee: "Rejoice, O Sovereign Lady, Inexhaustible Cup that quenchest our spiritual thirst!"

Ikos II

Angelic hosts and multitudes of the righteous glorify Thee without ceasing, O Theotokos, Queen of all, the mediatress for the greatly sinful Christian race which hath wallowed in lawlessness and remaineth in sins, for it is unto consolation and salvation that Thou grantest us Thy mercy through Thy miraculous icons many in name, which we behold like the stars of heaven throughout all our land. Falling down before one of these, named the Inexhaustible Cup, from the depth of our heart we cry to Thee:

Rejoice, dwelling-place of the unapproachable Godhead!
Rejoice, constant wonder to people!
Rejoice, Thou who cleansest our sins through afflictions!
Rejoice, Thou who healest our infirmities through our sorrows!
Rejoice, Thou who sendest us Thy mercy from on high through Thy wonderworking icons!
Rejoice, Thou who dost gladden our grieving hearts through their appearance!
Rejoice, most wondrous reconciliation for all with God!
Rejoice, redemption from eternal Gehenna!
Rejoice, O Sovereign Lady, Inexhaustible Cup that quenchest our spiritual thirst!

Kontakion II

On seeing the heartfelt sorrow and spiritual torment of people possessed by the destructive vice of drunkenness, and also their true repentance, Thou hast willed, O most holy Sovereign Lady, to show Thy mercy to the God-saved city of Serpoukhov by the appearance of Thy miraculous image "The Inexhaustible Cup," that all who fall down before it with faith and a contrite heart, on receiving healing from their grievous illness, may cry to God from the depth of their soul: Alleluia!

Ikos II

Having understood the meaning of the threefold apparition of St. Barlaam and his command to go to the God-saved city of Serpoukhov, a certain man, possessed by the passion of drunkenness, found in a monastery there Thy holy icon called "The Inexhaustible Cup." And we, seeing such concern bestowed on us sinners, with reverence cry out to Thee:

Rejoice, Thou who through pious people dost reveal to us sinners the glory of Thy wonders!
Rejoice, clairvoyant guide who showest them the way of salvation!
Rejoice, our all-good teacher, who dost draw us by Thy love!

Rejoice, Thou who dost teach us gratitude for Thy great benevolence!
Rejoice, Thou who dost turn our sorrow into joy!
Rejoice, Thou who dost gladden us with hope beyond doubt!
Rejoice, Thou who dost destroy our destructive passions!
Rejoice, Thou who dost further good intentions!
Rejoice, O Sovereign Lady, Inexhaustible Cup that quenchest our spiritual thirst!

Kontakion III

The power of the Most High and the Grace of the Sovereign Lady strengthened a certain man suffering from the disease of drunkenness, when he, having paralyzed legs, set out for the city of Serpoukhov in obedience to a command of the Mother of God, given to him by St. Barlaam. And having arrived in this city, he found the icon of the most pure Mother of God, and straightway was healed of the sickness of his soul and body, and from the depth of his soul gratefully he cried unto God: Alleluia!

Ikos III

Having an ever-flowing fountain, an inexhaustible cup of heavenly gifts, not only the people of the city of Serpoukhov, but also all Orthodox Christians of other cities and villages who hasten to Thy most wondrous icon, "The Inexhaustible Cup," and have received healing before it, falling down, with grateful lips cry out to Thee:

Rejoice, font in which all our sorrows are drowned!
Rejoice, cup by which we shall receive the joy of our salvation!
Rejoice, Thou who healest our spiritual and bodily infirmities!
Rejoice, Thou who tamest our passions by the power of Thy prayers!
Rejoice, Thou who grantest what is profitable to whosoever asketh in all kind of need!

Rejoice, Thou who bestowest upon all countless
  compassions!
Rejoice, Thou who openest for us the treasury of mercy!
Rejoice, Thou who showest compassion to the fallen!
Rejoice, O Sovereign Lady, Inexhaustible Cup that
  quenchest our spiritual thirst!

Kontakion IV

Those having a storm of doubting thoughts within, but also sincere repentance, those possessed by the passion of drunkenness, hastening to Thine inexpressible compassion, receive healing, and from the depth of their heart they cry to our Saviour born of Thee: Alleluia!

Ikos IV

The Lord, on hearing the heavy sorrows, tears, and cries of wives, aged women and children, whose kindred are possessed by the passion of drunkenness, gave them Thine icon, O Sovereign Lady, and all who hasten to it find in it consolation and spiritual joy, and they cry out to Thee with tears:

Rejoice, O ewe who gavest birth to the Lamb that takest
  away the sin of the world!
Rejoice, cup that drawest up joy for us from the fountain
  of immortality!
Rejoice, consolation of grieving mothers!
Rejoice, hope of the hopeless!
Rejoice, Grace-filled protection of those who hasten to
  Thee!
Rejoice, delight and gladness of those in grief!
Rejoice, Thou who dost quiet the waves of the passion of
  drunkenness!
Rejoice, Thou who dost stretch out Thy helping hand to
  those in need!
Rejoice, O Sovereign Lady, Inexhaustible Cup that
  quenchest our spiritual thirst!

Kontakion V

O Sovereign Lady of the world, Thou hast shown us Thy precious icon to be like a divinely moving star, which, as we behold it, and pray with heartfelt faith to Thee, O Theotokos, we say: heal those who are suffering from drunkenness and other illnesses of soul and body, and teach the faithful to sing in praise to God: Alleluia!

Ikos V

On seeing the most glorious wonders and most marvelous signs occurring not only from Thine icon that appeared in the city of Serpoukov, O Mother of God, but also from depictions that were copied in the likeness of this icon, falling down before them, humbly we cry out to Thee:

Rejoice, speedy intercessor, helper of those who fervently hasten to Thee!

Rejoice, kind-hearted hearer of our supplications!

Rejoice, Thou who hast overshadowed the city of Serpoukhov with Thy blessing!

Rejoice, Thou who hast shown the glory of Thy miracles in the region of Moscow!

Rejoice, inexhaustible treasure for all who are in need of healing!

Rejoice, O almighty protrectress of those who struggle well in sobriety!

Rejoice, O good helper of those who do battle against the world, the flesh, the devil, and drunkenness!

Rejoice, fervent defender of those who lead a life of piety in the world!

Rejoice, O Sovereign Lady, Inexhaustible Cup that quenchest our spiritual thirst!

Kontakion VI

Proclaiming Thy wonders, O Birthgiver of God, that occur from Thine icon called "The Inexhaustible Cup," we pray to Thee, O pure one, with tears: Deliver us all from the passion of wine drinking and from other falls into sins, and teach us temperance, as we strive to sing unto God: Alleluia!

Ikos VI

Thou hast shone forth in the brightness of Divine Glory, O Virgin Maiden of God, looking upon the Child, the pre-eternal God, our Lord Jesus Christ Who standeth in the chalice as if in an inexhaustible cup, as we see Thee depicted on Thine icon mysteriously called "The Inexhaustible Cup," from which Thou givest deliverance from the passion of drunkenness to those who hasten to Thee with faith. Therefore with tears we offer to Thee unceasing voices thus:

Rejoice, for in Thee the angelic hosts and the race of man Rejoice and exult!

Rejoice, for Thy glory surpasseth both earthly and heavenly praise!

Rejoice, Thou who dost reveal to us the mystery of the Divine Eucharist through the mystical depiction of Thy Son in the chalice!

Rejoice, Thou who dost wondrously show us the Lamb born of Thee Who is always eaten but never consumed!

Rejoice, O cup of life and immortality that leadest us to the gates of life eternal!

Rejoice, Thou who dost give thirsty souls to drink from the fountain of incorruption and joy!

Rejoice, Thou who in Thy measureless goodness dost not abandon even the most despised and rejected!

Rejoice, Thou who in Thy compassion dost snatch the hopeless out of the pit of destruction!

Rejoice, O Sovereign Lady, Inexhaustible Cup that quenchest our spiritual thirst!

Kontakion VII

A certain man desiring to thank Thee, O Sovereign Lady, for his healing from the disease of drunkenness, adorned Thy most wondrous icon, O Mother of God, that is in the city Serpoukhov, singing from the depth of his heart to God: Alleluia!

Ikos VII

We see a new miracle from Thy holy icon, O Sovereign Lady. For a certain servant of God, Stephen, suffering from the disease of drunkenness, fleeing to Thy maternal intercession, was delivered from his serious disease, and in thanks to Thee, he adorned Thine icon with majestic gifts, and falling before it, with tears he cried to Thee:

> Rejoice, Lifegiving Spring of healings!
> Rejoice, heavenly cup of divine gifts!
> Rejoice, river ever-flowing with healings!
> Rejoice, sea that drownest all our passions!
> Rejoice, Thou who with Thy maternal hands dost raise up those who fall under the heavy sin of drunkenness!
> Rejoice, Thou who dost not reject gifts of thanksgiving!
> Rejoice, Thou who dost gladden the hearts of pious people!
> Rejoice, Thou who dost fulfill all our good petitions!
> Rejoice, O Sovereign Lady, Inexhaustible Cup that quenchest our spiritual thirst!

Kontakion VIII

Strange and doubtful is it to unbelievers to hear how Thy holy icon, "The Inexhaustible Cup," poureth forth the miracle of divine healing. But we, believing in Thy words, O Sovereign Lady, spoken concerning Thy first-painted icon, "May the Grace of the One born of Me and Mine own be with this icon," believe that this icon of Thine also poureth forth Thy Grace. Wherefore, reverently worshipping, we kiss it, crying to God: Alleluia!

Ikos VIII

People suffering from the illness of drunkenness place all their hope in Thee, O Sovereign Lady. Bend down to our weaknesses and passions, for who shall pull us sinners out of the pit of destruction and bodily and spiritual misery if not Thee, O Sovereign Lady? Therefore, having bent our knees before Thy most pure image, we cry out to Thee thus:

> Rejoice, Thou who dost not reject the supplications of sinners!
> Rejoice, Thou who dost send down Thy heavenly help to those who call upon Thee!
> Rejoice, Thou who dost show the depth of Thy compassion for sinners!
> Rejoice, Thou who makest bold the despairing and hopeless!
> Rejoice, Thou who extendest a helping hand to those possessed by the passion of drunkenness!
> Rejoice, Thou who consolest with gifts of Grace those who suffer patiently!
> Rejoice, Thou who healest our spiritual and bodily ills!
> Rejoice, Thou who teachest us to despise the vain joys of this world!
> Rejoice, O Sovereign Lady, Inexhaustible Cup that quenchest our spiritual thirst!

Kontakion IX

All angelic nature was amazed at the act of Thy mercy, O Lord, for Thou hast given to the sinful race of man a steadfast intercessor and helper, who condescendeth to our infirmities and freeth from the bitter disease of drunkenness, and teacheth the faithful to sing unto God: Alleluia!

Ikos IX

Human orators are at a loss worthily to praise the glorious appearance of Thine icon, O Sovereign Lady. Nor can we sinners offer from our defiled lips a praise worthy of our Protectress. Yet having seen innumerable miracles revealed through Thine icon, rejoicing in soul and heart, we say to Thee:

> Rejoice, Thou who pourest forth miracles from Thy sacred image!
> Rejoice, Thou who dost speedily deliver from misfortunes and sorrows!
> Rejoice, Thou who dost put to shame those who reject Thee!
> Rejoice, Thou who dost preserve from every evil those who flee unto Thee!
> Rejoice, Thou who by Thy gentle radiance dost disperse the darkness of our sins and the gloom of our passions!
> Rejoice, Thou who fillest our hearts with love for Thee and Thy Son!
> Rejoice, Thou who wisely guidest us to the path of repentance!
> Rejoice, fervent mediatress, good defence for us before the Righteous Judge!
> Rejoice, O Sovereign Lady, Inexhaustible Cup that quenchest our spiritual thirst!

Kontakion X

Desiring to save many who suffer from the disease of drunkenness, Thou hast given us Thy wondrous icon, O Mother of God, so that all who are possessed by this passion might hasten to Thy wonderworking image, and having received healing, might cry out in compunction to God: Alleluia!

Ikos X

Thou art a wall and a shield, O Mother of God, for people who suffer from the disease of drunkenness, and for all who fervently hasten to Thee and who reverently honour Thy holy icon. For the Lord, the Giver of good things, gave it to us as a help and healing from this destructive passion, and through this He inspireth us to sing to Thee:

Rejoice, hope of the despairing and solace in our sorrows!

Rejoice, healing of our spiritual and bodily sicknesses!

Rejoice, Thou who dost cleanse our defilement by Thy purity!

Rejoice, Thou who dost enlighten our unworthiness by Thy Grace!

Rejoice, Thou who dost clothe our corruptible clay with incorruption!

Rejoice, Thou who dost fortify our supplications by Thine intercession!

Rejoice, Thou who dost strengthen us in our weakness!

Rejoice, Thou who dost quickly disperse the cloud of passions that surround us!

Rejoice, O Sovereign Lady, Inexhaustible Cup that quenchest our spiritual thirst!

Kontakion XI

O pure one, disdain not our humble song that we bring to Thee with love and zeal; and turn not away Thy face from those who suffer from despair and the illness of drunkenness, but do Thou help them and us, that we may be cleansed from every sinful defilement, that we might be able worthily and justly to sing to God: Alleluia!

Ikos XI

We see Thee, O most holy Virgin, as a lightbearing candle, for Thine image dispelleth the gloom of sin through the rays of Thy Grace, and guideth on the radiant path of the virtues those who with faith cry out to Thee:

Rejoice, Thou who through Thine intercession dost deliver us from the vanity of this greatly troubled world!

Rejoice, Thou who dost help us to resist the approach of passions of the flesh!

Rejoice, Thou who dost place a good thought in our heart!

Rejoice, Thou who dost enlighten our impure conscience!

Rejoice, Thou who dost deliver those who suffer from the tormenting disease of drunkenness!

Rejoice, Thou who dost summon to sincere repentance and understanding!

Rejoice, Thou dost soften the souls of those who have become hardened!

Rejoice, Thou who savest those who call upon Thee for help and who glorify Thy name!

Rejoice, O Sovereign Lady, Inexhaustible Cup that quenchest our spiritual thirst!

Kontakion XII

The Grace inherent in Thine icon, "The Inexhaustible Cup," draweth to it, O Sovereign Lady, all those who sorrow, all the unfortunate widows and orphans, and especially those who suffer from the disease of drunkenness. And they go not away empty-handed from the inexhaustible cup of Thy divine gifts, O pure one, but receiving healings without end from Thy wonderworking image, O all-good one, in gratitude they sing to God: Alleluia!

Ikos XII

Praising Thy wonders and great mercy shown to people possessed by the passion of drunkenness, we pray Thee, O Sovereign Lady: save and have mercy and direct us on the right path, and forsake us not who seek Thy protection and cry to Thee:

Rejoice, Thou who dost impel all to abstain from the sin of drunkenness!

Rejoice, Thou who dost free from addiction to wine with the dew of Thy mercy!

Rejoice, constant healing of those who suffer from the grievous sin of drunkenness!

Rejoice, speedy helper of those who languish in passions!

Rejoice, wondrous emboldenment of the fainthearted!

Rejoice, great joy of the courageous!

Rejoice, Thou who dost humble the proud!

Rejoice, Thou who dost exalt the humble and desire salvation for all!

Rejoice, O Sovereign Lady, Inexhaustible Cup that quenchest our spiritual thirst!

Kontakion XIII

O all-merciful Mother of our sweetest Lord Jesus Christ! Hear our present supplication and deliver us from all ills of soul and body, and especially free Thy servant(s) [name(s)], who suffer(eth) from the disease of drunkenness, that he (she, they) might not perish in evil, but that saved by Thee he (she, they) might ever sing to God: Alleluia! Alleluia! Alleluia!

This Kontakion is recited thrice; whereupon Ikos I and Kontakion I are repeated.

Prayer

O most merciful Sovereign Lady, we flee now to Thy protection. Disdain not our supplications, but mercifully hear us — wives, children, mothers, and those possessed with the grievous disease of drunkenness, and heal our brethren and sisters and kindred who for this cause have fallen away from their mother, the Church of Christ, and from salvation. O merciful Mother of God, touch their hearts and speedily raise them up from their sinful falls, and lead them to salutary temperance. Implore Thy Son, Christ our God, that He forgive us our offences and turn not away His mercy from His people, but that He strengthen us in sobriety and chastity.

Accept, O Most Holy Theotokos, the prayers of mothers shedding tears over their children, wives weeping for their husbands, children, orphans, beggars forsaken by those who have gone astray, and all of us who fall down before Thine icon. And through Thy prayers may this our cry be presented before the throne of the Most High.

Protect us, and keep us from the net of the evil one and all the snares of enemies, and at the dreadful hour of our departure, help us to pass through the aerial tollhouses without stumbling. By Thy prayers, deliver us from eternal condemnation, that the mercy of God may protect us unto the endless ages of ages. Amen.

Akathist Hymn
to the Protection of the All-Holy Theotokos

The Protection of the Theotokos

Akathist Hymn
to the Protection of the All-Holy Theotokos

Kontakion I

Offering worthy veneration and thanksgiving unto Thee, the Queen of heaven and earth, who art more exalted than all creation, who wast chosen by the preeternal King, and once did enter the Church of Blachernae to make supplication, with faith and compunction we flee beneath Thy radiant omophorion as ones who are in darkness. As Thou hast might which is invincible, free us from all misfortunes, that we may cry unto Thee:

> Rejoice, O our joy! Protect us from all evil by Thy precious omophorion!

Ikos I

A multitude of archangels and angels, together with the Forerunner, the Theologian, and the choir of all the saints, stood with Thee, their Queen, in the Church of Blachernae; and hearing Thy compunctionate entreaties in behalf of all the world, with amazement they cried out such things as these:

> Rejoice, preëternal good pleasure of God, the unoriginate Father;
> Rejoice, all-pure receptacle of God, the timeless Son!
> Rejoice, chosen dwelling-place of God, the most Holy Spirit;
> Rejoice, unceasing amazement of the ranks of angels on high!

Rejoice, most dread affrighting of the dark powers of hades;

Rejoice, Thou whom the many-eyed cherubim meet in the air!

Rejoice, Thou to whom the six-winged seraphim send up hymns of praise;

Rejoice, those before whose all-good protection we who are born on earth do bow down!

Rejoice, O our joy! Protect us from all evil by Thy precious omophorion!

Kontakion II

The holy Andrew, standing with Epiphanius in church and beholding Thee in the air, praying to God for Christians, knew that Thou wast the Mother of Christ our God Who had ascended to heaven; and falling down to the ground, they joyfully bowed down before Thine all-good protection, crying: Alleluia!

Ikos II

O Virgin Theotokos, in the defense of the Orthodox people Thou art incomprehensible understanding; wherefore, our enemies know not how mighty is the supplication of the Mother of God. But we, knowing well of Thine almighty aid, cry out to Thee thus with compunction:

Rejoice, all-merciful comforter of all who sorrow and are heavy laden;

Rejoice, sleepless guide for all who are lost and blind!

Rejoice, Thou who by thine entreaty dost quickly assuage the wrath of God which is justly directed against us;

Rejoice, Thou who by Thine almighty gesture dost quell our evil passions!

Rejoice, mighty arousal of sleeping consciences;

Rejoice, easy conquest of iniquitous habits!

Rejoice, Thou because of whom hades groaneth and the
    spirits of evil do tremble;
Rejoice, Thou for whose sake the gates of paradise are
    opened unto us all!
Rejoice, O our joy! Protect us from all evil by Thy pre-
    cious omophorion!

Kontakion III

The power of the Most High overshadoweth those who with faith and reverence flee to Thy most precious protection; for unto Thee alone, the all-holy and all-pure Mother of God, hath it been given that Thine every petition be fulfilled. Wherefore, the faithful of all ages glorify Thee and Thy Son, crying: Alleluia!

Ikos III

Possessed of an inexhaustible wealth of loving kindness, Thou stretchest forth Thy helping hand to all the ends of the earth, O Mistress, granting healing to the sick, cessation to the suffering and sight to the blind; and Thou dost give whatsoever is needful unto all who cry out with thanksgiving:

Rejoice, unbreakable might and bulwark of the domin-
    ions of the Orthodox;
Rejoice, foremost ornament of the holy temples and
    sanctuaries!
Rejoice, surest protection of the thrones of kings;
Rejoice, ever-vigilant helper of good hearted governors!
Rejoice, invincible commander of Christian officers and
    soldiers;
Rejoice, holy reflection of justice for incorruptible
    judges!
Rejoice, perfect knowledge of instructors and the teach-
    ers of children;
Rejoice, blessing of pious homes and families!
Rejoice, O our joy! Protect us from all evil by Thy pre-
    cious omophorion!

Kontakion IV

O Mistress, Thou helpest us who are beset by the storm of many misfortunes; for Thou standest before the altar of the Lord, lifting up Thine arms, and Thou prayest that the Lord, the King of glory, not disdain our unworthy supplication. And Thou dost hearken unto the entreaties of those who call upon Thy holy name, crying out to Thy Son: Alleluia!

Ikos IV

The Lord hearkened to Joshua, son of Nun, when he prayed and commanded the sun to stand still until he wrought vengeance upon his enemies; and the Lord Jesus hearkeneth now also unto Thine entreaties, O chosen palace of the Holy Spirit. Wherefore, we sinners, trusting in Thy protection, dare to say unto Thee, as the Mother of God:

> Rejoice, Thou who wast illumined by the noetic Sun and dost shine upon us light unapproachable;
> Rejoice, Thou who hast shed upon the whole earth the radiance of Thine all-pure soul!
> Rejoice, Thou who hast gladdened all the heavens with the purity of Thy body;
> Rejoice, protection and safekeeping of the holy monasteries of Christ!
> Rejoice, vigilance and admonition of the faithful pastors of the Church;
> Rejoice, instructor of God-fearing monks and nuns!
> Rejoice, untroubled serenity of reverent elders;
> Rejoice, mystic gladness of virgins and widows!
> Rejoice, O our joy! Protect us from all evil by Thy precious omophorion!

Kontakion V

Of old, whenever Moses the God-seer lifted up his arms during the battle against Amalek, Israel prevailed; and whenever he lowered his arms, Amalek prevailed. But supported by those who held up his arms, Moses conquered the enemy. But when Thou, O Mother of God, dost lift up Thine arms in supplication, without being supported by anyone, Thou dost ever vanquish the enemies of Christians, and art an invincible shield for us who cry: Alleluia!

Ikos V

Seeing Thee in the air within the Church of Blachernae, stretching forth suppliant hands unto Thy Son and God, the assemblies of the saints, together with the archangels and angels, joyously chanted a hymn unto Thee; and, strengthened by Thine arms, which are far stronger than the arms of Moses, we cry out with compunction:

> Rejoice, those whose love and loving kindness alone support Thine arms for all of us;
> Rejoice, Thou before whom our enemies, visible and invisible, cannot stand!
> Rejoice, Thou who drivest away the dark horde of our passions and lusts;
> Rejoice, Thou who holdest in Thine arms, without being consumed, Christ, the divine Fire, and thereby dost set us aflame who are cold!
> Rejoice, excellent crowning of those who wage war upon the flesh through chastity;
> Rejoice, constant conversor with those who struggle in fasting and stillness!
> Rejoice, speedy consoler of those who languish in despair and grief;
> Rejoice, Thou who preservest through the grace of humility and patience!
> Rejoice, O our joy! Protect us from all evil by Thy precious omophorion!

Kontakion VI

A proclaimer of thine inexhaustible grace and mercies was the holy Romanus the Sweet-singer shown to be, when in a dream he received from Thee a scroll to eat; and rendered wise thereby, he began to chant unto Thy glory with understanding, and to compose hymns of praise unto the saints, crying out with faith: Alleluia!

Ikos VI

Thou didst shine forth as a ray from the true Sun of righteousness, O divine Maiden and Virgin, enlightening all with the wisdom of God Thy Son, and leading to a knowledge of the truth those who cry to Thee such things as these:

> Rejoice, Thou who gavest birth in the flesh unto Christ, the Power of God and the Wisdom of God;
> Rejoice, Thou who hast put the foolish wisdom of this age to shame and guidest those who have been blinded by it to the right path!
> Rejoice, preservation of the Holy Faith and teacher of Orthodox dogmas;
> Rejoice, uprooter of ungodly heresies and corrupting schisms!
> Rejoice, Thou who knowest well all secret things hard to foresee, and dost relate them to those who ought to know them;
> Rejoice, Thou who puttest false seers and vain divinations to shame!
> Rejoice, Thou who in the hour of confusion dost place a good thought in one's heart;
> Rejoice, Thou who dost thwart perilous undertakings and senseless desires!
> Rejoice, O our joy! Protect us from all evil by Thy precious omophorion!

Kontakion VII

Desiring to reveal the unfathomable depth of the compassions of His love for mankind, the long suffering Lord Who seeth all things chose Thee alone to be His mother, and made Thee an invincible defense for His people, that even though one of them may appear worthy of condemnation by the righteous judgment of God, yet shall he be preserved for repentance by Thy mighty protection, crying out: Alleluia!

Ikos VII

Thou didst show forth Thy wondrous works in Thine all-pure Mother, O Lord, when the all-wondrous omophorion in Her hands appeared to shine more brightly than the rays of the sun; and she covered therewith the people who were in the Church of Blachernae. And having heard of such a sign of Her loving assistance, all said, held fast by awe and joy:

> Rejoice, Thou who spread forth thine omophorion not made by men's hands, as it were a cloud, over all the earth;
> Rejoice, Thou who holdest the sign of Thy Son, the eternal High Priest, in Thy hands!
> Rejoice, Thou who revealest new mercy and new grace unto those in the Orthodox Church;
> Rejoice, pillar of cloud protecting us all from the temptations and scandals of the world!
> Rejoice, pillar of fire showing to all of us the path of salvation in the midst of the gloom of sin;
> Rejoice, manifest strengthening of those who manifestly struggle for piety!
> Rejoice, secret encouragement of the secret servants of God amid the world;
> Rejoice, Thou who in Thy protection and grace dost not forsake even me, who am devoid of good works!
> Rejoice, O our joy! Protect us from all evil by Thy precious omophorion!

Kontakion VIII

Thee who appeared from the heavens in the Church of Blachernae did the angels wondrously hymn, the apostles glorify, the choir of holy hierarchs and the venerable, and the company of holy women praise. The Forerunner and the Theologian bowed down before Thee, and all the people in the church cried out with gladness: Alleluia!

Ikos VIII

Beholding His own Mother standing in the Church and praying to Him with compunction, the Lord, Who hath dominion over all on high and all below, said: "O My Mother, ask what Thou desirest, for I will not deny Thee, but will fulfill all Thy petitions, and will teach all to sing hymns of thanksgiving unto Thee thus!"

Rejoice, ark of the covenant wherein the sanctification of the whole human race is preserved;

Rejoice, O all-holy jar wherein the Bread of life everlasting is kept for those who hunger after righteousness!

Rejoice, vessel all of gold wherein the flesh and blood of the divine Lamb were prepared for our sake;

Rejoice, Thou who takest into thine almighty hands those abandoned by their physicians!

Rejoice, those who dost raise up from their bed of sickness those paralyzed in body but not in soul and faith;

Rejoice, Thou who givest new and better sanity unto those suffering from mental illness!

Rejoice, Thou who dost all-wisely hinder us on the crooked path of sin and the passions;

Rejoice, Thou who dost soften the hardness of our unrepentant hearts!

Rejoice, O our joy! Protect us from all evil by Thy precious omophorion!

Kontakion IX

All the nature of the angels offereth hymns of praise unto Thee, the true Mother of God and helper of all who have recourse unto Thee, knowing that with thine unbreakable protection Thou makest glad the righteous, helpest sinners, deliverest the unfortunate and prayest for all the faithful, who cry: Alleluia!

Ikos IX

Like mute fish the most eloquent of orators are at a loss how to praise the great feast of Thy most honored protection as is meet; for all the things said of Thee by them do not suffice for even a listing of Thy compassions. And we, seeing thine innumerable benefactions, cry out with gladness:

>Rejoice, Thou who dost preserve us from plague and
>>deadly pestilence;
>
>Rejoice, Thou who protectest cities and towns from the
>>sudden quaking of the earth!
>
>Rejoice, Thou who with Thy mighty hand dost turn
>>away the deluge and floods of water;
>
>Rejoice, Thou who with the dew of Thy prayers dost
>>deliver from fiery conflagration!
>
>Rejoice, Thou who by the Bread of life dost safeguard
>>against starvation, spiritual and bodily;
>
>Rejoice, Thou who dost deflect bolts of lightning and
>>thunder from our heads!
>
>Rejoice, Thou who savest from invasions of aliens and
>>those who slay in secret;
>
>Rejoice, Thou who with peace and love dost guard
>>against domestic strife and enmity among kin!
>
>Rejoice, O our joy! Protect us from all evil by Thy precious omophorion!

Kontakion X

Desiring to save the human race from the deception of the enemy, the Lord Who loveth mankind gave Thee, His own Mother, to us mortals as an aid, protection and defense, that Thou mayest be the comfort of the grieving, the joy of the sorrowful and the helper of the oppressed, and that Thou mayest raise all up from the depths of sin who cry: Alleluia!

Ikos X

"O King of heaven," the most immaculate Queen said in prayer as she stood with the angels in the air, "accept every man who prayeth unto Thee and calleth upon Thy name for help, that he not depart from before my face empty and unheard!" And hearing this all-good prayer, the assemblies of the saints cried out in thanksgiving:

> Rejoice, Thou who with blessed fruits dost crown husbandmen who are pure of hand and heart;
> Rejoice, help and just recompense for all who conduct trade with honesty!
> Rejoice, universal denunciation of oath-breaking and unjust acquisition;
> Rejoice, unexpected help of those who encounter misfortune while journeying on dry land and by water!
> Rejoice, Thou who dost gladden childless couples with the fruits of faith and the Spirit;
> Rejoice, unseen nurturer of motherless orphans!
> Rejoice, mighty helper of those in captivity and exile;
> Rejoice, Thou who dost unsleepingly watch over those who sit in fetters and prison!
> Rejoice, O our joy! Protect us from all evil by Thy precious omophorion!

Kontakion XI

Hearing most compunctionate hymnody and attending unto Thy fervent supplication in our behalf, O Virgin Theotokos, we beseech thee: Disdain not the voice of Thy servants, for unto Thee do we flee amid perils and tribulations, and before Thee do we shed tears amid our misfortunes, crying: Alleluia!

Ikos XI

Beholding Thee in the air, like a radiant lamp burning in prayer, the Church of Blachernae, together with a multitude of the people who were in it, exclaimed: "Whence is it to me, that the Mother of my Lord hath come to me?" And the holy Andrew and Epiphanius prayed fervently unto Thee, crying:

> Rejoice, unstinting bestower of all the gifts of the spirit and the body;
> Rejoice, faithful intercessor for sinners who make a beginning of repentance!
> Rejoice, trusted ally of those who do battle against the passions and the assaults of the enemy;
> Rejoice, invisible tamer of cruel and bestial masters!
> Rejoice, mystical rest and joy of meek and sufferings servants;
> Rejoice, most desired perfecter of good marriages!
> Rejoice, speedy and painless release for mothers in childbirth;
> Rejoice, sole helper for all of us at the hour of death!
> Rejoice, O our joy! Protect us from all evil by Thy precious omophorion!

Kontakion XII

Ask divine grace of Thy Son and God for us; stretch forth unto us a helping hand; drive from us every enemy and adversary; and bring peace to our life, that we not perish grievously, without repentance; but receive us into the everlasting mansions, O our protectress, that rejoicing we may cry out to Thee: Alleluia!

Ikos XII

Hymning Thy mighty protection, we all praise Thee as our steadfast intercessor; and we bow down before Thee who prayest for us. For we believe and hope that Thou wilt ask of Thy Son and God good things, eternal and temporal, for all who with love cry out to Thee thus:

> Rejoice, mighty help of the whole world;
> Rejoice, sanctification of all the elements of earth and heaven!

Rejoice, blessing of all the seasons of the year;
Rejoice, trampling down of all assaults and temptations which come from the world, the flesh and the devil!
Rejoice, unexpected reconciliation of those hardened in enmity;
Rejoice, unknown amendment of unrepentant sinners!
Rejoice, Thou who dost not reject those who have been spurned and rejected by all;
Rejoice, Thou who dost snatch the most desperate from the pit of destruction!
Rejoice, O our joy! Protect us from all evil by Thy precious omophorion!

Kontakion XIII

O most hymned Mother, all-pure Lady, Virgin Theotokos! Unto Thee do I lift the eyes of my soul and body; unto Thee do I stretch forth my paralyzed hands; and from the depths of my heart I cry out: Look upon the faith and humility of my soul, and cover me with Thine almighty omophorion, that I may be delivered from all misfortunes and perils. And at the hour of my death, O most good one, stand before me, and deliver me from the torment which hath been prepared for me because of my sins, that continually bowing down before Thee, I may cry out: Alleluia! Alleluia! Alleluia!

This Kontakion is recited thrice, whereupon Ikos I and Kontakion I are repeated.

Prayer to the All-holy Theotokos

O All-Holy Virgin, Mother of the Lord of the hosts on high, Queen of heaven and earth, almighty helper of our city and land! Accept this hymnody of praise and thanksgiving from us, thine unworthy servants, and bear our supplications to the throne of God Thy Son, that He may treat our injustices with mercy and shed His grace upon those who honor Thy most precious name and venerate Thy miraculous image with faith and love. For we are unworthy to receive mercy from Him, except Thou move Him to take pity on us, O Mistress, for all things are made possible for Thee by Him. Wherefore, we flee unto Thee as to our certain and speedy helper. Hearken unto us who pray to thee; overshadow us with Thine almighty protection; and ask of God Thy Son: for pastors zeal and vigilance for souls; wisdom and power for the municipal authorities; justice and impartiality for judges; understanding and humility of mind for teachers; love and concord for married couples; obedience for children; the fear of God for oppressors; courage for the sorrowful; restraint for those who rejoice; and for all of us the spirit of understanding and piety, the spirit of loving kindness and meekness, the spirit of purity and righteousness. Yea, O All-Holy Lady, have pity upon thine ailing people: gather those who have been scattered; guide those who are lost to the right path; support the elderly; impart chastity to the young; nurture the infants; and regard all of us with the gaze of Thy merciful aid; raise us up from the depths of sin, and enlighten the eyes of our hearts for the sight of salvation; be merciful unto us here and in the world to come, in the land of our earthly sojourn and at the dread judgment of Thy Son; and cause our fathers and brethren who have passed unto everlasting life from this life, in faith and repentance, to dwell with the angels and all the saints. For Thou, O Lady, art the glory of those in heaven and the hope of those on earth; for after God Thou art the hope and helper of all of us who have recourse unto Thee with faith. Unto Thee, therefore, do we pray, and to Thee, as our omnipotent helper, do we commit ourselves, and each other, and all our life, now and ever, and unto the ages of ages. Amen.

Prayer to the All-Holy Theotokos by One Who is in Trouble and Affliction

O mine all-good Queen, mine all-holy hope, receiver of orphans and assister of strangers, helper of the unfortunate and protection of the afflicted! Thou seest my peril, Thou seest my tribulation: I am beset by temptations on every side, but there is no one to help me. Wherefore, do Thou Thyself help me, for I am sick; feed me, for I am a stranger; guide me, for I am lost; heal and save me, for I am beyond hope. I have none other help, I have none other intercession or consolation, save Thee, O Mother of all who are troubled and heavily burdened. Wherefore, look upon me, a sinner in affliction, and cover me with Thine all-holy omophorion, that I may be delivered from the evils which compass me round about, and may continually praise Thine all-hymned name. Amen

Akathist Hymn to the All-Holy Theotokos, in Honor of Her Miraculous Icon Known as "She Who Healeth"

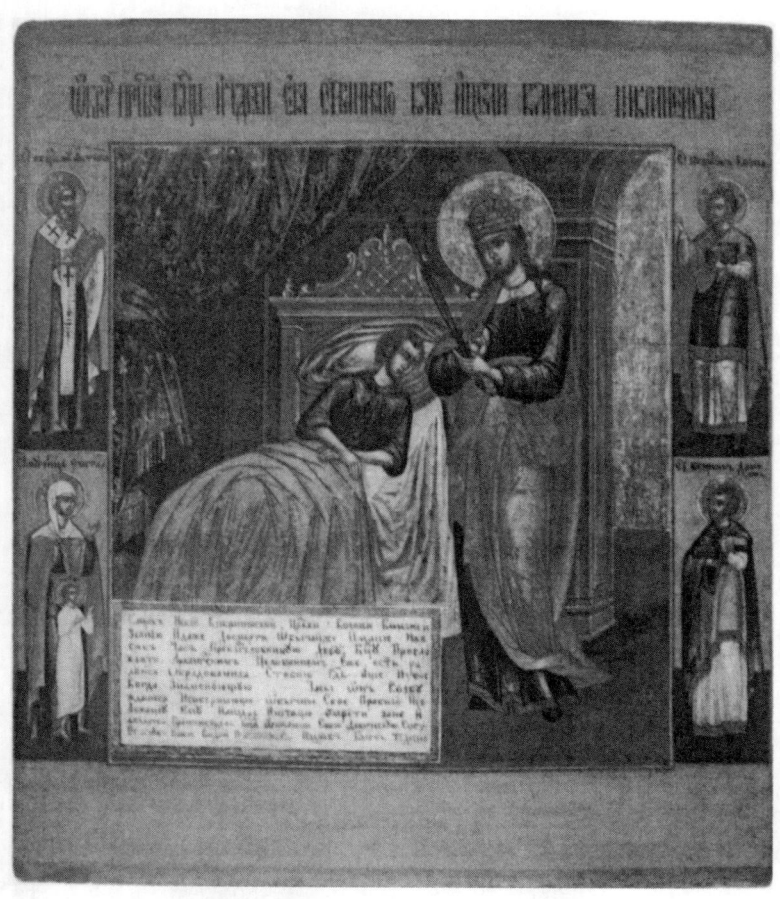

She Who Healeth

Akathist Hymn
to the All-Holy Theotokos,
in Honor of Her Miraculous Icon
Known as "She Who Healeth"

*The Memory of Which the Holy Church Doth Celebrate
On the 18th of September*

Kontakion I

Unto the All-Holy Virgin Theotokos, chosen from among all generations, who once appeared to an ailing cleric, to heal him of a grievous malady, let us offer up hymns of praise. As Thou hast might which is invincible, O most merciful Mistress, from all misfortunes and tribulations free us who cry to thee:

>Rejoice, O Thou who art full of grace, healer of our souls
>   and bodies!

Ikos I

The Archangel Gabriel, announcing to the All-Holy Virgin Mary the seedless conception of the Son of God from Her, said: "Rejoice, O Thou who art full of grace! The Lord is with Thee! Blessed art Thou among women!" And we sinners, daring to imitate the voice of the archangel, with faith, love and reverence cry out such hymns as these:

>Rejoice, Thou who wast chosen from the beginning of
>   time for the beginning of our salvation;
>Rejoice, Thou who wast proclaimed beforehand by the
>   prophets in many images!

Rejoice, Thou who without hesitations didst submit Thy will to the will of God;

Rejoice, unwedded Bride, who didst conceive the Son by the Holy Spirit!

Rejoice, Thou who wast a mother in giving birth, yet didst remain a virgin even after birthgiving;

Rejoice, Thou who didst wrap in swaddling bands Him Who clotheth Himself in light as in a garment!

Rejoice, Thou who with Thy milk didst nourish Him Who with His grace nourisheth that which is above and that which is below;

Rejoice, Thou who didst bear the Almighty in Thine arms!

Rejoice, Thou who with maternal love didst watch over Him as He increased in wisdom and stature;

Rejoice, Thou who hast been exalted by Him above all others!

Rejoice, Thou who art incomparably more honorable and glorious than all the hosts of heaven;

Rejoice, Thou who standest on high before the throne of Thy Son and God!

Rejoice, O Thou who art full of grace, healer of our souls and bodies!

Kontakion II

Seeing the diligent and reverent prayers which the cleric Vincent offered up every day, kneeling before Thine image and greeting Thee with the salutation of the archangel, O All-Holy Mistress, Thou didst accept his well-pleasing supplications and didst grant him to rise speedily and miraculously from his bed in the time of his illness. Wherefore, we also bend the knees of our souls and bodies before Thy healing image, O our Lady Theotokos, and, mindful of the wondrous healing of the ailing cleric, cry out to Thy Son and our God: Alleluia!

Ikos II

Becoming aware of his miraculous healing from his grievous malady, the cleric Vincent arose from his wretched bed, went to church, and there with hymns of praise glorified Thee, the healer of all the sick. Wherefore, accept also from us, O Mother of God, these goodly praises:

> Rejoice, Thou who from the gates of death returnest to life those incurably ill;
> Rejoice, Thou who aboundest with sympathy for the suffering!
> Rejoice, Thou who dost wondrously heal those stricken with divers illnesses;
> Rejoice, Thou who dost mercifully dispel all maladies!
> Rejoice, Thou who dost banish all lamentation from the hearts of men;
> Rejoice, Thou who pourest heavenly joy into our heart amid all sorrows and griefs!
> Rejoice, Thou who dost inspire us with love for God and our neighbors;
> Rejoice, Thou who preservest from the temptations of this world, which corrupt soul and body!
> Rejoice, Thou who dost swiftly and diligently hearken to those who pray to thee;
> Rejoice, Thou who pourest forth great mercies and compassions upon those who love thee!
> Rejoice, Thou who grantest all things needful in this life unto those who set their hope on thee;
> Rejoice, Thou who dost not forsake those who bless Thee at the dread hour of death!
> Rejoice, O Thou who art full of grace, healer of our souls and bodies!

Kontakion III

By the power imparted from Thee, O Lady, Queen and Mistress, Thy holy icon poureth forth healings in abundance upon those suffering from divers diseases, who have recourse unto Thee with undoubting faith, and cry out unto God: Alleluia!

Ikos III

Possessed of surpassing love for the Christian race and maternal care therefor, Thou dost quickly fulfill every good petition for all who ask aid and assistance of thee; wherefore, unto Thee, our most mighty helper and speedy aid do we offer these praises:

> Rejoice, consolation of the sorrowful;
> Rejoice, hope of the hopeless!
> Rejoice, help and strengthening of those who labor;
> Rejoice, clothing of the poor!
> Rejoice, feeding of the hungry;
> Rejoice, aid of those who are reviled and persecuted!
> Rejoice, Thou who dost frighten offenders;
> Rejoice, instructress in the Christian Faith!
> Rejoice, search for the lost;
> Rejoice, surety of salvation for sinners!
> Rejoice, mighty defense against evil demons;
> Rejoice, Thou who dost break asunder all the snares of Belial!
> Rejoice, O Thou who art full of grace, healer of our souls and bodies!

Kontakion IV

Deliver us from the storms of the passions and lusts, and from the temptations of the demons, O All-Merciful Theotokos; and strengthen and preserve in us, to the end of our life, the Orthodox Faith and devotion to the Holy Church, that we may chant unto the Lord God without hindrance: Alleluia!

Ikos IV

Hearkening in heaven to Thine entreaties concerning us, O All-Good Mistress, the Lord speedily fulfilleth Thine every petition; and bringing such maternal boldness to Thy Son, Jesus Christ, we flee unto Thee and earnestly beseech thee: Intercede for us, Thy greatly sinful servants, before our omnipotent Creator, that we not perish in our iniquities, but that He grant remission of the transgressions unto us who cry out to Thee from the depths of our soul:

> Rejoice, intercessor before God, who savest the world from misfortunes;
> Rejoice, Thou who dost incline Thy Son to mercy for us, the unworthy!
> Rejoice, Thou who by the dew of Thy supplications dost deliver from fiery conflagration;
> Rejoice, Thou who dost avert from our heads bolts and lightning and claps of thunder!
> Rejoice, Thou who puttest to shame the foolish wisdom of this age;
> Rejoice, Thou who showest the foolishness of the faithful to be true wisdom!
> Rejoice, Thou who showest the paths of salvation to the lost;
> Rejoice, Thou who unto sinners givest boldness before God!
> Rejoice, Thou who dost swiftly help those languishing amid perils, tribulations and temptations;
> Rejoice, Thou who dost ever abide with those who abide in prayer and the contemplation of God!
> Rejoice, Thou who teachest us to spurn the vain and quickly passing good things of this earth;
> Rejoice, Thou who leadest our minds and hearts up to heavenly and eternal treasures!
> Rejoice, O Thou who art full of grace, healer of our souls and bodies!

Kontakion V

A heavenly light illumined the room of the ailing cleric when Thou stoodest before him, O All-Good Mistress, to grant him healing of his grievous infirmity. O All-Holy Lady Theotokos, enlighten our souls, which are darkened by many sins, and grant healing unto our sick bodies, that, glorifying Thy mercies, we may cry out to God with joy: Alleluia!

Ikos V

Seeing Thee, the Mistress Theotokos, standing before the fiery throne of the All-Holy Trinity and praying for Christians, the heavenly hosts and all the saints who have been pleasing to God from times past bless Thee with unceasing glorification. And we sinners on earth, moved by love for Thee, dare to chant to Thee thus:

> Rejoice, Thou who unitest the whole Christian world with Thy maternal love;
> Rejoice, good helper of all the faithful!
> Rejoice, excellent ally of those who do battle with worldly and soul-destroying temptations;
> Rejoice, Thou who by peace and love dost provide protections against all evil and enmity!
> Rejoice, Thou who takest in all who flee beneath Thy shelter;
> Rejoice, instructress in chastity and temperance!
> Rejoice, guide to the heavenly Jerusalem for strugglers for piety;
> Rejoice, uprooter of heresies and schisms!
> Rejoice, imparter of knowledge which profiteth souls;
> Rejoice, speedy comforter amid misfortunes and sorrows!
> Rejoice, our advocate before Thy Son and God;
> Rejoice, Thou who makest continual supplication for us before the Most High!
> Rejoice, O Thou who art full of grace, healer of our souls and bodies!

Kontakion VI

The Holy Orthodox Church proclaimeth the multitude of the miracles of Thy great mercy, O All-Good Mistress; for Thou art a rampart protecting cities and villages, dost defend monastic houses and the dwellings of Thy pious servants, dost help the oppressed, and sendest down all good and spiritual profitable things upon all who glorify Thee and chant unto Thy Son: Alleluia!

Ikos VI

Thy miraculous icon, known as "the Healer," which dispelleth from all the faithful the darkness of temptations and perils, and poureth forth healings in abundance, is here adorned with splendor, O Lady Theotokos. Wherefore, we cry out to Thee in compunction:

> Rejoice, Thou who grantest swift healing of incurable illnesses;
> Rejoice, Thou who deliverest from all manner of misfortunes and tribulations!
> Rejoice, Thou who tamest sinful passions;
> Rejoice, Thou who strengthenest in the Orthodox Faith those who waver!
> Rejoice, Thou who pourest the consolation of grace into God-loving hearts;
> Rejoice, Thou who delightest the souls of the faithful with the hope of the good things of heaven!
> Rejoice, Thou who helpest us to excel in good deeds;
> Rejoice, Thou who defendest us against enemies, visible and invisible!
> Rejoice, Thou who restorest the fallen with Thy grace;
> Rejoice, Thou who dost plant the fear of God in our hearts!
> Rejoice, Thou who dost quickly fulfill all our good petitions;
> Rejoice, Thou who shalt lead us into the abodes of the saints!
> Rejoice, O Thou who art full of grace, healer of our souls and bodies!

Kontakion VII

Desiring to reveal Thine ineffable lovingkindness, O All-Good Virgin Theotokos, Thou hast given us Thy miraculous icon, known as "the Healer," that all who have recourse to Thee with faith may be freed of sicknesses and found worthy of every consolation; wherefore, we cry out to God for Thy sake: Alleluia!

Ikos VII

Wondrous and all-glorious are Thy works, O All-Immaculate Mistress; for to the measure of their faith and love Thou grantest every good thing, in accordance with the need of each, unto the rich and the poor, the healthy and the sick, who hasten to Thy healing icon with earnest prayer; wherefore, we also do not conceal Thy benefactions, but, glorifying Thy mercies with thanksgiving, we say to Thee thus:

Rejoice, hearing for the deaf;
Rejoice, recovery of sight for the blind!
Rejoice, voice of the mute;
Rejoice, mobility of the lame!
Rejoice, cleansing of lepers;
Rejoice, strengthening of those who are paralyzed!
Rejoice, freedom from evil and wicked spirits;
Rejoice, our refuge and help, after God!
Rejoice, certain deliverance from needs, griefs and misfortunes;
Rejoice, Thou who uprootest the passionate attachment to corrupting wealth!
Rejoice, Thou who teachest us to seek incorruptible riches in heaven;
Rejoice, Thou who dost enrich us with the treasures of grace divine!
Rejoice, O Thou who art full of grace, healer of our souls and bodies!

Kontakion VIII

Strangers and sojourners in this world of sorrow and great turmoil, we seek the eternal heavenly homeland, and humbly beseech Thee, the omnipotent Queen, the Ever-Virgin Theotokos: Guide us by the paths of the saving commandments of Thy Son, Christ our God, that we may avoid the snares of the invisible foe, and may chant without hindrance to Almighty God Thy hymn: Alleluia!

Ikos VIII

The whole Christian world blesseth Thee, the All-Immaculate Virgin, with voices of laudation, for it is a comfort for all the faithful, and especially for the sick, to gaze upon Thy most venerable icon, known as "the Healer," O All-Wondrous Lady Theotokos. Wherefore, accept also these our goodly and compunctionate praises:

>Rejoice, O our joy;
>Rejoice, ineffable beauty!
>Rejoice, summit of the virtues;
>Rejoice, depth of humble-mindedness!
>Rejoice, inexhaustible outpouring of mercies and compassions;
>Rejoice, fragrant blossom of virginity and purity!
>Rejoice, confirmation of the Christian Faith;
>Rejoice, reproof of unbelief!
>Rejoice, boast of the heavenly hosts;
>Rejoice, glory of all the righteous!
>Rejoice, model for those who run the good race of piety;
>Rejoice, champion of those who fight the good fight of the virtues!
>Rejoice, O Thou who art full of grace, healer of our souls and bodies!

Kontakion IX

All our hope do we place in Thee, O Mother of God, and with reverence and faith we hasten to Thy holy icon amid sorrow and sickness, hoping that we may receive through it speedy consolation and healing. O All-Holy Queen and Theotokos, regard with mercy us, Thy lowly servants, and hasten Thou to fulfill all things profitable for us in this life and that which is to come, that, glorifying Thy lovingkindness, we may chant unto God in Trinity: Alleluia!

Ikos IX

Even the most eloquent of orators are unable fittingly to praise Thee, the All-Pure Virgin, who art more honorable than the cherubim and beyond compare most glorious than the seraphim, who gavest birth without seed to the Saviour of our souls. But even though we are infirm, yet, overcome with love for Thee, we open our unworthy mouths to sing such praises unto thee:

> Rejoice, first among the miracles of Christ;
> Rejoice, fulfillment of all the prophecies!
> Rejoice, Thou who dost surpass the angels in purity;
> Rejoice, Thou who in Thyself hast wondrously united virginity and childbirth!
> Rejoice, Thou who in holy and immaculate manner didst preserve Thyself in both;
> Rejoice, Mother of the Son of God, Who is God Most High!
> Rejoice, Thou who givest entry into the heavenly kingdom to fallen mankind;
> Rejoice, calm haven from storms for those who sail the sea of life!
> Rejoice, joy bestowed by God upon the suffering;
> Rejoice, Thou who art resplendent with the grace and glory of Thine all-wondrous knowledge and miracles!
> Rejoice, gladness of the Christian martyrs;
> Rejoice, jubilation of venerable ascetics!
> Rejoice, O Thou who art full of grace, healer of our souls and bodies!

Kontakion X

Desiring to save the whole human race from iniquities and everlasting torments, the Lord Who loveth mankind gave Thee, His Mother, as a help, protection and defense unto all who believe in Him; and glorifying such lovingkindness toward us sinners, we cry out to him with thankful hearts and lips: Alleluia!

Ikos X

Thou art an invincible rampart and mighty help for all who flee to Thee in prayer, O Virgin Theotokos; wherefore, be Thou a bulwark for us, the unworthy, against grievous sicknesses and every evil circumstance, and grant timely aid and strengthening in all our works unto us who cry out to Thee:

Rejoice, our helper and boast;

Rejoice, our preserver and confirmation!

Rejoice, our joy and wondrous care for us;

Rejoice, our renowned refuge amid all troubling circumstances!

Rejoice, upraising of children;

Rejoice, instructress in chastity for the young!

Rejoice, Thou who givest love and concord to husbands and wives;

Rejoice, Thou who bringest the life of the reverent elderly to a peaceful end!

Rejoice, Thou who dost strengthen and admonish the faithful pastors of the Holy Church;

Rejoice, mediatress of everlasting joy for those who struggle in the angelic image!

Rejoice, Thou who in Thine aid dost not forsake those who live piously in the world;

Rejoice, Thou who beneath Thy precious omophorion dost shelter all who reverence thee!

Rejoice, O Thou who art full of grace, healer of our souls and bodies!

Kontakion XI

Our hymns and most compunctionate supplications, offered up before Thy healing image, do Thou accept, O Ever-Virgin Theotokos; and vouchsafe that, until the end of our life, we may chant to the one God: Alleluia!

Ikos XI

Thy miraculous icon shineth forth with radiance, O Mother of God, emitting steams of grace-bearing healings for the faithful, guiding those lost in the darkness of sin to the luminous path of the virtues and salvation. Wherefore, we cry out to Thee such hymns of praise:

> Rejoice, Thou who by the overshadowing of Thine icon dost drive the power of the enemy away from everyone;
> Rejoice, Thou who dost impart speedy consolation and healing to all who have recourse to Thee amid sorrow, need and pain!
> Rejoice, wonder of wonders, Directress and Mistress, who guidest all to the path of salvation;
> Rejoice, Thou who givest a peaceful disposition to those bestormed by perils!
> Rejoice, Thou who by Thy purity teachest us how to live in purity;
> Rejoice, Thou who dost admonish the wicked, prideful and wrathful!
> Rejoice, Thou who dost instill the right faith and the fear of God within us;
> Rejoice, Thou who by the light of the teaching of Christ dost drive away the darkness of unbelief!
> Rejoice, Thou who dispellest the turmoil of doubting thoughts;
> Rejoice, compassionate bestower of all spiritual gifts!
> Rejoice, rose whose sweet scent perfumeth the universe;
> Rejoice, lily of purity, filling our souls with goodly fragrance!

Rejoice, O Thou who art full of grace, healer of our souls
and bodies!

Kontakion XII

In Thy grace and compassions Thou dost not forsake Orthodox Christians, O All-Loving Mistress, giving consolation to the sorrowful, help to the oppressed, and deliverance to the sick and all who find themselves amid divers misfortunes; wherefore, glorifying Thee, we cry out to God with thanksgiving: Alleluia!

Ikos XII

Hymning Thine ineffable mercies and the miracles revealed to us, the unworthy, we bend our knee before Thy healing image, O Ever-Virgin Theotokos; and we beseech Thee earnestly: Grant us peace, serenity and a good end; and at the Second Coming of Thy Son and our God leave not bereft of Thy help and aid all who with compunction offer Thee these praises:

Rejoice, Thou who with the hope of salvation dost
strength those fallen into despair and
despondency;
Rejoice, Thou who rendest asunder the bonds of sin!
Rejoice, Thou who turnest to mercy the just wrath of
God directed at us;
Rejoice, Thou who dost order well our earthly life!
Rejoice, Thou who deliverest us from perilous
circumstances;
Rejoice, speedy helper for all the faithful at the time of
our end!
Rejoice, Thou who dost help those who honor Thee to
pass through the aerial toll-houses;
Rejoice, Thou who dost open the gates of paradise for
those who love Thee!
Rejoice, Thou who dost vouchsafe those who glorify
Thee everlasting blessedness in the kingdom of
heaven;

Rejoice, Thou who dost shame in the sight of all, those who honor Thee not!
Rejoice, our mighty and swift helper in times of grievous trials;
Rejoice, Thou who recallest all men to the bliss of Eden!
Rejoice, O Thou who art full of grace, healer of our souls and bodies!

Kontakion XIII

O most hymned Mother of our Lord Jesus Christ most sweet, mercifully accept this our meager supplication, deliver us from every danger, sickness, and from sudden death, and account us worthy to inherit the kingdom of heaven, and with all the saints to chant unto Thy Son and our God: Alleluia! Alleluia! Alleluia!

This Kontakion is recited thrice, whereupon Ikos I and Kontakion I are repeated.

Prayer to the All-Holy Theotokos before Her Icon, Known as "The Healer"

O most blessed and omnipotent Lady and Mistress, O Virgin Theotokos, accept these prayers, offered to Thee with tears by us, Thine unworthy servants, who with compunction send up hymnody before Thy healing image, as to Thee who art here present and dost hearken to our supplication. For Thou dost fulfill the petition of each, dost ease sorrows, curest the sick, healest the paralyzed and infirm, drivest the demons away from the possessed, cleansest lepers and hast mercy on children; and what is more, O Lady, Mistress and Theotokos, Thou grantest release from bonds and prison and dost cure all the multifarious passions: for all things are possible through Thy mediation before Thy Son, Christ our God. O most hymned Mother, All-Holy Theotokos, never cease to pray for us, Thine unworthy servants, who glorify and honor Thee, and who bow down with compunction before Thine all-pure image, and have sure hope and undoubting faith in Thee, the all-glorious and immaculate Ever-Virgin, now and ever, and unto the ages of ages. Amen.

Troparia to the All-Holy Theotokos
Chanted before Her Icon, Known as "The Healer"

Troparion, in Tone IV

As Thy holy image, "The Healer", shineth forth like an all-radiant star with divine miracles, O Mary Theotokos, grant also unto us the healing of infirmities of soul and body, salvation and great mercy.

Troparion, in Tone I

Unto those who venerate Thy holy image with love, who glorify Thee, the true Mother of God, and bow down before Thee with faith, O pure Virgin, Thou hast been shown to be a healer, driving far from them every evil and sickness, in that Thou art omnipotent.

The Icon of the All-Holy Theotokos
Known as "The Healer"

The icon of the Mother of God, "The Healer", is one of the most ancient, dating from the 6th century. Another icon with the same name was glorified by miracles in the 18th century. St. Dimitri of Rostov's book, *The Fleece Bedewed*, contains the following account of a miraculous sign wrought by the Mother of God. It was the pious habit of Vincent Vul'vinensky, a clergyman of the church in Navarninsk, on entering and leaving church, to bow down before the image of the Mother of God and to utter the short prayer "Rejoice, O Thou who art full of grace! The Lord is with thee. Blessed is the Fruit of Thy womb, which bore Christ, and the breasts which nourished our Lord, God and Saviour."

One day, this pious clergyman fell ill of a dangerous malady: his tongue became gangrenous, and the pain from this was so great that he went out of his mind. When he recovered his senses, the sick man consciously recited his usual prayer to the Theotokos, and straightway beheld a most comely youth standing at the head of his bed. This was his guardian angel. Gazing at the ailing man with sympathy, the angel called upon the All-Holy Theotokos, addressing to Her a prayer for the recovery of his charge. Suddenly, the Mother of God Herself appeared and in Her ineffable mercy provided a sign. The sick man sensed that he had completely recovered his health; went to church, and stood in the choir with the chanters.

Akathist Hymn to the All-Holy Theotokos in Honor of Her Wonder-working Icon "Unexpected Joy"

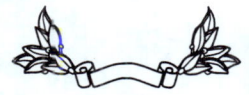

Unexpected Joy

Akathist Hymn
to the All-Holy Theotokos
in Honor of Her Wonder-working Icon
"Unexpected Joy"
Which the Holy Church Celebrates on the 9th of December

Kontakion I

To Thee, O Theotokos, the Mother of God and Queen, who wast chosen from among all generations, and who once appeared to an iniquitous man to turn him from the path of ungodliness, do we offer hymnody of thanksgiving. As Thou art possessed of ineffable loving-kindness, free us from all misfortunes and sins, that we may cry to thee: Rejoice, O Thou who givest unexpected joy to the faithful!

Ikos I

The angels and the souls of the righteous were amazed when Thou didst stand forth before Thy Son and God, and with great entreaty didst mediate for a man who ever abode in sins; and gazing with the eyes of faith upon Thy great compassion, with compunction we cry out to Thee thus:

> Rejoice, Thou who dost accept the prayers of all Christians;
> Rejoice, Thou who dost not reject the entreaties even of the most wretched sinners!
> Rejoice, Thou who intercedest with Thy Son for them;
> Rejoice, Thou who givest them the unexpected joy of salvation!

Rejoice, Thou who by Thine intercession savest the whole world;

Rejoice, Thou who dost assuage all our grief!

Rejoice, Mother of the God of all, who dost comfort the souls of the afflicted;

Rejoice, Thou who settest our life in good order!

Rejoice, Thou who hast brought deliverance from sins to all men;

Rejoice, Thou who for the whole world gavest birth unto Joy!

Rejoice, Thou who with compassion dost regard Thy sinful children;

Rejoice, Thou who with joy leadest the penitent into the kingdom of God!

Rejoice, O Thou who givest unexpected joy to the faithful!

Kontakion II

Beholding a man who, though he was iniquitous, yet cast himself down before Her honored icon every day with faith and hope and offered Her the salutation of the archangel, the All-Holy One hearkened to the glorification even of such a sinner, that, beholding Her maternal loving-kindness, all in heaven and on earth may cry out to God: Alleluia!

Ikos II

Thy love for the Christian race truly surpasseth the understanding of man, for Thou didst not cease Thy mediation for the iniquitous man even when Thy Son showed Thee the wounds of the nails which pierced Him because of men's sins. And seeing Thee making such tireless intercession for us sinners, we cry out to Thee with tears:

Rejoice, fervent helper of the Christian race, given us by God;

Rejoice, O our guide, who leadest us up to the heavenly homeland!

Rejoice, fortress and refuge of the faithful;
Rejoice, help of all who call upon Thy holy name!
Rejoice, Thou who from the pit of destruction dost rescue those who have been despised and rejected by all;
Rejoice, Thou who returnest them to the right path!
Rejoice, Thou who dispellest incessant despondency and darkness of soul;
Rejoice, Thou who givest a new and higher understanding to those whose intelligence hath been devastated by infirmity!
Rejoice, Thou who takest into Thine own omnipotent hands those who have been abandoned by their physicians!
Rejoice, Thou who makest of Thy compassions vesture for those stripped naked of the virtues!
Rejoice, Thou who dost draw forth life-giving water from the well of Thy loving-kindness, to give as drink to those who thirst!
Rejoice, merciful Lady who dispenseth the grace of Thy Son as alms to the destitute!
Rejoice, O Thou who givest unexpected joy to the faithful!

Kontakion III

The power of grace abounded where sin was rife, that all the angels in heaven might rejoice over one penitent sinner, chanting before the throne of God: Alleluia!

Ikos III

Possessed of maternal loving-kindness for the Christian race, O Mistress, Thou extendest a helping hand unto all who have recourse to Thee with faith and hope, that with one heart and one mouth they all might offer Thee such glorification as this:

Rejoice, for through Thee doth the blessing of God descend upon us;

Rejoice, for through Thee do we have even greater boldness before God!

Rejoice, for in the midst of all our misfortunes and evil circumstances Thou offerest up earnest supplication to Thy Son in our behalf;

Rejoice, Thou who dost render our prayers pleasing unto God!

Rejoice, for Thou drivest the invisible foe away from us;

Rejoice, for Thou deliverest us from visible enemies!

Rejoice, for Thou dost soften the hearts of wicked men;

Rejoice, for Thou removest us from slander, reproach and insults!

Rejoice, for by Thee are all our good desires fulfilled!

Rejoice, for Thy supplication is able to accomplish much before Thy Son and God;

Rejoice, for Thy maternal entreaties move Him to temper justice with pity;

Rejoice, for through Thee doth His infinite love for man come down upon us sinners!

Rejoice, O Thou who givest unexpected joy to the faithful!

Kontakion IV

While a tempest of sinful thoughts raged within him, the iniquitous man prayed before Thine honored icon; and seeing blood flow in streams from the wounds of Thy preëternal Son, as it flowed forth when Christ was on the Cross, he fell down in fear and cried out thus to Thee with lamentation: "Have mercy on me, O Mother of loving-kindness, that my wickedness may not prevail over Thine ineffable goodness and loving-kindness: for Thou art the only hope and refuge of all sinners! Wherefore, incline Thy Son and my Creator to mercy, O good Mother, and entreat Him, that I may unceasingly cry out to Him: Alleluia!"

Ikos IV

Hearing of the salvation of their earthly brother who was perishing, which was miraculously accomplished by Thy supplications, the inhabitants of heaven glorified Thee, the kind-hearted Queen of heaven and earth; and having learned of this aid given a sinner like us, even though our tongue is at a loss how to praise Thee as is meet, we sinners cry out to Thee thus from the depths of our compunctionate hearts:

>Rejoice, surety of the salvation of sinners;
>Rejoice, search for the perishing!
>Rejoice, unexpected joy of the sinful;
>Rejoice, Thou who settest aright the fallen!
>Rejoice, intercessor before God, who savest the world from tribulations;
>Rejoice, mediator for the wretched and lowly!
>Rejoice, for the demons tremble at the sound of Thy supplications;
>Rejoice, for the angels rejoice thereat!
>Rejoice, for the power of Thy prayers filleth us mortals with gladness;
>Rejoice, for the strength of Thine entreaties in our behalf moveth us to jubilation!
>Rejoice, for thereby dost Thou pull us from the mire of sins;
>Rejoice, for Thou dost extinguish the flame of our passions!
>Rejoice, O Thou who givest unexpected joy to the faithful!

Kontakion V

Thou hast shown us the wonder-working icon of Thy Mother as a divinely moving star, O Lord; for, gazing upon Her image with our bodily eyes, we are upborne to Her, the prototype, in mind and heart, and through Her we hasten unto Thee, chanting: Alleluia!

Ikos V

The guardian angels of Christians, seeing that the Mother of God aideth them in instructing, helping and saving them, hastened to cry out thus unto Her who is higher in honor than the cherubim and more glorious beyond compare than the seraphim:

Rejoice, Thou who reignest eternally with Thy Son and God;
Rejoice, Thou who ever offerest unto Him entreaties for the Christian race!
Rejoice, instructor in Christian faith and piety;
Rejoice, uprooter of heresies and corrupting schisms!
Rejoice, Thou who preservest from temptations which ruin soul and body;
Rejoice, Thou who deliverest from perilous circumstances and sudden death without repentance and Holy Communion;
Rejoice, Thou who grantest an unashamed ending of life unto those who trust in thee;
Rejoice, Thou who dost unfailingly mediate before Thy Son even after death for a soul which hath departed unto the judgment of the Lord!
Rejoice, Thou who deliverest it from everlasting torment by Thy maternal intercession;
Rejoice, Thou who seest it washed whiter than snow by the blood of Christ!
Rejoice, Thou who dost rejoice greatly in its salvation;
Rejoice, Thou who dost abide with it in the mansions of heaven!
Rejoice, O Thou who givest unexpected joy to the faithful!

Kontakion VI

The holy Demetrius of Rostov was a proclaimer of the wondrous loving-kindness which Thou didst show a certain iniquitous man, for, describing the great and glorious and excellent works of God revealed in Thee, he also committed to writing this act of Thy mercy, for the instruction and consolation of all the faithful, that amid their sins, misfortunes, sorrows and afflictions, with faith they might bend their knees in prayer before Thine image many times each day, and, delivered therefrom, may cry out to God: Alleluia!

Ikos VI

Thy wonder-working icon hath shone forth upon us like an all-radiant beam, O Mother of God, driving away the darkness of misfortunes and tribulations from all who with love cry out to Thee thus:

Rejoice, O our healer amid the ailments of our bodies;
Rejoice, good comforter amid the griefs of our souls!
Rejoice, Thou who dost transform our sorrow into joy;
Rejoice, Thou who dost gladden the hopeless with certain hope!
Rejoice, feeder of the hungry;
Rejoice, vesture of the naked!
Rejoice, consoler of widows;
Rejoice, unseen nurturer of motherless orphans!
Rejoice, helper of those unjustly persecuted and oppressed;
Rejoice, Thou who dost wreak just vengeance upon persecutors and oppressors!
Rejoice, ally of Christians in the war against wickedness;
Rejoice, Thou who grantest us victory over the hordes of the evil one!
Rejoice, O Thou who givest unexpected joy to the faithful!

Kontakion VII

The just Bestower of the law, the Lord Himself, desiring to be a fulfiller of the law and to show forth the abyss of His loving-kindness, inclined Himself to Thy fervent entreaty concerning the iniquitous man, O all-blessed Virgin Mother, saying: "The law commandeth that a son honor his mother. I am Thy Son, and Thou art My Mother. I must needs honor Thee, acceding to Thine entreaty. Wherefore, be it as Thou desirest: his sins are now forgiven for Thy sake." And, seeing the power of the prayer of our Mediatress to accomplish the forgiveness of our offenses, we glorify Her loving-kindness and ineffable compassions, crying out: Alleluia!

Ikos VII

A new, wondrous and glorious sign hath been revealed to all the faithful, for Thou, O Lord, hast imparted the power of miracles not only to Thy Mother, but to Her all-pure countenance depicted upon a board; and marvelling at this mystery, in compunction of heart we cry out to Her such things as these:

> Rejoice, manifestation of the wisdom and goodness of God;
> Rejoice, confirmation of the Faith!
> Rejoice, revelation of grace;
> Rejoice, gift of spiritually profitable understanding!
> Rejoice, easy victory over sinful habits;
> Rejoice, Thou who givest wisdom of speech unto those who ask!
> Rejoice, Thou who makest the senseless wise;
> Rejoice, Thou who givest facility of mind to children who have difficulty learning!
> Rejoice, guardian and instructor of youth;
> Rejoice, guide to piety for Christian parents!
> Rejoice, preserver of Orthodox families;
> Rejoice, support of those bowed down by old age!
> Rejoice, O Thou who givest unexpected joy to the faithful!

Kontakion VIII

A strange and awesome vision did that iniquitous man receive, showing him the goodness of the Lord, which forgave his sins through the intercession of the Mother of God; and thus, having thenceforth corrected his way of life, he lived in a God-pleasing manner. Wherefore, seeing the glorious works and great and varied wisdom of God in the world and our life, let us put away from us earthly vanities and the excessive cares of life, and lead our mind and heart up to the heavens, chanting unto God: Alleluia!

Ikos VIII

Though Thou abidest wholly in the highest, Thou hast never forsaken those below, O All-Loving Queen of heaven and earth; for even though Thou didst ascend into the heavens with Thine all-pure flesh after Thy dormition, yet Thou hast not abandoned the sinners of earth, showing thyself to be a participant in the providence of Thy Son concerning the Christian race. Wherefore, as is fitting, we call Thee blessed:

>Rejoice, Thou who hast enlightened the whole earth with the radiance of Thine all-pure soul;
>Rejoice, Thou who hast gladdened all the heavens with the purity of Thy body!
>Rejoice, holy one who servest the providence of Thy Son for the Christian race;
>Rejoice, ardent intercessor for the whole world!
>Rejoice, Thou who adopted us all at the Cross of Thy Son;
>Rejoice, Thou who ever showest Thy maternal love for us!
>Rejoice, generous bestower of all gifts, spiritual and bodily;
>Rejoice, Mediatress of temporal good things!
>Rejoice, Thou who openest the gates of the kingdom of Christ to the faithful;
>Rejoice, Thou who even on earth fillest their hearts with pure gladness;
>Rejoice, Thou who takest away their griefs and sorrows;

Rejoice Thou who dost cause them to rejoice exceedingly!
Rejoice, O Thou who givest unexpected joy to the faithful!

Kontakion IX

Every angelic being was amazed at the workings of Thy lovingkindness, O Lord, for Thou hast given so steadfast and fervent a helper and aide to the Christian race, who dwelleth invisibly with us, hearkening unto those who chant unto Thee: Alleluia!

Ikos IX

Orators most eloquent, yet unenlightened by God, vainly say that the veneration of a holy image is like unto the worship of an idol, for they do not understand that the honor accorded a holy image ascendeth to its prototype. And we, not only knowing these things well, but hearing from faithful people of the many miracles wrought through the countenance of the Mother of God, and ourselves receiving through the veneration thereof those things needful for this transitory life and that which is eternal, cry out with gladness to the Theotokos:

Rejoice, for miracles are wrought through Thy sacred visage;
Rejoice, for this wisdom and grace is hidden from the wise and learned of this age!
Rejoice, for it is revealed to those of childlike faith;
Rejoice, for Thou dost glorify those who glorify thee!
Rejoice, for those who reject Thee are put to shame in the sight of all;
Rejoice, for they are cast down in the imagination of their heart!
Rejoice, for those who have recourse unto Thee Thou deliverest from flood, fire and the sword;
Rejoice, for they who flee to Thee are cured of every deadly disease!

Rejoice, for Thou dost mercifully heal every sickness of
    man, spiritual and bodily;
Rejoice, for Thou dost protect those who venerate Thee
    from every evil!
Rejoice, for Thou art a calm shelter against tempest for
    those who sail the sea of life;
Rejoice, for even at the end of our life's journey it is
    hoped that Thou wilt lead us to the land of the
    kingdom of Christ, which is untroubled by
    storms!
Rejoice, O Thou who givest unexpected joy to the
    faithful!

Kontakion X

Desiring to save that iniquitous man from straying from the path of life, Thou didst show him a wondrous vision through Thine all-honorable icon, O all-blessed one, that, beholding the miracle, he might repent and, lifted up from the depths of sin by Thy loving forethought, might cry out to God: Alleluia!

Ikos X

Thou art the bulwark of virgins and of all who have recourse unto Thee, O Virgin Theotokos, for the Creator of heaven and earth, Who dwelt within Thy womb and was born of Thee, hath revealed Thee, the Ever-Virgin, as the guardian of virginity, purity and chastity and the vessel of every virtue, and He hath taught all to cry out to Thee:

Rejoice, pillar and ground of virginity;
Rejoice, invisible guardian of purity and chastity!
Rejoice, good instructor of virgins;
Rejoice, excellent adorner and surety of brides!
Rejoice, most desired perfecter of good weddings;
Rejoice, easy delivery for mothers giving birth to
    children!
Rejoice, nurture and gracious protection of children;

Rejoice, Thou who gladdenest childless parents with the fruits of faith!
Rejoice, consolation of grieving mothers;
Rejoice, secret joy of pure virgins and widows!
Rejoice, for by Thine entreaty Thou dost speedily allay the just wrath of God directed against us;
Rejoice, for through Thee doth His loving-kindness descend upon mankind!
Rejoice, O Thou who givest unexpected joy to the faithful!

Kontakion XI

Offering most compunctionate hymnody unto Thee, O Virgin Theotokos, we, the unworthy, beg Thee: Disdain not the cry of Thy servants, for unto Thee do we flee amid perils and tribulations, and before Thee do we pour forth tears amid our misfortunes, chanting: Alleluia!

Ikos XI

We perceive the holy Virgin to be a light-giving lamp revealed to those in the darkness of sin and the vale of tears; for the spiritual fire of Her prayers, shedding the light of instruction and consolation, leadeth to the never-waning Light all who honor Her with these cries:

Rejoice, ray emitted by Christ our God, the Sun of righteousness;
Rejoice, Thou who dost cast light upon the unclean conscience!
Rejoice, Thou who knowest well all things secret and hard to foresee, and relatest them to those to whom it is proper;
Rejoice, Thou who puttest to shame lying seers and vain predictions!
Rejoice, Thou who dost place a goodly thought in man's heart in time of doubt;
Rejoice Thou who dost resolve every perplexity!

Rejoice, Thou who ever dwellest with those who abide in fasting, prayer and the contemplation of God;

Rejoice, sure consolation of God-fearing monks and nuns!

Rejoice, Thou who dost encourage and enlighten the faithful pastors of the Church!

Rejoice, Thou who through them impartest the grace of Thy Son!

Rejoice, unashamed helper of sinners who repent before God;

Rejoice, fervent mediatress of all Christians!

Rejoice, O Thou who givest unexpected joy to the faithful!

Kontakion XII

Ask divine grace for us from Thy Son and God; stretch forth to us a helping hand; drive from us every enemy and adversary; and bring peace to our life, that we may not meet an evil end, without repentance. But accept us into the mansions of heaven, O Theotokos, that, rejoicing, we may chant unto God Who saveth us through Thee: Alleluia!

Ikos XII

Hymning Thine ineffable maternal loving-kindness for the iniquitous man, we all praise Thee as the steadfast intercessor for us sinners; and we bow down before Thee who prayest for us. For we believe and trust that Thou dost ask of Thy Son and God good things, temporal and eternal, for all who with love cry out to Thee thus:

Rejoice, trampling down of all the assaults and temptations which come from the world, the flesh and the devil;

Rejoice, unexpected reconciliation of those at bitter enmity!

Rejoice, incomprehensible correction of unrepentant sinners;

Rejoice, speedy consoler of those sick with despondency!

Rejoice, Thou who keepest us safe by the grace of humility and patience;
Rejoice, universal denunciation of oath-breaking and theft!
Rejoice, Thou who with peace and love dost protect kinsmen from domestic strive and enmity;
Rejoice, Thou who invisibly turnest us away from destructive pursuits and senseless desires!
Rejoice, sure aid in our goodly intentions;
Rejoice, Thou who dost assist us in God-pleasing works!
Rejoice, Thou who makest us worthy to be called Christians!
Rejoice, helper of us all at the hour of death!
Rejoice, O Thou who givest unexpected joy to the faithful!

Kontakion XIII

O most hymned Mother, who contained the uncontainable God in Thy womb and gavest birth to Joy for the whole world! Accept this present hymnody, transform all our griefs into joy, and from all perils and future torment deliver all who cry out to Thee: Alleluia! Alleluia! Alleluia!

Prayer to the All-Holy Theotokos before Her Icon, "Unexpected Joy"

O All-Holy Virgin, most good Mother of the most good Son, protectress of the royal city of Moscow, faithful intercessor and helper of all who find themselves amid sins, tribulations, misfortunes and sickness! Accept this hymnody of supplication which is offered unto Thee by us, Thine unworthy servants; and as of old Thou didst not disdain the sinner who prayed many times each day before Thine honored icon, but gavest him the unexpected joy of repentance, and by Thy great and ardent mediation before Thy Son didst incline Him to forgive that errant sinner: so now do Thou not disdain the entreaties of us, Thine unworthy servants; and beseech Thy Son and our God, that He grant unexpected joy unto all of us who with faith and compunction worship before Thy healing image, unto each according to his need: to sinners bemired in the pit of evils and the passions, all-effective admonition, repentance and salvation; to those in sorrow and grief, consolation; to those who find themselves in misfortunes and afflictions, complete deliverance therefrom; to the hopeless and those who have lost courage, hope and endurance; to those who live in joy and abundance, unceasing gratitude to the Benefactor; to the poor, loving-kindness; to those long ill and in sickness, who have been abandoned by the physicians, unexpected healing and fortitude; to those who have lost their mind through illness, the return and restoration of their sanity; to those who are departing to the everlasting and never-ending life, the memory of death, compunction and contrition for their sins, a watchful spirit and steadfast hope in the compassion of the Judge. O All-Holy Lady! Have pity on all who venerate Thy most precious name, and show Thine omnipotent protection and aid unto all: those who abide in piety, purity and an honorable manner of life do Thou preserve in goodness until their final departure; make the evil good; guide the lost to the right path; assist every good deed which is pleasing to Thy Son; destroy every evil deed which is contrary to God; send down invisible help and admonition from heaven upon those who find themselves in perplexity and difficult and perilous circumstances; save them from temptations, stumbling-blocks and destruction; defend and preserve them from all wicked men and from enemies visible and invisible; sail with those who journey by water; accompany those who travel by land; nurture those who hunger and are in need; be Thou a shelter and refuge for those who have no roof or haven; clothe Thou the naked; help those who are oppressed and unjustly persecuted; invisibly vindicate those who are subject to slander, reproach and calumny; unmask the slanderers and calumniators in the sight of all; to those who are at bitter enmity give unexpected reconciliation; and unto all of us give love one for another, peace, piety, health and length of days. Preserve marriages in love and oneness of mind; pacify spouses who are separated and at enmity, unite them to one another, and render their bond of love unbreakable; to mothers who are giving birth to children grant a quick delivery; nurture infants; make chaste the youth, and open their minds to accept every profitable teaching and the fear of God, and teach them moderation and industry; and with peace and love preserve them all from domestic strife and the malice of kinfolk. Be Thou a mother to motherless orphans; turn them away from every fault and defilement, and teach them every good and God-pleasing thing. Taking away the defilement of sin, lead Thou the deceived and those who have fallen into sin and impurity up from the pit of destruction. Be Thou the comforter and helper of widows, and a staff for the elderly. Deliver us all from sudden death without repentance, and grant us all a Christian ending to our life, peaceful, without fear and shame, and furnish us with a good defense at the dread tribunal of Christ. Cause those who have departed this life in faith and repentance to dwell with the angels and all the saints; beg Thy Son to be merciful unto those who have died a sudden death; and for all the departed who have no kinfolk to entreat Thy Son for their repose, be Thou a tireless and fervent advocate and mediatress: that all in heaven and on earth may see Thee to be the steadfast and unashamed intercessor of the Christian race, and knowing this may glorify Thee, and with Thee Thy Son, and His unoriginate Father and His consubstantial Spirit, now and ever, and unto the ages of ages. Amen.

Akathists to Various Saints

Akathist Hymn to Our Venerable Father Ambrose of Optina

Saint Ambrose of Optina

Akathist Hymn to Our Venerable Father Ambrose of Optina

Whose Memory the Holy Church Celebrates on October 10th

Kontakion I

O chosen favorite of God and wonder-worker, great elder Ambrose, boast of Optina and wondrous instructor of all Russia! Glorifying thy life, which is excellent in struggles, we offer thee hymnody of great praise. As thou hast boldness before the Lord, pray for all of us, thy children, who cry out with compunction:

Rejoice, O venerable Ambrose, divinely wise teacher of faith and piety!

Ikos I

Emulating the life of the angels, thou didst spurn all the beautiful and quickly passing things of this corrupt world, and didst direct thy steps to the Elder Hilarion, that he might guide thee in truth to the path of life and bless thee to undertake the struggle for salvation. And foreseeing thy future God-pleasing life, he sent thee to the Monastery of Optina, which thou didst find to be a spiritual haven for thyself. And seeing that such was the will of God for thee, we say such things as these:

> Rejoice, scion of pious parents, chosen by God;
> Rejoice, thou who didst love the Lord from thy childhood years!
> Rejoice, thou who from thy youth wast inclined to study;

Rejoice, thou who didst accept the Spirit-bearing teaching of the holy fathers!

Rejoice, rejection of the good things of this world which quickly perish;

Rejoice, strong desire for treasures which do not decay!

Rejoice, thou who didst seek the will of God for the salvation of thy soul;

Rejoice, thou who didst receive a blessing for the monastic path!

Rejoice, O venerable Ambrose, divinely wise teacher of faith and piety!

Kontakion II

Seeing the goodly intention of thy heart, Christ traced out for thee the narrow and thorny path of thy salvation; and when thou didst suddenly find thyself nigh unto death on a bed of pain, thou didst make a vow unto the Lord: that if He would heal thee, thou wouldst give thyself wholly over to the struggles of monasticism. Wherefore, lifted up by the mercy of God from thy bier of pain, thou didst straightway glorify the most compassionate God, the Physician of souls and bodies, crying: Alleluia!

Ikos II

Having acquired an understanding of the divine Scriptures, thou didst wonder in godly fear how the Lord would arrange the future way of thy salvation, and how thou shouldst undertake to tread the laborious and sorrowful path of the monastic life. And marveling at thy goodly intention, we chant unto thee:

Rejoice, thou who didst set all thy hope on our provident God;

Rejoice, thou who didst seek His good will alone!

Rejoice, thou who wast ready to bear every trial for salvation;

Rejoice, thou who didst follow the dictates of thy
    conscience!
Rejoice, thou who didst disdain worldly amusements;
Rejoice, thou who hadst no love for earthly riches!
Rejoice, thou who wast moved to enslave thyself wholly
    to God alone;
Rejoice, thou whose only desire was to please Him!
Rejoice, O venerable Ambrose, divinely wise teacher of
    faith and piety!

Kontakion III

Made steadfast by the power of love, in faith thou wast zealous to acquire the life of the Gospel, following the example of the venerable fathers of the ancient Church; and when the Lord gave thee an understanding of how to please Him, thou didst chant with compunction: alleluia!

Ikos III

Possessed of a mighty faith in the good providence of God for the salvation of man, thou didst hasten to the precious Tambov icon of the all-holy Theotokos, which was a blessèd hierloom of thy family; and thou didst pray humbly to our Mistress, that She direct thy path. And, seeing thy steadfast hope in the mercy of the Queen of heaven, we chant unto thee:

Rejoice, faithful and beloved child of the Mother of
    God;
Rejoice, mystic acquisition of the power of Her sacred
    protection!
Rejoice, thou who didst faithfully cherish thine ancestral
    blessing in Her icon.
Rejoice, blessed venerator of our zealous helper!
Rejoice, thou who many times during the night didst
    with tears offer up prayers unto Her;
Rejoice, thou who didst receive heavenly help from Her
    without disappointment!

Rejoice, thou who thus didst find sweet consolation for thy heart;
Rejoice, for thou didst receive right peaceful compunction!
Rejoice, O venerable Ambrose, divinely wise teacher of faith and piety!

Kontakion IV

Impelled by a storm of thoughts, thou didst go to the Monastery of Saint Sergius of Radonezh, that the wonder-worker of all Russia and teacher of monastic activity, who poureth forth streams of gracious aid from the shrine of his precious relics, that he might fortify thy heart for the struggles of the monastic contest which lay before thee. And moved there to compunction of heart, thou didst cry out with joy: Alleluia!

Ikos IV

Hearing of the great life and piety of the divinely wise fathers and elders of the Optina Hermitage, thou didst secretly abandon the world and all that it is in it, and undaunted didst arrive at the monastery in humility of soul, that thou mightest find salvation and please God. And perceiving the exceeding great zeal of thy soul, we offer thee hymnody of praise:

Rejoice, thou who didst consider the corruptible good things of this world to be naught;
Rejoice, thou who didst recognize the sweetness of the Church!
Rejoice, thou who madest thine abode in a holy monastery;
Rejoice, thou who gavest thyself wholly to God!
Rejoice, thou who didst truly fulfill the commandments of God;
Rejoice, thou who didst sweetly taste the fruits of Christ's teaching!

Rejoice, lover of the struggles of the holy fathers;
Rejoice, tireless maintainer of purity of soul!
Rejoice, O venerable Ambrose, divinely wise teacher of faith and piety!

Kontakion V

The divinely given hermitage took thee into its fatherly embrace, and there thou didst meekly dwell and didst first undertake the labors of obedience in the cell of that great elder, the divinely enlightened Leo, by whom thou wast instructed in spiritual activity; and having come to know the sweetness of the denial of thine own will, thou didst cry out: Alleluia!

Ikos V

Seeing thy success in monasticism, the fathers of the hermitage invested thee in the habit of the great schema; and Christ, the Judge of the contest, vouchsafed that thou acquire angelic grace. Wherefore, we cry unto thee:

Rejoice, thou who didst love God with all thy heart;
Rejoice, thou who didst serve Him with all thy soul!
Rejoice, thou who didst immutably make thy faith firm through many labors;
Rejoice, thou who through hope didst arm thyself with hope from on high!
Rejoice, treasury of evangelical love;
Rejoice, dwelling-place of the Holy Spirit!
Rejoice, warrior valiant in monastic struggles;
Rejoice, all-wondrous emulator of the life of the angels!
Rejoice, O venerable Ambrose, divinely wise teacher of faith and piety!

Kontakion VI

Thou wast shown to be a preacher of the Orthodox Faith and the true life in Christ Jesus, rejecting teachings contrary to the Gospel and the Church; and unto Christ, the Bestower of life, thou didst turn many who had strayed from the path, chanting with thanks: Alleluia!

Ikos VI

Thou didst shine forth like a lamp of great radiance in the land of Russia, enlightening with the light of Truth everyone who came unto thee; and those weighed down with sins and many sorrows have found in thee a divinely wise guide of piety and a good father to all the afflicted, the suffering and the downtrodden, who chant such things as these:

> Rejoice, luminary of the Orthodox land of Russia;
> Rejoice, mirror of love divine!
> Rejoice, tower of apostolic faith;
> Rejoice, rock of hope for everlasting life!
> Rejoice, divinely inspired guide out of all evil circumstances;
> Rejoice, loving preacher of repentance!
> Rejoice, physician of bodily ailments;
> Rejoice, healer of sicknesses of soul!
> Rejoice, O venerable Ambrose, divinely wise teacher of faith and piety!

Kontakion VII

Desiring to follow Christ Himself, thou didst emulate Him with all thy heart, taking His yoke upon thee; and having learned of Him meekness and humility, thou didst find peace for thy soul, which ever crieth out: Alleluia!

Ikos VII

Thou wast shown to be a new and wondrous star of sanctity in the firmament of the Church when thou didst ascend the spiritual ladder to angelic perfection; and thou didst spread the rays of thy love over the face of the whole land of Russia, and hast drawn to thyself the high-born and those of low estate, the wise of this age and the unlearned, who cry to thee such things as these:

Rejoice, city standing on the peak of a mountain;
Rejoice, beacon driving away the gloom of ignorance!
Rejoice, thou who healest all the infirm;
Rejoice, thou who deliverest from misfortunes and the delusions of the enemy!
Rejoice, comforter of the grieving;
Rejoice, thou who givest spiritual drink to the thirsty!
Rejoice, denouncer of the blasphemous philosophies of this age;
Rejoice, thou who settest many of the lost on the path of the Truth!
Rejoice, O venerable Ambrose, divinely wise teacher of faith and piety!

Kontakion VIII

In the earthly world thou didst stand before the strangers and sojourners seeking the city of heaven, and thou didst bear the burdens and weaknesses of thy neighbor who sought thy help, and didst thus fulfill the law of Christ, chanting with thanksgiving: Alleluia!

Ikos VIII

Wholly filled with the fire of divine love, all throughout thy monastic life thou didst bear the most burdensome cross of bodily pangs, possessing thy soul in patience, in the words of the Gospel of Christ; and thou hast taught us all to bear our cross without complaint, for which we cry out to thee:

Rejoice, leader for those seeking salvation;
Rejoice, model of true obedience!
Rejoice, thou who thyself didst endure grievous infirmities;
Rejoice, thou who hast taught forbearance amid sickness and grief unto those who have recourse unto thee!
Rejoice, thou who givest excellent care to thy flock;
Rejoice, feeder of those who hunger for life everlasting!

Rejoice, protector of the oppressed;
Rejoice, rebuker of those who refuse to submit to the will of God!
Rejoice, O venerable Ambrose, divinely wise teacher of faith and piety!

Kontakion IX

Thou didst thoroughly test thy human nature amid sicknesses and bodily weaknesses, crucifying thy flesh with its passions and lusts; and with tireless prayer thou didst drive away perils and the temptations of evil spirits, and thus didst teach all to withstand the wiles of the demons, crying out with faith: Alleluia!

Ikos IX

With the word of God and thy pure manner of life thou didst cast into confusion orators, the vain-minded, and those who knew not the power of the Orthodox Faith, and didst truly shine forth like a radiant pillar of piety and a keeper of the traditions of the holy fathers, earnestly setting forth the works of the ancient fathers in easily comprehensible form. And, marveling at thy labors, we chant such things as these:

Rejoice, diamond of the right Faith;
Rejoice, might of life lived according to the Faith!
Rejoice, instiller of the spirit of piety;
Rejoice, sower of the Christian virtues!
Rejoice, inheritor of the struggles of eldership;
Rejoice, spiritual enlightenment of a multitude of monks!
Rejoice, thou who leddest them to salvation;
Rejoice, thou who didst turn many sinners to repentance!
Rejoice, O venerable Ambrose, divinely wise teacher of faith and piety!

Kontakion X

Helping those seeking the kingdom of heaven to find salvation, thou didst show thyself to be a faithful guide, pointing the way for laymen and for the clergy; and at the end of thy days thou didst lay aside thy many labors, founding the Shamordino Convent for the poor that the nuns thereof might find rest and salvation for their souls, chanting the hymn of praise: Alleluia!

Ikos X

Thou wast a bulwark and refuge for thy children, protecting them from demonic assaults by thy tireless prayers; and thou didst inspire them to wage war invisibly against the spirits of malice, setting pride and love of glory at naught by humility. Wherefore, rejoicing, we cry unto thee:

> Rejoice, thou who didst quench the burning arrows of the enemy;
> Rejoice, thou who didst conquer the hosts of the demons!
> Rejoice, thou who didst free those held captive by the spirits of evil;
> Rejoice, thou who leddest forth many souls from the prison of the passions!
> Rejoice, thou who through love and prayer didst turn to God those gone astray;
> Rejoice, good guardian of orphans and widows!
> Rejoice, God-bearing giver of guidance to monks and nuns;
> Rejoice, eloquent preacher of humble-mindedness and meekness!
> Rejoice, O venerable Ambrose, divinely wise teacher of faith and piety!

Kontakion XI

Compunctionate hymnody do we offer unto thee, the speedy helper of all who with faith and love have recourse to thee amid need and grief: for to the end of thy days thou wast a solicitous father for the suffering and oppressed who sought consolation for their souls. Wherefore, God is truly glorified by thee, for He is wondrous in His saints who cry out unceasingly: Alleluia!

Ikos XI

All the ends of the earth saw in thee a beacon of the virtues, O Ambrose our father: for thou didst finish thine earthly sojourn in patience and humility, didst fulfill all the commandments which Christ left us in His teaching, and didst pass from earth to heaven, in bliss beholding thy Lord, in that thou art a faithful servant of Christ. Wherefore, rejoicing, we chant to thee such things as these:

> Rejoice, diligent servant who carried out the will of thy Lord;
> Rejoice, warrior of Christ, who forsook the vanity of life!
> Rejoice, thou who didst serve God alone;
> Rejoice, thou who didst fulfill all the commandments of God!
> Rejoice, thou who wast accounted worthy of a dwelling-place in heaven;
> Rejoice, thou who sharest in glory on high!
> Rejoice, inheritor of life everlasting;
> Rejoice, all-praised favorite of God!
> Rejoice, O venerable Ambrose, divinely wise teacher of faith and piety!

Kontakion XII

Thou hast inherited a treasure of grace that cannot be stolen and hast found a peaceful haven in the heavens. And through the action of the providence of God in these latter days thou hast been reckoned among the choir of the saints. Wherefore, blessing thy holy memory we all chant: Alleluia!

Ikos XII

Chanting thy glorification, we offer thee our humble prayers, like incense of sweet savor. Forget not thy children, who honor thy holy name and cry out to thee in thanksgiving:

Rejoice, O Ambrose, namesake of heavenly sustenance;
Rejoice, honored boast of the Orthodox Church!
Rejoice, thou who hast joined the choir of the holy favorites of God;
Rejoice, thou who servest the mysteries with the company of the venerable fathers!
Rejoice, our steadfast intercessor before the throne of God Most High;
Rejoice, our fervent mediator before the judgment seat of God!
Rejoice, guide for us who wander in the vale of tears;
Rejoice, tireless advocate for the whole Russian land!
Rejoice, O venerable Ambrose, divinely wise teacher of faith and piety!

Kontakion XIII

O wondrous favorite of Christ and wonder-worker, our venerable elder Ambrose! Accept now the meager supplication of thine unworthy servants: Abandon us not amid tribulations and pain. Come thou and extend thy helping hand. Guide us to the path of repentance and salvation, that we may be delivered from everlasting torment, that through thee we may ever glorify God, crying out: Alleluia! Alleluia! Alleluia!

This Kontakion is recited thrice; whereupon Ikos I and Kontakion I are repeated.

Prayers to the Venerable Ambrose, Elder of Optina

Prayer I

O great elder and favorite of God, our venerable father Ambrose, boast of Optina and teacher of piety to all Russia! We glorify thy humble life in Christ, whereby God exalted thy name while thou wast yet on earth, and hath even more crowned thee with heavenly honor since thy departure to the bridal-chamber of everlasting glory. Accept now the entreaty of us, thine unworthy children, who honor thee and call upon thy holy name. By thine intercession before the throne of God deliver us from all grievous circumstances and sickness of body, from attacks of malice, and corrupt and wicked temptations. From our most generous God send down upon our homeland peace, tranquility and prosperity. Be thou the perpetual protector of the monastery, wherein thou didst make progress in struggles, by all of which thou didst please our God Who is glorified in Trinity—the Father, the Son and the Holy Spirit—to Whom is due all glory, honor and worship, now and ever, and unto the ages of ages. Amen.

Prayer II

O our venerable and God-bearing father Ambrose! Desiring to labor for the Lord, thou didst make thine abode in Optina, and tirelessly didst struggle in labors, vigils, prayers and fasting, and wast a guide for monastics and a zealous teacher for all men. Wherefore, standing now, since thy departure from earthly things, before the King of heaven, entreat His goodness, that He have pity on the place of thy sojourn, the holy Monastery of Optina, where thou abidest forever in the spirit of thy love, and that He fulfill the goodly petitions of all thy people who with faith fall down before the shrine of thy relics. Beseech our merciful Lord, that He send down upon us an abundance of the good things of the earth, and even more that He grant us those things that are for the profit of our souls, and that He vouchsafe that we may finish this transitory life in repentance, and that on the day of judgment he count us worthy of a place and bliss in His kingdom, unto the ages of ages. Amen.

Prayer III

O most honored elder of the all-glorious and wondrous Hermitage of Optina, our venerable and God-bearing father Ambrose, goodly adornment of our Church and beacon of grace illumining all with heavenly light, beauteous spiritual fruit of Russia and the whole world, abundantly delighting and gladdening the souls of the faithful! With faith and trembling we now fall down before thy holy icon [the healing shrine of thy holy relics], which thou hast mercifully bestowed as a consolation and help for the suffering, and we humbly entreat thee, O holy father, with heart and mouth, as the guide of all Russia and teacher of piety, our shepherd, the physician of our bodily and spiritual ailments: Look upon thy children, who have sinned greatly in word and deed, and visit us with thy great and holy love, wherein thou didst gloriously excel in thy days on earth, and even more since thy righteous repose, instructing us in the canons of the holy and divinely illumined fathers, teaching us the commandments of Christ, for which thou wast wholly zealous to the last hour of thine onerous monastic life. Ask for us, who are weak in soul and afflicted with sorrows, a right-acceptable and salvific time for repentance, true correction and renewal of our way of life, for therein we sinners have become vain in mind and heart and have given ourselves over to unprofitable and grievous passions, lusts and iniquities without number. Wherefore, accept, preserve and protect us under the shelter of thy great mercy; send down upon us blessing from the Lord, that we may bear the easy yoke of Christ in longsuffering until the end of our days, hoping for the life which is to come and the kingdom where there is no grief, no sighing, but life and the endless joy which floweth from the one, most holy and blessed Well-spring of immortality: God—the Father, the Son and the Holy Spirit—Who is worshiped in Trinity, now and ever, and unto the ages of ages.

Akathist Hymn
to Our Venerable and God-bearing Fathers Anthony and Theodosius of the Caves of Kiev

Sts. Anthony and Theodosius

Akathist Hymn
to Our Venerable and God-bearing Fathers
Anthony and Theodosius of the Caves of Kiev

Kontakion I

O our venerable and God-bearing fathers, Anthony and Theodosius of the Caves, ye elect of the Holy Spirit, who are filled with Him, excellent scions of the Russian land, all-wondrous adornments of the Russian people! As I, the unworthy one, am about to chant hymns of laudation unto you, I humbly entreat you: With the light of the grace given you by God illumine my benighted mind, enlighten the darkness of ignorance, release me from vexation and hindrance, strengthen my weakness, and as our fathers free us all from every misfortune and peril, from tribulations and sickness, that in fervor of heart we may all cry out to you from the depths of our souls:

> Rejoice, O Anthony and Theodosius, ye founders of the
> monastic life in Russia!

Ikos I

Desiring a way of life like unto that of the angels, in your youth ye straightway consciously rejected all the beautiful things of this world, and casting them from thee as though they were refuse, ye trampled them under your youthful feet and sanctified yourselves wholly unto Christ God as a gift and offering. Wherefore, considering this, your holy and God-pleasing will, we offer you such hymns as these:

> Rejoice, O God-bearing fathers who spurned all the
> good and beautiful things of the world;

Rejoice, ye who from your youth loved Christ with all your heart and all your soul!

Rejoice, ye who accounted the house, estates and all the acquisitions of your parents as but nought;

Rejoice, ye who, while yet in your childhood, took the easy and sweet yoke of Christ upon your shoulders!

Rejoice, for ye emulated the God-pleasing sacrifice of the righteous Abel;

Rejoice, for ye were imitators of the God-loving Noah in his offering upon leaving the ark!

Rejoice, ye who offered your Creator your bodies instead of fat lambs and bulls;

Rejoice, ye who offered Christ the Saviour your souls instead of sweet-smelling incense!

Rejoice, ye who prepared your hearts well for perpetual service to God and His all-pure Mother, and who committed yourselves wholly unto them;

Rejoice, ye who, like unto Samuel, did beautifully spend your whole life in the service of God, pleasing Him even unto your final breath!

Rejoice, ye who taught a great multitude of men and women, young men and virgins, to emulate your manner of life;

Rejoice, ye who sweetened the easy and light yoke of Christ from many!

Rejoice, O Anthony and Theodosius, ye founders of the monastic life in Russia!

Kontakion II

The all-seeing eye of the Father of lights, beholding your undertaking, which greatly pleased Him, and your soul-saving intention, even though He did not straightway arrange for you to dwell together, yet in a short time thus united and joined you together as He had united and joined together Peter and Paul, that bearing a single yoke, ye might lead many to the mansions of heaven. Wherefore, marvelling at this, in thanksgiving we chant unto God Who so arranged it: Alleluia!

Ikos II

Eager to acquire a God-pleasing understanding spiritually beneficial for thyself and for others, O most lauded Anthony, day and night, with fervent tears, thou didst earnestly entreat it of the most merciful God, exclaiming with the prophet: "O Lord, tell me the way wherein I should go!" Wherefore, God, Who loveth mankind, attending to thy tearful entreaty, instilled in thy heart the thought that thou shouldst depart without delay for Mount Athos; and like a second Abraham thou didst undertake the journey with great diligence, fulfilling the commandments of God. We therefore cry out to thee such things as these:

>Rejoice, O father Anthony, who wast like unto Abraham of old, who following the word of God readily and obediently, without sorrow or grief forsook his kinfolk;
>
>Rejoice, thou who didst joyously leave thine own land for a far and unknown country, to acquire the monastic life!
>
>Rejoice, thou who undisturbed didst tread the long, hard and difficult road;
>
>Rejoice, thou who, like Tobit, didst have an angel of God as thy companion on the way!
>
>Rejoice, thou who didst successfully reach Mount Athos, according to thy desire and the will of God;
>
>Rejoice, thou who there didst acquire the good and spiritually profitable treasures of the Spirit!
>
>Rejoice, thou who there didst astonish many by thy loving life, in fasting and prayer, unceasing labor, vigils and unquestioning obedience;
>
>Rejoice, thou who in monastic labors and struggles didst make thyself the equal of the great elders of the Holy Mountain!
>
>Rejoice, O Anthony, who like a divinely wise bee didst gather monastic sweetness from the fathers who labored there, as from divers flowers;

Rejoice, thou who didst bring this very sweetness to thy homeland and there didst successfully lay it up and increase it an hundredfold!

Rejoice, thou who by this sweetness didst in word and deed draw many, and among them the great Theodosius, to monasticism;

Rejoice, for thou didst abundantly satisfy thine assembled brethren with this sweetness and didst strengthen them in the virtues!

Rejoice, O Anthony and Theodosius, ye founders of the monastic life in Russia!

Kontakion III

When the power of the Most High dwelt in thy pure and blameless heart, O all-blessed Theodosius, it so enflamed thee wholly with the love of God that thou didst withdraw from all earthly and transitory things, and it taught and enlightened thee to seek continually those things which are eternal and never-ending. Wherefore, beholding thy zeal and diligence for the salvation of thy soul, we chant with compunction to Almighty God: Alleluia!

Ikos III

O all-blessed father Theodosius, thou didst have the all-great desire to visit the holy places in Jerusalem, and when thou didst find an opportunity to fulfill this desire, thou didst join with those going to the Holy City. But the malicious enemy caused hindrance unto thee, for he stirred up thy mother, who pursued and overtook thee, and dragged thee back home, bound like a malefactor; and after inflicting upon thee many blows, locked thee in thy chamber. Yet thou didst patiently bear this ill treatment with steadfastness, and when thou wast released from incarceration didst again devote thyself to the baking of bread fit for use in the Eucharist. Wherefore, marvelling at this, we cry out to thee thus:

Rejoice, O father Theodosius, thou unshakable and indestructible pillar of patience;

Rejoice, O all-wondrous and all-beauteous model of humility and meekness!

Rejoice, thou who didst cheerfully and manfully bear thy mother's heavy beatings and tramplings;

Rejoice, thou who didst account her blandishments and kisses as deadly harm!

Rejoice, thou who with all thy soul didst love to serve God and the Mother of God;

Rejoice, thou who from childhood didst attend the services of the Church with all diligence!

Rejoice, thou who didst reckon the mockeries and laughter of thy peers as honor;

Rejoice, thou who for old and young alike wast a model of humility and meekness!

Rejoice, thou who with all thy soul didst forgive all who offended thee;

Rejoice, thou who are praised, loved and honored by all virtuous men more than all thy generation!

Rejoice, thou who didst adorn thyself with goodly morals and piety more beautifully than with splendid raiment;

Rejoice, thou who didst regard the vesture of thy mother and guardian as abominable filth!

Rejoice, O Anthony and Theodosius, ye founders of the monastic life in Russia!

Kontakion IV

Thou didst show thyself to be immune to pleasures and ragings abominable to God, O Theodosius our venerable father; for having ever in thy mind and heart the will to labor unceasingly for the Lord, every day thou didst undertake great labors, and every day didst strive to please and love God the more. And vanquishing love of honor and every passionate attachment to the world, thou didst continually chant unto the one God: Alleluia!

Ikos IV

Having heard, O all-blessed father Theodosius, of the strict and onerous way of life which the holy Anthony was living in the solitude of his cave, like a deer to springs of water thou didst secretly flee to him from thy mother's home; and when thou didst come to him, thou didst earnestly entreat him to receive thee into his community and enter thee among the number of his monastics. And he, perceiving in thee the living grace of God, commanded that thou be invested with the monastic habit without delay. Wherefore, giving thanks for this to God thy Benefactor, thou didst lay hold of the monastic life with both hands, and together with Anthony didst labor unceasingly. And we, pondering this, cry out to you thus:

Rejoice, O Anthony and Theodosius, founders of the monastic life;
Rejoice, ye first guides of the first monks of Russia!
Rejoice, ye who led those who had recourse to you unto the stillness of monasticism, as to a safe ship;
Rejoice, all-good helmsmen for those tossed about upon the abyss of this world!
Rejoice, ye who wisely transformed the storms, billows and upheavals of this world into tranquility;
Rejoice, ye who lovingly guide all to the good harbor of salvation!
Rejoice, ye who wisely lay low the raging arrogance of the enemy;
Rejoice, ye who easily save those who flee to you from all dire tempests!
Rejoice, ye who paternally receive all under your protection and defense;
Rejoice, ye who impartially defend all against every peril and misfortune!
Rejoice, ye who ever and everywhere intercede well for the unfortunate;
Rejoice, ye who ever mediate for the oppressed, the afflicted and the downtrodden!
Rejoice, O Anthony and Theodosius, ye founders of the monastic life in Russia!

Kontakion V

The universal Sun revealed you on the firmament of Russia as divinely manifest stars enlightening many with the rays of your exalted holiness, directing many to the way of the knowledge of God, guiding many to monasticism, and confirming and strengthening many in the virtues and in a strict and sorrowful manner of life. And beholding this, the will of God, fulfilled so well within you, with thanksgiving we chant unto our most merciful God: Alleluia!

Ikos V

Beholding your God-pleasing manner of life, when ye confined yourselves to caves as to tombs, many were moved to compunction of soul and to contrition of heart; and, seeking salvation, they hastened to you with all speed, humbly asking that, having made them to share in such a life, ye might sanctify them for the perpetual service of God. And remembering Him Who said: "Him that cometh to Me I will in nowise cast out," ye lovingly received all who came unto you and instructed them paternally. Wherefore, we crown you with such hymnody as this:

>Rejoice, all-blessed fathers, who led many from the yoke of slavery to the sweet freedom of the Spirit;
>Rejoice, ye who taught many to labor truly for Christ and to serve Him sincerely!
>Rejoice, ye who by your virtues revealed to many the path to salvation, as Moses once revealed the way to the promised land;
>Rejoice, ye who led many not to any promised land, but to the very mansions of heaven!
>Rejoice, ye who taught your disciples and followers not by word alone, but more by your deeds and your earnest prayer unto God;
>Rejoice, ye who beautifully and divinely directed the fellow members of your community by the canons of monasticism!
>Rejoice, ye who quickly assist those weighed down by divers temptations and trials;

Rejoice, ye who ever help those who are assailed and grievously oppressed by the adversary!

Rejoice, ye who by your speedy aid strengthen those who are conquered by the enemy, yet who do not despair and with goodly hope call upon you in prayer;

Rejoice, ye who mightily set at nought every assault of the enemy!

Rejoice, ye who with your vigilant eyes watch continually over the spiritual flock ye assembled;

Rejoice, ye who unceasingly guide your disciples and heirs to the way of God's commandments!

Rejoice, O Anthony and Theodosius, ye founders of the monastic life in Russia!

Kontakion VI

Proclaimed and everywhere greatly praised was your God-pleasing life of solitude, O venerable fathers. For who, having merely seen or heard of your life of non-acquisition spent in the fortress of caves, did not consider you to be more like angels than men? And each, marvelling at your patience and your mortification of your bodies, chanted with you the hymn: Alleluia!

Ikos VI

Ye shone forth in the firmament of the province of the Church of Russia, O all-blessed ones; for even though ye enclosed yourselves in dark caves, as under a bushel, yet with the rays of your struggles and virtues ye illumined and enlightened all the surrounding lands, as the material sun illumineth and sheddeth light; and thus ye warmed and moved the hearts of many toward the God-pleasing life, and made them fit for virtue, just as the sun, warming the earth, maketh it fit to produce divers trees and fruits, herbs of the fields and all manner of plants for the use of men and cattle. And giving thanks unto God for this, we offer you this hymnody:

Rejoice, enlighteners of those who abide in the darkness of the passions;

Rejoice, upbraiders of those who dwell in vanity and self-neglect!

Rejoice, guides for those who find themselves in perplexity and error;

Rejoice, directors of those who begin to live a life of goodness!

Rejoice, strengtheners of those who are weak in what is good and waver through cowardice and despondency;

Rejoice, rousers of those who sleep in indifference!

Rejoice, all-good teachers of vigilance and watchfulness;

Rejoice, renowned dispellers of neglect and slothfulness!

Rejoice, most fervent lovers of the industriousness which is the beginning and confirmation of every good work;

Rejoice, never-tiring preservers of the pure and blameless life!

Rejoice, excellent and faithful guides for all to salvation;

Rejoice, wise instructors of all who desire to live the pious and God-pleasing life!

Rejoice, O Anthony and Theodosius, ye founders of the monastic life in Russia!

Kontakion VII

The most evil enemy, desiring to hinder and thwart your good beginning, thus enflamed the prince with wrath against you, and he burned with anger against your tonsuring of his servants as monks, especially those he loved more than all others—a certain eunuch and the son of a nobleman; and it became necessary for you to leave the caves in which ye dwelt and to move to another place. Yet not for long did the malicious one revel in his machinations, for the noble prince, reproved by his God-fearing spouse, quickly recognized your innocence and, perceiving the wiles and perfidy of the enemy, sent after you, begging you to return to your former place of residence. And rejoicing over this, in thanksgiving ye chanted unto God: Alleluia!

Ikos VII

A new labor and a new struggle did ye undertake after your return to your dwelling-place in the caves, O venerable fathers; for ye energetically set about the expansion of the monastic cells and the construction of a temple of prayer, that ye might trample down the pride of the malicious enemy, put to shame his blatant mindlessness, more readily move the assembled brethren toward the God-pleasing and virtuous life, and struggle for a more zealous ministry to Christ God. And we, beholding this with spiritual eyes, cry out to you thus:

Rejoice, ye industrious discoverers and lovers of monastic cave-dwelling;
Rejoice, all-glorious and fervent defenders of the monastic life!
Rejoice, vigilant and tireless preservers of your communities;
Rejoice, most humble tamers of the wrath and anger of the prince!
Rejoice, true and unfeigned lovers of your ill-wishers and enemies;
Rejoice, righteous lovers of those who committed offenses against you and caused you temptations!
Rejoice, most earnest fulfillers of the commandments and precepts of God;
Rejoice, able guides to the pure and blameless life!
Rejoice, most excellent teachers of good morals and reverence;
Rejoice, almighty ones who with the power of Christ help those who struggle in piety and labor in doing good!
Rejoice, never-tiring strugglers in monastic labors;
Rejoice, champion in all for the flock ye assembled!
Rejoice, O Anthony and Theodosius, ye founders of the monastic life in Russia!

Kontakion VIII

Your strange and greatly sorrowful life amazed not only men on earth, but even the angels in heaven; for, having enclosed yourselves in caves, as in dark tombs, ye labored with all diligence for God alone, in fervor of heart and soul, that the service ye offered up day and night to your Creator might be unknown to the world, but known to the Creator Himself. Wherefore, we ever chant unto God Who thus taught and instructed you: Alleluia!

Ikos VIII

It was all your zeal and all your care continually to oppose the most evil foe of the Christian race, O all-blessed and God-bearing fathers: and ye trampled and ground his prideful head underfoot. Ye glorified the common Creator of all in your souls and bodies with His disciples, and in this your good volition and God-pleasing struggle ye so succeeded that ye were able to accomplish all things in Christ Jesus, Who strengtheneth you. Wherefore, the glory of God hath shone forth from your caves and illumined all the ends of the earth; for which cause we offer up to you such hymnody of praise:

> Rejoice, lovers and proclaimers of the inexhaustible praise and worship of God in the world;
> Rejoice, mighty humblers of the haughty-minded pride of the enemy!
> Rejoice, right laudable ones, who set at nought the assaults and oppressions of the adversary;
> Rejoice, courageous ones who foil the snares and pernicious wiles of the foe!
> Rejoice, ye who adorned yourselves with profound humility and meekness, as with precious pearls;
> Rejoice, ye who made many steadfast in these same God-loving virtues!
> Rejoice, ye who emulated the fasting and asceticism of the ancient desert-dwellers;
> Rejoice, ye who passed your days and nights in unceasing prayer, without wearying or despondency!

Rejoice, ye who taught your followers well to abide in
   this same prayer;
Rejoice, ye who have shown us a model and path for
   keeping vigilant against the assaults of the enemy and vanquishing them!
Rejoice, ye who instead of swords wielded fasting, prayer
   and prostrations against the noetic foe ;
Rejoice, ye who increased the glory of God in the world
   by your strict and onerous way of life!
Rejoice, O Anthony and Theodosius, ye founders of the
   monastic life in Russia!

Kontakion IX

Looking upon your poor, humble and exceeding strict way of life, every rank of human nature—rich men and paupers, baseborn and noble—offered great thanks unto God and glorified exceedingly His goodness and ineffable lovingkindness, in that He had thus arranged for you to pass through so strict and difficult a life, that, leading many away from soul-destroying ways, ye might like shepherds guide them to the path of salvation, teaching them ever to chant unto the omniscient Creator: Alleluia!

Ikos IX

Ye were shown to be chosen rhetors, O our all-glorious fathers, yet not in the image of those who are the rhetors of this world, for the things which this world loveth ye hated with all diligence, and the things which it doth bless and greatly esteem, ye despised and, casting them far from you like some useless and unprofitable refuse, ye trampled them under your feet. Wherefore, ye receive from all such laudatory honors as these:

Rejoice, staunch haters of the world and all its pleasures,
   beauties and allurements;
Rejoice, most fervent lovers of monastic non-acquisition
   and poverty!

Rejoice, stern mortifiers of your bodies and all bodily senses;

Rejoice, true zealots of meekness, humility and abstinence!

Rejoice, ye who set all your consolation and blessedness in poverty and non-acquisition;

Rejoice, ye who adorned yourselves exceedingly with stillness and withdrawal from the world!

Rejoice, ye who wholly entrusted yourselves to the providence and care of God;

Rejoice, ye who never desired sweet foods and delicious beverages!

Rejoice, ye who never wore soft and splendid clothing;

Rejoice, ye who all throughout your lives lovingly wore patched and tattered rags as though they were priceless raiment!

Rejoice, ye who instead of choice foods nurtured yourselves with prolonged fasting and severe mortification of the body;

Rejoice, ye who instead of sweet beverages drank the tears of your heart!

Rejoice, O Anthony and Theodosius, ye founders of the monastic life in Russia!

Kontakion X

Desiring to save many, our most loving God, Who mercifully awaiteth the conversion and salvation of all, showed you to Russia as new apostles, that through you He might enlighten many and guide them to the straight path of salvation. And laboring like the apostles, diligently teaching those in ignorance the truth of the Gospel, ye led them to the Orthodox Faith and moved them to keep the commandments of God and the pure and God-pleasing life, chanting unto God their helper: Alleluia!

Ikos X

Ye have been shown to be a firm rampart and a mighty bulwark for those who have recourse unto you, O most lauded fathers; for ye mercifully extended a helping hand not only to those who desired to become monks with you, but those weighed down and oppressed by the divers cares, perils and tribulations of this world ye consoled like parents consoling their children; and ye comforted them amid sorrowful circumstances and sickness, giving them joy by your care, and alleviating the heaviness of their griefs with paternal kindness. For this your benefactions we offer unto you these hymns of thanksgiving:

>Rejoice, speedy helpers of the afflicted and those assailed by divers temptations;
>Rejoice, renowned defenders of the downtrodden and oppressed!
>Rejoice, all-good helmsmen for those bestormed by the grievous assaults of this world;
>Rejoice, most compassionate enrichers of the impoverished and those in dire poverty!
>Rejoice, merciful feeders of the hungry and starving;
>Rejoice, all-wondrous ones, who refresh those who burn and are oppressed by unbearable thirst!
>Rejoice, ye who reveal to those bereft of clothing and shelter the protection and refuge which is in the bosom of the lovingkindness of God;
>Rejoice, most marvellous guides for the blind, and especially for those who err in the law of God!
>Rejoice, all-wise healers of those afflicted and oppressed by sickness and grievous ailments;
>Rejoice, mighty and powerful dispellers of all temptations, misfortunes and sorrows!
>Rejoice, bestowers of every good, temporal and eternal;
>Rejoice, ye who fervently defend those who have recourse to you with faith from all troubling circumstances!
>Rejoice, O Anthony and Theodosius, ye founders of the monastic life in Russia!

Kontakion XI

The hymnody we offer you, O god-bearing fathers, doth not suffice to praise your all-glorious struggles and superhuman labors; for as your life surpassed the life of men and was like unto that of the angels, so also the praises offered unto you should come from the angels rather than from men. Yet, regarding our heartfelt volition, lovingly accept the hymns we offer you, and cleanse us of sins and all defilements and impurities, that every day, and at every hour, we may chant unto God with a pure heart: Alleluia!

Ikos XI

Ye were shown to be light-giving luminaries in the earthly firmament, filling the whole world with the grace of God, O all-blessed fathers, clearly emitting splendor from beneath the bushel of your subterranean cave through your all-radiant virtues; for when your works shone forth from your underground fastness, ye became known and recognized throughout the whole world, for the East blesseth them, the West magnifieth them, the South praiseth them, and the North glorifieth them exceedingly. Wherefore, out of love we sing to you thus:

>Rejoice, ye eager fulfillers of all the virtues;
>Rejoice, all-good populators of many monasteries!
>Rejoice, all-radiant mirrors of all the virtues;
>Rejoice, mighty and invincible bulwarks of your communities!
>Rejoice, all-comely and all-wondrous abodes of the Holy Spirit;
>Rejoice, all-beauteous habitations of all God-pleasing and right acceptable works!
>Rejoice, ye who pleased your Creator and God well in this transitory life;
>Rejoice, ye who most beautifully prepared yourselves for your departure from this fleeting and exceeding difficult life!

Rejoice, ye who instructed your disciples in the God-pleasing life as children of the truth, not only in this life, but all the more in your departure;

Rejoice, ye who promised these same disciples that after your departure from hence ye would remain invisibly with them, and continually assist and help them!

Rejoice, ye who easily entered into the mansions of heaven, without any hindrance;

Rejoice, ye who have received from the most compassionate Bestower of rewards great recompense for the sufferings of evils ye endured as monks!

Rejoice, O Anthony and Theodosius, ye founders of the monastic life in Russia!

Kontakion XII

The grace which our most merciful and most compassionate God bestowed from His inexhaustible treasuries was in you never vain and empty, but continually bore abundant fruit, like good seed cast upon good earth. For having emulated the good and wise servants who received talents from their master, ye thus labored industriously through the powers given you from on high, that ye might be shown to be pleasing to and beloved of God; and ye have won for yourselves endless reward in the mansions of heaven, unceasingly chanting unto God: Alleluia!

Ikos XII

Hymning your serene life with God alone, far removed from the cares of this life and the world, we praise your exceeding strenuous labors and ascetic feats, we honor the vigils and prayers which ye made by day and throughout the night, we glorify your frequent prostrations and bows, we cherish your mortifications of the flesh and contrition of spirit which ye courageously undertook out of love for Christ, and we remember likewise the recompense which ye have received in abundance from God, the righteous Judge and Bestower of rewards, chanting thus:

Rejoice, ye who are like unto the angels in the endless glory of heaven;

Rejoice, ye who have received honor equal to that of the patriarchs!

Rejoice, ye who were enlisted in the rank of the prophets, in that ye possess the gift of prophecy;

Rejoice, ye who have joined the choir of the apostles and evangelists, in that by word and deed ye spread the glad tidings of Christ!

Rejoice, ye who piously enrolled in the assembly of the martyrs, in that ye endured much for the sake of Christ;

Rejoice, ye who in the company of the confessors were honored with the rank of confessor!

Rejoice, ye who as virgins were magnified with the virginal;

Rejoice, ye who have found a portion and inheritance with all the saints who have been well pleasing unto God!

Rejoice, ye who continually delight in the direct vision of the all-sweet and blessed All-Holy Trinity;

Rejoice, ye who enjoy endless peace after your monastic struggles and ascetic labors!

Rejoice, ye who have been rightly counted worthy to inherit the ineffable good things prepared from eternity for the righteous;

Rejoice, ye who have shown yourselves to share in and possess the kingdom of heaven, which holds all the sweetness and beauty, all the great and blessed things which pass human understanding!

Rejoice, O Anthony and Theodosius, ye founders of the monastic life in Russia!

Kontakion XIII

O all-blessed and God-bearing fathers who are worthy of all honor, Anthony and Theodosius of the Caves! Lovingly receiving this meager supplication, offered to you with love by us, the unworthy, preserve our native land unshaken and unharmed by every attack of the enemy and assault of the foe; and as our fathers deliver us, who have recourse unto you with filial faith and love, from all misfortunes, tribulations and perils, that we may continually chant with thanksgiving for you unto God our Saviour: Alleluia! Alleluia! Alleluia!

This kontakion is recited thrice, whereupon Ikos I and Kontakion I are repeated.

Prayer to Our Venerable and God-bearing Father Anthony of the Caves of Kiev

O our good pastor and guide, ever-memorable first instructor of the monks of Russia, venerable and God-bearing Anthony our father! Thou dwellest in heaven above, while we are on earth below, separated from thee not so much in place as by our sinful impurity. Yet, mindful of thy paternal love for thy kinsmen, we fall down and pray to thee with compunction and faith: Help us sinners to cleanse ourselves by repentance and to find mercy and forgiveness with the Lord our Creator. Entreat His goodness, that He grant us great and rich mercy, fertility to the earth, seasonable weather, peace profound, sincere love for our brethren, unfeigned piety, a sufficiency of life's necessities; and that we may not turn to evil the good things which He hath given us with His compassionate right hand, but may turn them instead to the glory of His holy name and to our salvation. By thy holy intercession, O favorite of God, keep our pious Orthodox hierarchs in health and length of days, causing them to triumph over all heresies and schisms. By thy right powerful supplications preserve the cities and lands where Orthodox Christians dwell unharmed by any evil. All those who dwell in this sacred monastery and those who repair to it for worship do thou cover with thy heavenly blessing, and grant them consolation, deliverance and healing amid their sorrow, tribulation and sickness, that with thanksgiving we may glorify, praise and magnify the Lord Who hath glorified thee and through thee doth shower wondrous benefits upon us: the unoriginate Father, and His only-begotten Son, and His consubstantial Spirit—the life-creating and indivisible Trinity—and thy holy aid, unto the ages of ages. Amen.

Prayer to Our Venerable and God-bearing Father Theodosius of the Caves of Kiev

O sacred one, earthly angel and heavenly man, our venerable and God-bearing father Theodosius, thou excellent servant of the all-holy Theotokos, in whose holy name thou didst establish an all-wondrous monastery upon the mountains of the Caves, and therein didst shine forth in a multitude of miracles! We beseech thee with great earnestness: Pray for us to the Lord God, and ask that He grant us great and rich mercies: right faith, unwavering hope of salvation, unfeigned love for all, unshaken piety, health of body and soul, a sufficiency of the needs of life, and that we may not turn to evil the good things given us by His generous right hand, but may turn them rather to the glory of His holy name and unto our salvation. Preserve, O venerable wonderworker, the Orthodox land of Russia [and our land], thy city and lavra, unharmed by any evil. And all the people who hasten thither to venerate thy precious tomb and those who abide in thy holy monastery, do thou overshadow with thy heavenly blessing, mercifully delivering them from all evils. Even more, at the hour of our death show us thy mighty aid, that through thy supplications to the Lord we may be delivered from the power of the cruel prince of this world and may be vouchsafed to inherit the kingdom of heaven. Show us thy kindness, O father, and leave us not orphaned and helpless, that we may unceasingly glorify thy holy assistance and God Who is wondrous in His saints—the Father, and the Son, and the Holy Spirit—unto the ages of ages. Amen.

Akathist Hymn
to All the Venerable Fathers of Athos, the Holy Mountain

All Saints

Akathist Hymn to All the Venerable Fathers of Athos, the Holy Mountain

Whose Memory the Holy Church Doth Celebrate on the Second Sunday after Pentecost

Kontakion I

O chosen favorites of the Lord, spiritually fragrant blossoms of the garden of Jesus, who have been transplanted from Athos, the Holy Mountain, to the garden of heaven, and have acquired boldness before the Lord! We beseech you, O God-bearing fathers: By your supplications free us from all misfortunes, that we may cry out to you in praise:

> Rejoice, O venerable fathers of Athos, fervent intercessors in behalf of our souls!

Ikos I

Ye were truly angels in the flesh and heavenly men, O God-bearing fathers who lived the angelic life in the wilderness of Athos. And ye have been shown to stand with the angels in heaven, from whence ye continually illumine the darkness of our souls with the radiant beams of your supplications through grace. By the example of your God-pleasing life do ye direct to the path of salvation us who cry out to thee from the depths of our soul:

> Rejoice, undimmed luminaries of the grace of God;
> Rejoice, unshakable pillars of the Holy Orthodox Church!

Rejoice, valiant ascetics, who have adorned Athos with
    your struggles;
Rejoice, divinely wise fasters who illumine the whole
    universe with your miracles!
Rejoice, spiritual pearls who have shone forth from the
    valleys of Athos to the heavenly Sion;
Rejoice, priceless gems of the treasury of the Mother of
    God!
Rejoice, O venerable fathers of Athos, fervent interces-
    sors in behalf of our souls!

Kontakion II

We see you, O venerable fathers Peter and Athanasius, as enjoying the first place among the assembly of the saints of Athos, and as ones exceedingly favored by the appearance of the All-Holy Theotokos to you; wherefore, as two of the divinely wise who served well the divine Trinity, we bless you with hymns of praise, O right wondrous fathers, and cry out unto the triune God Who hath glorified you: Alleluia!

Ikos II

Ye acquired heavenly understanding, O divinely wise fathers; and, having disdained all the beautiful things of this world, on Mount Athos found spiritual peace in Christ, and ye abide with Christ in the kingdom of heaven. From thence, by your supplications, do ye graciously grant peace unto us who are battered by the threefold waves of the sea of life, that in tranquillity of spirit we may chant unto you, our helpers, such hymns as these:

Rejoice, ye who by the steering of Christ traversed well
    the depths of the sea of the passions;
Rejoice, ye who safely reached the harbor of salvation!
Rejoice, ye who with the sail of faith, hope and love
    invisibly preserved the ship of your souls from
    the tempest of the passions;
Rejoice, ye who with the anchor of fasting and prayer
    made it fast with strength!

Rejoice, divinely radiant stars illumining our sinful night
    with grace;
Rejoice, ye who with the light of your virtues spiritually
    illumine our benighted souls!
Rejoice, O venerable fathers of Athos, fervent interces-
    sors in behalf of our souls!

Kontakion III

Replete with the power of Christ, O divinely wise and holy hierarchs Athanasius, Callistus, Niphon, Theonas, Gregory, and many others who shone forth on Athos, ye pastors of the Church of Christ, entreat Christ, the Chief Shepherd, we beseech you, that He shepherd us, who are lost sheep, unto salvation, and that He vouchsafe us to imitate your godly wisdom, that in this age we may live righteously and in a God-pleasing manner, may receive a blessed ending to our life, and with you may chant unto Him: Alleluia!

Ikos III

Having one desire, which was to be well-pleasing to Christ alone, to serve Him faithfully in holiness and righteousness, O most blessed fathers, ye were shown to be both boast and confirmation, and ye spiritually adorned well the portion of the Mother of God with your holy struggles. With her pray ye to the Lord, her Son and God, that we not be deprived of the goodly portion of those saved by Christ's love for mankind, that we may cry out to you in thanksgiving and praise:

Rejoice, invincible warriors of the King of heaven, who
    fought the invisible foe under the banner of the
    Cross;
Rejoice, chosen servants of the Queen of heaven, who
    through your virtues have glorified well Her
    earthly portion!
Rejoice, worthy heirs of the joy of heaven and the glory
    of the saints;

Rejoice, ye who share in the blessedness of paradise and
    never-waning light!
Rejoice, ye who mercifully regard those on earth from
    the heavenly heights of your glory;
Rejoice, ye who paternally visit us, your children and the
    reason-endowed sheep of your flock!
Rejoice, O venerable fathers of Athos, fervent intercessors in behalf of our souls!

Kontakion IV

Ye wisely fled the storm of life and exchanged well an earthly realm for a heavenly kingdom, O myrrh-streaming Symeon and holy hierarch Savva, boast of Serbia and renowned patrons of the Monastery of Hilandar; wherefore, Christ hath glorified you with all-glorious miracles, and instead of the good things which pass away, which ye forsook out of love for Him, He hath enriched you with eternal and incorruptible good things. Pray ye earnestly unto Him, O right laudable fathers, that we sinners may also receive salvation in Christ, for we right compunctionately cry unto Him: Alleluia!

Ikos IV

Hearing of your struggles, we marvel, O venerable fathers of Athos, who by your residence have made the Holy Mountain another heaven, and have easily ascended therefrom to the heavenly mountain, where in your souls ye now inhabit the Jerusalem on high and continually delight in the sweet sight of Christ. Yet as good imitators of the loving-kindness of the Saviour, with your supplications mercifully overshadow us, who are lowly and sinful, and guide us to the path of salvation, that with all joy we may cry unto you:

Rejoice, eagles with heavenly wings, soaring aloft to the
    mountain of heaven from the portion of Athos;
Rejoice, sweetly melodious larks, who filled the wilderness of Athos with prayerful hymns!

Rejoice, ye who were illumined from on high by the
    light of the threefold Sun;
Rejoice, ye who have been glorified by the Lord with the
    grace of miracles and the gift of healing!
Rejoice, for great is the fame of your sanctity on earth;
Rejoice, for great is your reward in the heavens!
Rejoice, O venerable fathers of Athos, fervent interces-
    sors in behalf of our souls!

Kontakion V

Ye were shown to be divinely radiant stars, O John, George and Euthymius of Iveron, Neophytus and Euthymius of Dochiariou, Symeon, Paul, Dionysius and Gregory, most honored abbots and founders of the monasteries of Athos, to whom we add the wonder-workers Gregory of Sinai, Dionysius of Olympus, Symeon, Theophanes and Eudocimus, and Gennadius and Nectarius the fasters, in that they were resplendent in the virtues. And we beseech you, O most blessed fathers who dwell now in the eternal mansions: In your supplications cease not to preserve and keep us, your spiritual children, from the pursuit and snares of the devil, that, saved by your holy intercessions, we may cry out to God our Saviour: Alleluia!

Ikos V

O God-bearing fathers, we look to you, who kept well all the commandments of Christ and diligently applied yourselves to the love of spiritual wisdom; and, guided by your example, we shake off the slothfulness which is harmful to the soul, and take up spiritual struggles, having you as teachers and guides to spiritual asceticism. Wherefore, we cry out to you in thanksgiving:

Rejoice, ye who, weeping, found the blessedness of
    paradise;
Rejoice, ye who pray tirelessly before God for the peace
    of the whole world!
Rejoice, ye who with fasting nourished your souls unto
    salvation;

Rejoice, ye who mightily cast down the invisible foe
through all-night vigils and prostrations!
Rejoice, ye who quenched the burning arrows of the
devil's temptations with compunctionate
weeping;
Rejoice, ye who by sighs from the depths of your hearts
rendered the wilderness of Athos spiritually
fruitful!
Rejoice, O venerable fathers of Athos, fervent intercessors in behalf of our souls!

Kontakion VI

In the preaching of the Gospel of righteousness ye diligently imitated the apostles of Christ, the preachers of the Holy Faith, O Cosmas peer of the apostles, Damian, Nicetas, Cyprian, and James, with thy two disciples, who contended even unto the shedding of your blood for the name of Christ and received martyrdom, O right victorious crowned ones; and ye now reign eternally with Christ in the mansions of paradise. Him do ye earnestly beseech, that we also be not deprived of the inheritance of heaven, who cry unto Him; Alleluia!

Ikos VI

Ye shone forth on Athos like divinely radiant luminaries, O all-blessed fathers, and fill the whole universe with the radiance of your miracles; for from the east even unto the north your holy names are glorified, and the struggles of your angelic life are blessed with such goodly praises as these:

Rejoice, most joyous heralds of the omnipotence and
power of Christ;
Rejoice, ascetics mighty of soul, who crushed the head
of most prideful Belial!
Rejoice, good healers of infirmities of soul and body;
Rejoice, renowned placators of Christ God, the King of
heaven!

Rejoice, spiritual warriors, arrayed in holiness and righteousness;

Rejoice, ye who received from the Lord authority over unclean spirits!

Rejoice, O venerable fathers of Athos, fervent intercessors in behalf of our souls!

Kontakion VII

Desiring to live piously in Christ, ye showed forth in yourselves a model of the God-pleasing life of stillness, O venerable desert-dwellers Maximus, Cosmas and Acacius, and ye myrrh-streamers Nilus and Theophilus, who struggled angelically in the wilderness of Athos; and ye joined the venerable Anthony of the Caves, who was trained spiritually on Athos, and became the founder of the monastic life in Russia. Entreat ye the Lord, O God-bearing fathers, that we, the lowly, may be vouchsafed to inherit with you the kingdom of heaven, and may chant forever to our Creator, in the joy of the saints: Alleluia!

Ikos VII

Athos, the Holy Mountain, hath been shown to be a new Sion, to which spiritual children came from the east, the north and the south, blessing the Lord therein with hymns of praise; for, lo! the divinely radiant assembly of the venerable fathers who dwelt in holiness on Athos call us today to honor their struggles and labors, and to cry out to them thus:

Rejoice, great favorites of God, who amazed the angels by the magnitude of your struggles;

Rejoice, all-glorious wonder-workers, who help men amid misfortunes and tribulations!

Rejoice, grace-bearing plants of the wilderness of Athos;

Rejoice, spiritual beauty and joy of the Holy Orthodox Church!

Rejoice, fervent mediators of joy and glory for us;

Rejoice, speedy fulfillers of our goodly desires!

Rejoice, O venerable fathers of Athos, fervent intercessors in behalf of our souls!

Kontakion VIII

In a strange and all-glorious fashion thou didst walk dryshod over the sea, O venerable Gabriel, and didst carry the icon of the divine Keeper of the Portal as a blessing and sanctification for Athos; and to thee, O God-bearing John Kukuzelis, did the All-Holy Theotokos herself appear, and from Her all-pure hands wondrously gave thee a golden coin, that thou mightest unceasingly chant hymns of praise unto Her. Wherefore, marveling at so many divine miracles, let us cry out to God: Alleluia!

Ikos VIII

The whole of Mount Athos, its wilderness and all its valleys, reveal the blessing of God, for from them right fruitful trees formed the paradise of Jesus, the great assembly of our venerable fathers of Athos; and nourished by their spiritual fruits, let us give thanks to them with the such words of our hearts and mouths as these:

> Rejoice, earthly angels and heavenly men;
> Rejoice, fragrant lilies produced by the wilderness!
> Rejoice, ye who made Mount Athos heaven by your
>   celestial virtues;
> Rejoice, ye who continually mediate before the Lord for
>   the whole Christian world!
> Rejoice, chosen ones of God, who bore witness to your
>   election by many miracles;
> Rejoice, right victorious crown-bearers, who were
>   crowned by the right hand of Christ!
> Rejoice, O venerable fathers of Athos, fervent intercessors in behalf of our souls!

Kontakion IX

All the inhabitants of heaven were amazed by your contest, O martyred monks of Zographou, venerable Thomas and those with thee, who were burned alive by the Latins for the Orthodox Faith, and were shown to be sacrifices right acceptable to God; for your names have been inscribed in the heavens, in the book of everlasting life, and are confessed by Christ God before the heavenly Father, to Whom ye chant with joy among the choir of the martyrs: Alleluia!

Ikos IX

Vain-minded human orators, who say that spiritual asceticism is foolishness, have been put to shame by your struggles and miracles, O our venerable fathers of Athos; for who is not moved to compunction by how, having disdained all earthly things, ye hastened with all your soul toward what is heavenly, and sought and found it in the all-radiant sight of the countenance of Christ. Wherefore, we praise you thus:

>Rejoice, O holy nation, royal sanctity, restoration of men;
>Rejoice, spiritual salt of the whole earth, which shall never lose its savor!
>Rejoice, proclaimers of the righteousness of Christ, who forsook the world for the service of God;
>Rejoice, ye who were called forth from every generation for the sweet servitude of the Lord!
>Rejoice, ye who took the easy yoke upon you and sincerely followed after Christ the Master;
>Rejoice, ye who have received from Christ, the Judge of the contest, everlasting peace for your souls in the heavens!
>Rejoice, O venerable fathers of Athos, fervent intercessors in behalf of our souls!

Kontakion X

Sending up hymnody of praise to God the Saviour, Who led you forth from the bitter slavery of sin, ye hastened to suffer for Christ, O most valiant venerable-martyrs Macarius, Hilarion, Pachomius, Constantine, Onuphrius, Procopius, Luke, Timothy, Agathangelus, and many others who issued forth from Athos and confessed Christ before the Moslems. Ye suffered for Him even to the shedding of your blood, and laid down your lives for Him; and now ye rejoice with the martyrs and chant sweetly to Him: Alleluia!

Ikos X

O God-bearing fathers, ye were shown to be valiant warriors of Christ, the King of heaven; and having received the reward of your labors from Him, by the example of your faith ye guide your spiritual children directly to Him, and hear from us such worthy praises of you as these:

> Rejoice, ye for whom the angels rejoice and men glorify God;
> Rejoice, ye by whom Athos, the Holy Mountain, is spiritually adorned from generation unto generation!
> Rejoice, dew-bearing clouds which cool the burning of our passions;
> Rejoice, fruitful olive trees, anointing our hearts with the oil of your labors!
> Rejoice, diamonds of patience, resplendent with rays of grace divine;
> Rejoice, pillars of Orthodoxy, who by your miracles make steadfast those wavering in faith!
> Rejoice, O venerable fathers of Athos, fervent intercessors in behalf of our souls!

Kontakion XI

Offering up hymnody to the All-Holy Trinity, a trinity of new martyrs shone forth spiritually on Athos—the most valiant Euthymius, Ignatius and Acacius—who put to shame the ungodliness of Islam and all-gloriously confessed the name of Christ before the Moslems; and having received martyrdom from them, they now dwell with Christ, chanting to Him the hymn of victory: Alleluia!

Ikos XI

By the radiant beams of your miracles is Mount Athos spiritually illumined, O most blessed fathers, and it blesseth you as is meet, as its heavenly helpers and protectors; and, honoring your struggles and sufferings, out of spiritual love we offer you these praises with humility and faith:

> Rejoice, healing myrrh of the grace of God, which is poured forth upon us in abundance;
> Rejoice, all-good physicians of infirmities of soul and body!
> Rejoice, ye who require of us only faith for the healing of ailments;
> Rejoice, ye who freely receive and freely impart to us the grace of healing!
> Rejoice, good bestowers upon us of spiritual gifts beneficial to the soul;
> Rejoice, our speedy helpers and comforters amid misfortunes and sorrows!
> Rejoice, O venerable fathers of Athos, fervent intercessors in behalf of our souls!

Kontakion XII

All ye, our venerable fathers of Athos, O chosen vessels of the grace of God, both those whose names are known and those whose are unknown: in your splendid assembly hasten quickly to aid us when we are helpless, and by your right acceptable intercession before the Lord from sudden and violent death deliver those who honor you, that we may cry out to Him in thanksgiving: Alleluia!

Ikos XII

Hymning your holy, angelic life and your many miracles, O our venerable fathers of Athos, we praise, glorify and magnify Christ God, Who hath glorified you, the Sanctifier of the saints and Author of miracles, Who hath showered you with an abundance of the gifts of grace; and we bless you, O our holy and most mighty intercessors, with such sayings as these:

Rejoice, instructors of monks and conversers with the angels;
Rejoice, friends of all the saints and intimates of God!
Rejoice, citizens of the shining city of the heavenly Jerusalem;
Rejoice, celestial protectors of our communities on earth!
Rejoice, confirmation and help of Orthodox monastics;
Rejoice, tireless mediators for the whole world!
Rejoice, O venerable fathers of Athos, fervent intercessors in behalf of our souls!

Kontakion XIII

O our all-venerable fathers of Athos, who have been given to us by God as helpers and protectors: ye dwell in heaven on high, while we are on the earth, below, far removed from you not so much by place as through our sinful impurity. Yet even so, we make bold to offer you this meager hymnody of praise, entreating and asking you for one thing only: Beseech Christ the Saviour, that He deliver us from everlasting torment and vouchsafe us the kingdom of heaven, that with you we may chant unto Him forever: Alleluia! Alleluia! Alleluia!

This Kontakion is recited thrice, whereupon Ikos I and Kontakion I are repeated.

Prayer to All the Venerable Fathers of Athos, the Holy Mountain

O our venerable and God-bearing fathers of Athos, all-radiant luminaries of the earth, who shone forth gloriously upon the Orthodox Church from the wild valleys of Athos, the Holy Mountain, who by the beauties of your life rendered heavenly the Holy Mountain, our dwelling-place, and amazed the whole world with the splendors of your exalted virtues and the effulgence of divine miracles! Having now bodily set for a time in the grave, through the sunset of death, as righteous ones ye are with Christ, the Sun of righteousness, in your souls, and shine like the sun in the kingdom of heaven. There, spreading forth your prayers like rays unto God, the true Light, forget us not, your spiritual children, who languish in the night of the passions and in sorrows; but send down from on high beams of grace, that, walking aright the path of the commandments of Christ in the light of your virtuous life, we may be vouchsafed to gaze upon the light of the unapproachable glory of God, together with you praising God, Who is glorified and worshiped in the Holy Trinity—the Father, the Son and the Holy Spirit—time without end. Amen.

Akathist Hymn
to Our Father Among the Saints Basil the Great, Archbishop of Cæsaria of Cappadocia

Saint Basil the Great

Akathist Hymn
to Our Father Among the Saints Basil the Great, Archbishop of Cæsaria of Cappadocia
Whose Memory the Holy Church Doth Celebrate on the 1st of January

Kontakion I

O chosen minister of the King of heaven and great hierarch of the Church of Christ, who didst shine forth throughout the whole world in the confession of the right Faith, and art possessed of great boldness before the Holy Trinity! From all misfortunes shield us who cry out to thee with compunction:

    Rejoice, O Basil, great and holy hierarch, universal lamp of Orthodoxy!

Ikos I

The Creator of the angels, Who from the ages chose thee beforehand to be a great luminary of His Church, O all-blessed father Basil, revealed thee to be angelic in thy manner of life; for having struggled in the wilderness with feats of asceticism and great contemplation of God, thou didst hasten to the heights of virtue. Wherefore, O thou who hast acquired glory in the heavens, accept from us, the lowly ones who dare to praise thee, these words of praise:

    Rejoice, O Basil, namesake of kingship;
    Rejoice, great hierarch of Christ!
    Rejoice, unshakable pillar of the Church;
    Rejoice, all-honorable scion of a holy family!

Rejoice, thou who from thy youth didst serve the King of heaven with all diligence;

Rejoice, thou who with all earthly wisdom, and even more with that of heaven didst enrich thy mind!

Rejoice, thou who with thy friend Gregory the Theologian didst excel in philosophy;

Rejoice, thou who with all-wise words didst convert Euplus, thy teacher, to Christ!

Rejoice, all-wondrous preserver of purity and chastity;

Rejoice, faithful guide to salvation!

Rejoice, refuter of soul-destroying heresies;

Rejoice, divinely wise teacher of the whole world!

Rejoice, O Basil, great and holy hierarch, universal lamp of Orthodoxy!

Kontakion II

Seeing the Church of Christ assailed by the storm of the heresy of Arius, and submitting to the call of God, O venerable father, thou didst come forth from the wilderness thou didst love, to the city of Cæsaria, where thou didst receive the grace of the priesthood and wast ordained archbishop, proclaiming aloud tidings of salvation to all the ends of the earth, and teaching the faithful all the days of thy life to chant as is meet unto the Creator of all: Alleluia!

Ikos II

Enlightening the understanding of the faithful with the knowledge of God, O Basil, holy hierarch of Christ, thou didst make clear the nature of things, and didst teach them to recognize the invisible God in the creations of His hands. Wherefore, illumined by thy divinely wise teachings, we cry out thus:

Rejoice, thou who didst enlighten the faithful with the knowledge of God Who created all things in six days;

Rejoice, thou who didst teach them to praise His wondrous works as is meet!

Rejoice, palace of wisdom, all-adorned;

Rejoice, treasure chest filled to overflowing with theology!

Rejoice, for thou hast taught us to see the mysteries of the wisdom of God in all the world;

Rejoice, for thou hast instructed us to see the majesty of God even in the least things!

Rejoice, thou who didst describe the beauty of the primal light;

Rejoice, thou who didst point out the mighty power of the first words of God in the universe!

Rejoice, thou who didst liken earthly glory to the grass which quickly withereth away;

Rejoice, thou who didst show that we are to see Christ, the Sun of righteousness, in the magnificence of the luminaries of the skies!

Rejoice, thou who by the industriousness of a little creature didst turn the people away from slothfulness;

Rejoice, thou who didst order man, the king of all creatures, to gain the rule over the passions!

Rejoice, O Basil, great and holy hierarch, universal lamp of Orthodoxy!

Kontakion III

Strengthened by the power of the Most High, O holy father Basil, thou didst contend against Julian, the apostate from God, and didst beseech the Lord and His All-Pure Mother to set at nought his plots against the Christians, that all might chant with thanksgiving to the one God: Alleluia!

Ikos III

Possessing great zeal for God Almighty, and taking His word in thy hand as a sword, thou didst swiftly cut down the tares of the pagan ungodliness of Julian, and didst make the faithful steadfast in piety. Teach us also, O venerable father, to serve the one God alone with a pure life, for we cry out to thee thus:

> Rejoice, thou who didst manfully denounce the prideful Julian for his apostasy from God;
> Rejoice, thou who didst set at nought his Christ-hating plots!
> Rejoice, thou who didst wound him with tearful prayer, as with a spear;
> Rejoice, thou who didst announce beforehand his speedy destruction!
> Rejoice, thou who didst free the people of God from idolatry, like as Moses of old did Israel;
> Rejoice, thou who didst uproot the tares of ungodliness!
> Rejoice, thou who hast abundantly provided the faithful with the food of divine words;
> Rejoice, thou who hast watered men's hearts with streams of grace!
> Rejoice, thou who hast admonished us to hold fast the tablets of the commandments of Christ;
> Rejoice, thou who with thy manner of life didst confirm the teaching of thy mouth!
> Rejoice, good and faithful servant;
> Rejoice, diligent workman of the vineyard of Christ!
> Rejoice, O Basil, great and holy hierarch, universal lamp of Orthodoxy!

Kontakion IV

By the power of the Spirit Who abode within thee, O saint of God, thou didst still the tempest of the rage of the Emperor Valens, who was stuck fast in the Arian heresy, and didst give peace to the Holy Church; and in thy holy labors and fervent supplications unto God thou didst chant to Him, rejoicing: Alleluia!

Ikos IV

Hearing that thou, O hierarch of God, didst stand firm in the Truth, and that all the faithful heeded thy voice, the impious Valens desired to turn thee away from the right Faith; and for this cause he sent to thee his governor, Modestus, and later came himself to Cæsaria. But thou, O God-bearing father, wast undaunted by either the wrath of the emperor or the threats of his dread general. And glorifying this thy steadfast confession, we cry out to thee:

Rejoice, invincible champion of the right Faith;
Rejoice, shepherd who wast ready to lay down thy life
for the faithful!
Rejoice, thou who didst show forth the steadfast confession of Peter;
Rejoice, thou who didst manifest Elijah's zeal for the
glory of the Holy Trinity!
Rejoice, thou who didst allay the rage of the impious
emperor with the divine magnificence of thy
sacred service;
Rejoice, thou who didst shut the mouth of the heretical
general with thy divinely wise words!
Rejoice, for thou wast not daunted by threats of banishment and tortures;
Rejoice, for thou didst even desire to receive death for
Christ!
Rejoice, thou who didst endure persecution for the
Faith;
Rejoice, thou who after many tribulations didst enter
into the joy of the Lord!
Rejoice, thou who didst fearlessly proclaim the Truth of
Christ in the face of kings and rulers;
Rejoice, thou who by a steadfast confession didst show
thyself to be a faithful servant of the King of
heaven!
Rejoice, O Basil, great and holy hierarch, universal lamp
of Orthodoxy!

Kontakion V

Thou wast shown to be a divinely guided star, O Basil, holy hierarch of Christ, illumining the dark night of tribulations with the all-radiant beams of lovingkindness, dispelling the gloom of misfortunes, and pointing out the straight path to the kingdom of heaven unto all who navigate the stormy sea of life, that, rejoicing, they may all chant unto the God Who saveth: Alleluia!

Ikos V

They who saw thee to be a solicitous father, O holy hierarch of God, diligently sought help of thee amid perils and sorrows; and thou didst treat them all with lovingkindness, in thyself providing them with a model of true faith. O all-good father, be thou a speedy helper for us also, who are tempest-tossed by sins and tribulations, but who cry out to thee with love:

>Rejoice, beacon of love shining forth from Christ;
>Rejoice, thou who didst imitate the heavenly Father in lovingkindness!
>Rejoice, rich treasure of those who have none;
>Rejoice, sure refuge amid necessities!
>Rejoice, thou who didst feed the starving, as did Joseph of old;
>Rejoice, thou who in Cæsaria didst found many hostels for the homeless and the poor!
>Rejoice, thou who, like the good Samaritan, didst bind up the sores of lepers with thine own hands;
>Rejoice, thou who didst heal the ailing Modestus, thy persecutor, and didst save him from being slain by the people!
>Rejoice, thou who didst defend a poor widow from the malice of the governor;
>Rejoice,. thou who didst ask of God forgiveness of sins for a sinful woman!
>Rejoice, father of orphans and consolation of the suffering;

Rejoice, thou who dost bring those perishing in sins to
    their senses and set them aright!
Rejoice, O Basil, great and holy hierarch, universal lamp
    of Orthodoxy!

Kontakion VI

Thou wast shown to be a preacher of the Truth of Christ to the whole world, O holy hierarch father Basil, who dost pierce sinful hearts with the grace-filled power of thy words, as with a sharp sword, and movest them to repentance, that all may chant to the Holy Trinity with a pure heart: Alleluia!

Ikos VI

Thou didst shine forth in the firmament of the Church, O father Basil, like a great and radiant luminary enlightening the whole world with the understanding of the true Faith, and driving away the darkness of the sinful passions, from which do thou also free us who cry out to thee thus:

Rejoice, faithful servant of the Holy Trinity;
Rejoice, divinely illumined elucidator of the mysteries of
    the Faith!
Rejoice, thou who didst loudly proclaim that the Son is
    consubstantial and the Spirit equally enthroned
    with the Father;
Rejoice, thou who didst make clear to the faithful the
    truth of the preëternal Light which shone forth
    from preëternal Light!
Rejoice, thou who didst confess the Lord Saviour to be
    God incarnate and the Creator of all the ages;
Rejoice, thou who didst disclose the mystery of the two
    natures and one hypostasis in Christ God!
Rejoice, thou who with the kingly power of thy words
    didst command the rich to throw open their
    granaries;

Rejoice, thou who by thy teaching didst turn many away from ill-gotten gains!

Rejoice, thou who like thunder didst smite soul-destroying drunkenness by thy words;

Rejoice, thou who didst uproot hard-heartedness and envy from the hearts of men!

Rejoice, zealous instructor in temperance;

Rejoice, tireless preacher of repentance!

Rejoice, O Basil, great and holy hierarch, universal lamp of Orthodoxy!

Kontakion VII

Desiring to protect the faithful from the assemblies of the Arians, O Basil, saint of God, thou didst adorn everything in the church, and didst wisely set down the compunctionate rite of the divine Liturgy. Many prayers poured forth from thy mouth like sweet-smelling myrrh, and thereby we ask forgiveness of sins for ourselves and our brethren who have fallen asleep, and we glorify the All-Holy Trinity, crying: Alleluia!

Ikos VII

The faithful saw in thee a new Aaron, O holy father Basil, when with divine majesty thou didst serve the bloodless Sacrifice, adorned with the gifts of the Spirit as with vestments glittering with precious stones. Intercede now for the Church at the altar on high, and be thou continually mindful also of us, who cry out to thee with compunction:

Rejoice, hierarch of God, who didst receive the abundant grace of the priesthood, as did Aaron;

Rejoice, thou who didst acquire great boldness in prayer for the people!

Rejoice, wise performer of the mysteries of God;

Rejoice, thou who didst adorn well the rites of the Church!

Rejoice, thou who didst learn the service of the Liturgy from Christ Himself, as had the Apostle James;

Rejoice, man of prayer enlightened by the Spirit of God!
Rejoice, thou who during the service was illumined with a heavenly light, as some perceived;
Rejoice, thou who wast surrounded by angels, as by certain all-radiant men!
Rejoice, for by thy first prayer do we prepare ourselves to partake of the Mysteries of Christ;
Rejoice, for with thy words on the evening of Pentecost do we send up our petitions on bended knee!
Rejoice, glory and adornment of the hierarchal throne of Cæsaria;
Rejoice, for to the priests of the whole Church dost thou impart from God gracious strength in their ministry!
Rejoice, O Basil, great and holy hierarch, universal lamp of Orthodoxy!

Kontakion VIII

An awesome and all-glorious vision was revealed to the venerable Ephraim the Syrian concerning thee, O holy hierarch Basil: for one day God showed thee to him as a pillar of fire extending up to the heights of heaven; and later, when he had come to Cæsaria, the venerable one beheld thee teaching with a tongue of fire, and with compunction he cried out to God: Alleluia!

Ikos VIII

Thou wast wholly aflame with the heavenly light of seraphic love, O God-bearing Basil; for thy words were as bolts of lightning, burning up heresies, but enlightening the souls of the faithful with flames of faith and love. Wherefore, by thy supplications, O father, grant that we may have if only the least spark of thy love, for we cry out such things as these:

Rejoice, pillar of fire reducing heresies to ashes;
Rejoice, warming fire of true faith and love unfeigned!
Rejoice, stern denouncer of the falsehood of the heresy of Arius;

Rejoice, ardent zealot of the Truth of Christ!
Rejoice, for thou didst put to shame the prideful Eunomius, who blaphemed the Son of God;
Rejoice, for thou didst dispute the blasphemy of Macedonius against the Holy Spirit!
Rejoice, thou who didst set at nought the vain belief of Nestorius;
Rejoice, earnest defender of the honor of the All-Holy Mother of God!
Rejoice, pastor illumined by the heavenly effulgence of love;
Rejoice, teacher of the Faith, who didst proclaim words bearing lightning!
Rejoice, divinely planted olive tree, which produced many saints for the Church;
Rejoice, vine which bore divinely wise champions of Orthodoxy!
Rejoice, O Basil, great and holy hierarch, universal lamp of Orthodoxy!

Kontakion IX

The whole assembly of the heretics was unable to withstand the power of the grace which abode within thee, O holy father; for by the power of thy prayer thou didst wrest from the snares of the enemy a certain youth who had fallen under the authority of Satan, and didst return him, penitent, unto Christ, chanting with thanksgiving to God our Saviour: Alleluia!

Ikos IX

Many heretics who were conquered by thy divinely inspired rhetoric and beheld the all-glorious miracle wrought upon the youth, united themselves to the Church, O holy hierarch Basil. Vouchsafe that we also may become faithful and obedient children thereof, who cry out to thee thus:

Rejoice, thou who didst enlighten all the ends of the
    earth with heavenly doctrine;
Rejoice, thou who didst overcome the dark powers of
    hell with the grace of Christ!
Rejoice, thou who didst free the youth from the snares
    of Satan;
Rejoice, thou who didst nourish him with the Body and
    Blood of Christ!
Rejoice, for thou didst not let a soul redeemed by the
    blood of Christ perish;
Rejoice, for thou didst beseech Christ to forgive the
    young man who had fallen into pernicious sin!
Rejoice, for thou didst amaze the people with this all-
    glorious wonder;
Rejoice, for by the conversion of the lost one thou didst
    cause the angels to rejoice!
Rejoice, thou who teachest us to ask protection of the
    Lord of the angels;
Rejoice, thou who by thy supplication dost cause our
    guardian angels to draw nigh unto us!
Rejoice, thou who bringest deliverance from the assaults
    of the enemy;
Rejoice, speedy defender in time of temptations!
Rejoice, O Basil, great and holy hierarch, universal lamp
    of Orthodoxy!

Kontakion X

Desiring to save His reason-endowed creatures, the Creator showed thee to be a steadfast defender of the faithful, O father Basil, and a preserver of His Church, that through thee the light of Orthodoxy might be revealed to the whole world, and all the faithful may chant with thanksgiving to the Holy Trinity: Alleluia!

Ikos X

Thou wast shown to be a bulwark of the Church and a strong wall of defense for the faithful, O Basil great among hierarchs, when in the city of Nicæa the doors of the church were opened by the power of thy prayer, and thou didst thereby reveal the Truth of the right Faith, and didst shut the mouths of those who blaspheme the name of Christ. For us who confess the Lord and Saviour in Orthodox manner do thou open the doors of the lovingkindness of God by thine aid, O father, that we may cry out to thee thus:

> Rejoice, earthly angel, preserver of the Church of Christ;
> Rejoice, defender of the faithful chosen beforehand by God!
> Rejoice, thou who by thy prayer didst open the doors of the Church, as of old Elijah opened the heavens;
> Rejoice, thou who didst return to the faithful the holy church which had been confiscated by heretics!
> Rejoice, thou who protectest the faithful from heresies;
> Rejoice, thou who didst preserve the Church of Christ unharmed by false doctrines!
> Rejoice, thou who didst magnify the all-great name of Christ in the heavens and His wonders on earth;
> Rejoice, thou who didst establish Orthodoxy throughout the world!
> Rejoice, for through thee was the pride of the ungodly cast down;
> Rejoice, for through thee was the humility of the faithful exalted!
> Rejoice, for through thee was the Holy Faith glorified;
> Rejoice, for through thee was the Church of Christ wonderfully adorned!
> Rejoice, O Basil, great and holy hierarch, universal lamp of Orthodoxy!

Kontakion XI

It is fitting rather that hymnody be offered thee from the heavens than from the earth, O all-wondrous Basil; for thou wast the revelation of the heavens upon the earth, and didst transport the minds of the faithful to heaven by thy divinely wise teachings. And now, with mercy thou lookest down from heaven upon us, and to all of us givest superabundant grace from Christ God, the Bestower of compassions, to Whom with the angels in the heavens thou dost continually chant: Alleluia!

Ikos XI

O radiant beacon, thou wast wholly illumined with many gifts of God and with the virtues, O Basil, saint of God. Therewith enlighten us also, instruct us in virtue, and guide us to the kingdom of heaven, who cry to thee thus:

> Rejoice, never-waning radiance and all-lustrous ornament of the Church of Christ;
> Rejoice, for to the Christians of all ages thou grantest strengthening in the right Faith!
> Rejoice, thou who didst perfect the talents entrusted thee by God;
> Rejoice, thou who didst glean from earthly wisdom all things profitable for salvation!
> Rejoice, thou who didst impart miraculous healing to the son of the emperor, unto the glory of the right Faith;
> Rejoice, thou who didst perceive the chaste life of the priest Anastasius and his wife!
> Rejoice, thou who didst meekly forgive those who offended thee;
> Rejoice, thou who by humility and patience didst set at nought the slanders made against thee!
> Rejoice, thou who for monks didst confirm the rule of the perfect life;
> Rejoice, thou who didst gather many monks in monasteries!
> Rejoice, thou who didst bequeath rules, canons and the doctrines of salvation to be the heritage of the Church;

Rejoice, thou who in thy divinely wise writings didst bestow a priceless treasure for the edification of Christians!

Rejoice, O Basil, great and holy hierarch, universal lamp of Orthodoxy!

Kontakion XII

Christ God gave thee great grace, O holy hierarch father Basil, not only to bring the lost to repentance, but to convert many infidels to Christ; for when thou wast already sick unto death, and drewest nigh unto thy blessed end, thou didst enlighten with holy baptism thy Jewish doctor, his wife and children, and with them didst chant the hymn of thanksgiving to the Holy Trinity: Alleluia!

Ikos XII

All the faithful sing great praises unto thee, O great hierarch Basil; for thou didst labor greatly on earth, to the end of thy life, for the glory of the right Faith, hast entered into the Holy of holies in the heavens, and as a faithful servant of God standest before the Holy Trinity, where do thou pray continually for us thy children, O all-good father, who cry out to thee thus with faith and love:

Rejoice, royal priesthood, all-praised Basil;

Rejoice, all adorned dwelling-place of the Holy Trinity!

Rejoice, thou who didst glorify the King of heaven with the working of miracles;

Rejoice, thou who didst not leave off thy zeal for the glory of the Faith even during thy fatal illness!

Rejoice, thou who didst ask God to prolong thy life miraculously for the sake of the conversion of one who did not believe;

Rejoice, thou who, rising from thy death-bed, didst with thine own hands enlighten him with baptism!

Rejoice, thou who didst vanquish the power of heresy by thine efforts and wisdom;

Rejoice, thou who didst ask victory over enemies for right-believing kings!
Rejoice, thou who in thy labors didst share in the ways of the apostles;
Rejoice, thou who with the holy hierarchs Gregory the Theologian and John Chrysostom art glorified with equal honor, according to thy command!
Rejoice, thou who hast shone forth in the incorruption of thy relics and been crowned with glory in the heavens;
Rejoice, great and fervent helper given us by God!
Rejoice, O Basil, great and holy hierarch, universal lamp of Orthodoxy!

Kontakion XIII

O Basil, all-holy and great hierarch of Christ, beacon of Orthodoxy and bulwark of the faithful! Look down from heaven upon this praise offered thee by us, and by thy supplications protect us against misfortunes and the passions, preserve us in the right Faith, and vouchsafe to us the kingdom of heaven, that with thee and all the saints we may chant forever to the Holy Trinity: Alleluia! Alleluia! Alleluia!

This Kontakion is recited thrice, whereupon Ikos I and Kontakion I are repeated.

Prayers to the Holy Hierarch Basil
Prayer I

O all-blessed father Basil, great among hierarchs, divinely wise teacher of the whole world! Great were the struggles and labors which thou didst make for the glory of the Holy Church! Thou wast a steadfast confessor and beacon of the Faith of Christ on earth, who didst illumine the faithful with the light of the knowledge of God, didst burn up false heresies, and didst announce tidings of the truth of salvation to all the world. And now, O thou who hast great boldness before the Holy Trinity in the heavens, help us who fall down before thee with humility, to preserve the holy Orthodox Faith steadfast and unchanged until the end of our life, and keep us from being of little faith, from doubts and wavering, lest we be deluded by the words of soul-destroying teachings opposed to God. By thine intercession enkindle with the spirit of the holy zeal wherewith thou wast aflame, O all-glorious shepherd of the Church of Christ, us also, whom Christ hath ordained to be pastors, that with all diligence we may enlighten and confirm in the right Faith the reason-endowed flock of Christ. O loving and holy hierarch, entreat the Father of lights, that unto all He grant every gift which is right profitable to each: for babes, a good upbringing in the fear of God; for the young, chastity; for the aged and infirm, strengthening; for the sorrowful, consolation; for the sick, healing; for those in error, understanding and correction; and for our fathers and brethren who have departed this transitory life, goodly repose. Yea, O saint of God, look down with mercy from the mansions of heaven upon us, the lowly, who are bestormed by temptations and perils, and lead up from the earth to the heights of heaven those who have been cast down. Bestow upon us, O all-good father, thine archpastoral and holy blessing, that, overshadowed thereby, we may, in this new age, and for the remaining time of our life, live in peace, repentance and obedience to the Holy Orthodox Church, diligently doing the commandments of Christ, and fighting the good fight of the Faith, that thus we may attain to the kingdom of heaven, where do thou account us worthy to hymn and glorify the holy, consubstantial and indivisible Trinity, with thee and all the saints, unto the ages of ages. Amen.

Prayer II

O great and all-holy hierarch father Basil, all-glorious teacher of the universal Church, most diligent champion of the all-holy Trinity, chosen confessor of the Mother of God and Her all-immaculate virginity, all-holy model of purity, humility and patience! Lo! I, who am greatly sinful and unworthy to gaze upon the heights of heaven, do humbly beseech thee, O all-wise teacher of the Church of Christ: teach me thus to lead a life without fear, that I may never stray or be drawn from the path contrary the commandments of God; by thy most mighty intercession preserve and deliver me from the temptations of the world and the snares of the devil, as thou didst deliver therefrom the youth who had apostatized from our Saviour most sweet, and fallen under the power of Satan; grant me the strength of soul to be a diligent imitator of thine exalted virtues; make me firm and unshakable in the right Faith; strengthen me, who am lacking in patience and trust in the Lord; make my heart fervid with true love for Christ, that I may desire the good things of heaven more than all else and take delight therein; and beseech the Lord to grant me contrition for my sins, that I may spend the rest of my life in peace, repentance and the fulfillment of the commandments of Christ. And when the time of mine end draweth nigh, do thou, O all-good father, with the All-Blessed Virgin Mary, then hasten to mine aid, to defend me from the malicious assaults of the enemy; and vouchsafe that I may be an inheritor of the mansions of paradise; that with thee and all the saints I may stand before the throne of the unapproachable majesty of God and glorify and hymn the life-creating, consubstantial and indivisible Trinity, always, time without end. Amen.

Prayer III

O great, all-glorious and holy hierarch of Christ, divinely wise teacher of the whole Church Universal, steadfast confessor and champion of Orthodoxy, most blessed father Basil! Look down from the heights of heaven upon us, who humbly fall down before thee, and entreat the Lord Almighty, Whose faithful servant thou wast on earth, that He grant us to keep the Faith steadfastly and without change, obedience to the Holy Church, correction for our life, speedy help amid all needs, sorrows and temptations, and patience and strength. Grant us thy holy blessing, that, overshadowed thereby, we may live in these new times, and all our days, in a God-pleasing manner, in peace and repentance, and may in the kingdom of heaven be vouchsafed to hymn and glorify the life-creating Trinity—the Father, the Son and the Holy Spirit—with thee and all the saints, unto the ages of ages. Amen.

Akathist Hymn
to the Holy Hieromartyr Cyprian

Hieromartyr Cyprian

Akathist Hymn
to the Holy Hieromartyr Cyprian
Whose Memory the Holy Church Doth Celebrate on the 2nd of October

Kontakion I

O hieromartyr Cyprian, who didst leave the service of the devil for the worship of the true God, and wast numbered among the saints! Entreat Christ God, that we be delivered from the snares of the evil one, and may vanquish the world, the flesh and the devil, that we may cry unto thee:

> Rejoice, O hieromartyr Cyprian, speedy helper and intercessor for our souls!

Ikos I

The angelic choirs were amazed at how thou didst turn from the sorcerous arts to divine knowledge, O divinely wise one, and through repentance didst find the angelic life of dispassion. And marveling at thy conversion, we cry out to thee such things as these:

> Rejoice, thou who didst astonish the angels with thy conversion;
> Rejoice, thou who didst gladden the choir of the saints!
> Rejoice, thou who didst manifest wisdom;
> Rejoice, thou who didst receive a crown from Christ!
> Rejoice, for by thee are the demons driven away;
> Rejoice, for by thee are all sicknesses healed!
> Rejoice, O hieromartyr Cyprian, speedy helper and intercessor for our souls!

Kontakion II

Seeing how from his earliest years Cyprian's ungodly parents committed him to the study of demonic worship, the Lord desired to turn him to Himself, that with the angels and all the saints he might chant: Alleluia!

Ikos II

Possessed of a mind as yet unsuited for higher understanding, O Cyprian, thou didst labor diligently, studying the wiles of the devil; but perceiving the weakness of the demons, that they feared Christ, thou didst turn to the knowledge of the true God. Wherefore, we magnify thee:

> Rejoice, thou who utterly overcamest the wiles of the demons;
> Rejoice, thou who denounced the deception of their worship!
> Rejoice, thou who didst put the evil serpent to shame;
> Rejoice, thou who hast glorified Christians!
> Rejoice, thou who art wiser than the wise of this world;
> Rejoice, thou who hadst more understanding than any sage!
> Rejoice, O hieromartyr Cyprian, speedy helper and intercessor for our souls!

Kontakion III

The power of the Most High enlightened thy mind, O blessed Cyprian, when, having failed to bewitch Justina, the demons said to thee: "We fear and tremble before the power of the Cross, whereby the virgin Justina driveth us away!" And thou didst say to them: "Ye fear the Cross, but He Who was crucified on the Cross is mightier than the Cross!" Wherefore, thou didst go to the temple of the Lord to chant with all the faithful: Alleluia!

Ikos III

His mind illumined with power from on high, Cyprian approached the priest and requested baptism; but the priest, fearing perfidy, drove him away. Then Cyprian went to the temple of the Lord and, standing at the liturgy, refused to leave the church when the deacon proclaimed: "Catechumens, depart!", but said: "I will not leave the church until I receive baptism!" And we, rejoicing that thou hadst come to thy senses, chant to thee such things as these:

> Rejoice, thou who wast illumined with power from on high;
> Rejoice, thou who was brought to thy senses by the Lord!
> Rejoice, thou who didst perceive the power of the Cross;
> Rejoice, thou who didst drive the demons away from thyself!
> Rejoice, thou who didst set thy life aright;
> Rejoice, thou who didst direct thy steps to the church!
> Rejoice, O hieromartyr Cyprian, speedy helper and intercessor for our souls!

Kontakion IV

A storm of thoughts beset Cyprian as to how to obtain baptism. Wherefore, first of all, taking his sorcerous books, he brought them to the center of the city and there made a bonfire of them, chanting to God: Alleluia!

Ikos IV

When the priest heard that thou didst indeed have the good intention to become a Christian, O most wise one, he baptized thee and made thee a reader in the church. Wherefore, we cry out to thee:

> Rejoice, thou who vanquished the spirits of evil;
> Rejoice, thou who burned up thy sorcerous books!
> Rejoice, thou who desired to become a Christian;
> Rejoice, thou who received holy baptism!

Rejoice, thou who wast adorned with struggles and the virtues;
Rejoice, thou who wast ordained to the priesthood!
Rejoice, O hieromartyr Cyprian, speedy helper and intercessor for our souls!

Kontakion V

Having received the divinely-woven robe of holy baptism, O most lauded Cyprian, thou didst pray fervently to God for the forgiveness of the sins thou hadst committed before, chanting unto God with all the Christians: Alleluia!

Ikos V

Seeing thy struggles and labors, thy fasting, thy keeping of vigils for many nights, thy prostrations, penitence, tears and prayers, the priest had thee ordained to the diaconate after examining thee, O hieromartyr Cyprian. And we, giving thanks unto God, praise thee:

Rejoice, thou who didst cry out to God in repentance day and night;
Rejoice, thou who didst pray for the forgiveness of sins!
Rejoice, thou who wast an example of correction;
Rejoice, thou who didst offer the Lord tearful prayers!
Rejoice, thou who didst indicate the way to salvation;
Rejoice, thou who didst show ardent love for Christ!
Rejoice, O hieromartyr Cyprian, speedy helper and intercessor for our souls!

Kontakion VI

Emulating the virgin Justina as a model of Christian piety, O hieromartyr Cyprian, thou didst truly show thyself to be a perfect Christian; for, having been baptized, thou didst abandon ungodly teaching, and in thanksgiving didst chant unto God with thy mouth and a pure heart: Alleluia!

Ikos VI

The light of divine perfection shone forth in thy heart, O divinely wise Cyprian, and thou didst attain the rank of priest, and later bishop. We entreat thee: By thy supplications illumine also the hearts of us who fervently pray to thee:

> Rejoice, thou who wast ordained to the rank of bishop;
> Rejoice, O eagle upborne on high!
> Rejoice, city standing on the height of a mountain;
> Rejoice, lamp burning before God!
> Rejoice, tireless intercessor before Christ;
> Rejoice, teacher given by God!
> Rejoice, O hieromartyr Cyprian, speedy helper and intercessor for our souls!

Kontakion VII

Desiring that all be saved, the Lord hath given us this advocate, helper and healer against the spirits of wickedness in high places. For by his teaching and words, the divinely eloquent one brought many to repentance and the correction of their sinful lives, teaching all to chant unto God: Alleluia!

Ikos VII

Thou hast been shown to the world as a new and most wise physician, O hieromartyr Cyprian, for the machinations of sorcery cannot withstand thy prayer, but the spells of evil men and wicked demons are straightway set at nought and dispelled. And we, seeing the power of God given thee, cry out to thee such things as these:

> Rejoice, destroyer of sorcerous wiles;
> Rejoice, dispeller of fearsome demons!
> Rejoice, thou before whom the spirits of evil vanish like smoke;
> Rejoice, thou who givest speedy aid to those suffering grievously!
> Rejoice, thou who deliverest from misfortunes and sorrows;

Rejoice, thou who turnest sufferings into joy!
Rejoice, O hieromartyr Cyprian, speedy helper and
    intercessor for our souls!

Kontakion VIII

A strange wonder is manifest upon those who have recourse unto thee with faith, O hieromartyr Cyprian; for by the grace given thee by God the demons which torment man are driven away, and the sick are healed, crying out to God: Alleluia!

Ikos VIII

O all-glorious one who lifted thyself up to God with all thy heart, and loved Him with all thy soul, thou didst have the zeal and desire to do His will; and as a good shepherd thou didst not turn away those weighed down by misfortunes, but intercedest before God in prayer, granting us healing and consolation. Wherefore, praising thy love for the Lord, we cry out to thee thus:

Rejoice, thou who didst love Christ with all thy heart;
Rejoice, thou who didst acquire all the virtues!
Rejoice, aid for those sick and paralyzed;
Rejoice, consolation amid sorrows and griefs!
Rejoice, repeller of the attacks and temptations launched
    by the world, the flesh and the devil;
Rejoice, healer of all ailments of soul and body!
Rejoice, O hieromartyr Cyprian, speedy helper and
    intercessor for our souls!

Kontakion IX

The whole army of the angels was glad, seeing thee, O father, to be an invincible warrior of the King of heaven, preaching Christ with boldness when thou wast led with Justina to the place of execution. For, fearful lest she renounce Christ when she see thee beheaded, thou didst say unto her: "Let them behead thee first." And bowing your heads beneath the sword, ye chanted unto God: Alleluia!

Ikos IX

The most eloquent of orators are unable worthily to hymn your sufferings for Christ, for ye were not afraid of the cruel threats, but stood before the emperor's tribunal with shining faces, moving all the faithful to say to you such things as these:

> Rejoice, unshakable confessors of the Faith of Christ;
> Rejoice, bold proclaimers of the all-holy Trinity!
> Rejoice, ye who laid down your life for Christ;
> Rejoice, ye who considered the cruel torments as nought!
> Rejoice, for your sufferings are glorified by the faithful;
> Rejoice, for your names are magnified in the churches of God!
> Rejoice, O hieromartyr Cyprian, speedy helper and intercessor for our souls!

Kontakion X

Desiring to save the souls of all under the sway of unclean spirits, cease thou never to cry out to the Lord, O divinely eloquent Cyprian; for unto thee hath been given the grace to pray for us, that, finding mercy and purification, we may chant unto God: Alleluia!

Ikos X

Be thou a firm rampart and mighty bulwark for us who flee unto thee with fervent faith and love, O hieromartyr Cyprian; for, protected against enemies, visible and invisible, we who are delivered by thee glorify thee thus:

> Rejoice, thou who didst vanquish the spirit of evil by humility;
> Rejoice, thou who didst extinguish the fiery arrows of the enemy by the fire of prayer!
> Rejoice, rampart and bulwark against enemies, visible and invisible;
> Rejoice, all-glorious adornment of the Orthodox Church!

Rejoice, all-wondrous help for those abandoned by their physicians;

Rejoice, loving consolation and gladness of the sorrowful!

Rejoice, O hieromartyr Cyprian, speedy helper and intercessor for our souls!

Kontakion XI

More than others, O hieromartyr Cyprian, didst thou offer unceasing hymnody to the All-Holy Trinity, Who out of mercy for fallen sinners hath been well-pleased to make the unworthy worthy and to number them among the flock of the saints. And, giving thanks to God for His mercy toward us sinners, we say unto Him: Alleluia!

Ikos XI

A radiant lamp in the Church of Christ wast thou, O divinely wise one, illumining the souls of the faithful with immaterial light. We beseech thee: Enlighten also our hearts, which have been darkened by sins, that we may chant unto thee such things as these:

Rejoice, thou who wast illumined by the thrice-radiant Light;

Rejoice, thou who hast been reckoned among the company of the saints!

Rejoice, for thou dost enlighten the souls of the faithful with immaterial light;

Rejoice, for thou guidest the lost to the straight path!

Rejoice, for like a lamb thou wast rescued by the Saviour from the pit of destruction;

Rejoice, thou who puttest the demons to shame and givest joy unto men!

Rejoice, O hieromartyr Cyprian, speedy helper and intercessor for our souls!

Kontakion XII

The grace was given thee by God to trample down the power of the enemy and every assault of Satan; for thou didst vanquish thine enemies, and didst seal thy faith in Christ by thy martyric struggle. And standing now before the throne of the King of glory, O most blessed Cyprian, pray that we may be delivered from diabolical captivity, and may cry out unto God: Alleluia!

Ikos XII

Hymning thy faithfulness to God and thy wondrous and all-glorious miracles, we magnify and praise thee, O hieromartyr Cyprian; for thou hast received such grace from God. Wherefore, we entreat thee: When the hordes of demons surround our souls at the hour of our death, show us thine aid, that, delivered by thee, we may cry out to thee thus:

Rejoice, speedy defense against the assailing foe;
Rejoice, deliverance from all manner of tribulations and griefs!
Rejoice, thou who didst love Christ to the end;
Rejoice, thou who didst lay down thy life for Him!
Rejoice, thou who wast washed in the blood of the Lamb;
Rejoice, thou who hast made thine abode in the courts of the Lord!
Rejoice, O hieromartyr Cyprian, speedy helper and intercessor for our souls!

Kontakion XIII

O all-wondrous and all-glorious favorite of God, hieromartyr Cyprian, speedy helper of all who have recourse unto thee! Accept from us, the unworthy, our hymnody of praise. Yea, O holy hierarch, we pray thee: Heal us of our multifarious ailments, help us against our enemies, visible and invisible, and entreat the Lord to deliver us from torment, that with thee we may chant: Alleluia! Alleluia! Alleluia!

This kontakion is recited thrice, whereupon Ikos I and Kontakion I are repeated.

Prayer to the Holy Hieromartyr Cyprian

O holy favorite of God, hieromartyr Cyprian, speedy helper and advocate for all who have recourse unto thee! Accept this laudation from us, the unworthy. Ask that the Lord God grant unto all of us strength amid our infirmities, consolation amid our griefs, and all things profitable in our life. Lift up to the Lord thy mighty supplication, that He protect us from the assaults of sin, that He teach us true repentance, that He deliver us from diabolical captivity and every action of the unclean spirits, and subdue those who oppress us. Be thou for us a mighty champion against all enemies, visible and invisible. Grant us patience amid temptations, and at the hour of our death show us thy help against those who will interrogate us in the aerial toll-houses: that led by thee, we may attain unto the heavenly Jerusalem, and be vouchsafed with all the saints in the kingdom of heaven to glorify and hymn the all-holy name of the Father, and the Son, and the Holy Spirit, unto the ages of ages. Amen.

Akathist Hymn to the Holy and Venerable New-martyr Elizabeth, Grand Duchess of Russia

New-Martyr Grand Duchess Elizabeth

Akathist Hymn
to the Holy and Venerable New-Martyr Elizabeth, Grand Duchess of Russia
Whose Memory the Holy Church Celebrates on the 5th of July

Kontakion I

O daughter of Russia, chosen from among the reigning dynasty, who served God and neighbor well with abundant love and kindness, who laid down thy life for thy faith in Christ our Lord, and hast been adorned with a crown of Christ's glory: Praising thy struggles and sufferings, we lovingly chant thus unto thee:

> Rejoice, O holy and venerable martyr Elizabeth, adornment of the Church of Russia, who wast counted worthy to be the bride of Christ!

Ikos I

O thou who loved Christ with angelic love and desired to serve Him alone: taught by thy mother, from childhood thou wast a model of the virtues in labors, prayers and the giving of alms. In the repose of thy mother and close kin thou didst perceive a way of the cross ordained by the Lord. Wherefore, marveling that thou wast thus chosen from thy youth, we cry out to thee with compunction:

> Rejoice, thou who loved Christ from thy youth;
> Rejoice, chosen ewe-lamb of Christ!

Rejoice, thou who received the seed of faith from thy parents;

Rejoice, thou who wast reared by them in the fear of God!

Rejoice, thou who didst inherit the virtues of thy mother;

Rejoice, thou who wast taught by her to be industrious and kind!

Rejoice, thou wast made steadfast in God by thy heart;

Rejoice, thou who bore thy cross with faith and hope, and followed after Christ!

Rejoice, fragrant blossom of thy native land;

Rejoice, thou who hast gladdened the heavens by the purity of thy soul!

Rejoice, thou who wast chosen by God to minister to the suffering;

Rejoice, O our advocate before God!

Rejoice, O holy and venerable martyr Elizabeth, adornment of the Church of Russia, who wast counted worthy to be the bride of Christ!

Kontakion II

The Lord saw the good disposition of thy heart, how from thy youth thou didst desire to lead thy life in piety and purity, uplifting the eyes of thy heart to the beauty of heaven and kindling within thyself the fire of love for God. By thy supplications enlighten our hearts with love for God, that with thee we may chant unto Him: Alleluia!

Ikos II

Enlightened by understanding from on high, O holy Elizabeth, thou wast not afraid to leave thy homeland, kin and the house of thy father, and to make thine abode in a new land, when thou wast united in matrimony with Grand Duke Sergius of Russia, that, serving God with thy spouse, thou mightest live with him in chastity, showing true love for the people of Russia. And we cry out with love to thee thus:

Rejoice, glorious sojourner who camest from the West;
Rejoice, thou who didst find a new home in the land of Russia!
Rejoice, right-believing princess who faithfully served our land;
Rejoice, instructor for us in good works!
Rejoice, thou who dwelt in the wedded state in love and chastity;
Rejoice, for thou wast a wise helper for thy spouse in the charitable deeds!
Rejoice, protectress of pious married couples;
Rejoice, thou who warmest us with maternal love!
Rejoice, thou who desired to fulfill the commandments of God;
Rejoice, thou who didst kindle zeal for God in our hearts!
Rejoice, thou who by the beauty of thy soul and body didst move all to rejoice;
Rejoice, adornment of the whole Christian world!
Rejoice, O holy and venerable martyr Elizabeth, adornment of the Church of Russia, who wast counted worthy to be the bride of Christ!

Kontakion III

Made wise unto salvation by the power of divine grace, with understanding thou didst recognize the true Faith, O merciful Princess Elizabeth; and while sojourning in the Holy Land, thou wast confirmed in thy desire to embrace Orthodoxy, chanting to God Who enlightened thee: Alleluia!

Ikos III

Possessed of a heart like unto good earth, thou didst readily receive the Orthodox Faith; wherefore, thou wast vouchsafed Holy Chrismation and the communion of the Holy Mysteries of Christ on the Sunday of the resurrection of the righteous Lazarus. And we, glorifying thine enlightenment by the grace of the Holy Spirit, magnify thee, saying:

Rejoice, thou who received the Orthodox Faith on the day of the resurrection of the righteous Lazarus;
Rejoice, blessed fruit of the Russian land!
Rejoice, thou who didst receive the seal of the Holy Spirit through Chrismation;
Rejoice, thou who in Orthodoxy didst retain the name given thee at birth!
Rejoice, namesake of the holy and righteous Elizabeth;
Rejoice, for thou didst assiduously emulate her life in thy struggles!
Rejoice, for to the children of the West thou showest the way to the True Faith;
Rejoice, for the pious people of Russia honor thy memory with love!
Rejoice, merciful mother who hast found mercy with the Master and Lord;
Rejoice, thou who prayest earnestly that we find mercy!
Rejoice, thou who bearest the divine Light in thy heart;
Rejoice, thou who with the light of the commandments of Christ dost illumine the darkness of our life.
Rejoice, O holy and venerable martyr Elizabeth, adornment of the Church of Russia, who wast counted worthy to be the bride of Christ!

Kontakion IV

The tempest of the evil of the enemy of the human race did not shake thee, O holy one, when thy right-believing spouse endured a martyr's death; and suffering with him, thou didst show great courage and Christian love. And, bearing aloft the soul of thy husband, the angels chanted: Alleluia!

Ikos IV

When the Russian people heard of the assassination of the right-believing Grand Duke Sergius, they prayed that God would give thee the strength, O holy Elizabeth, to bear this sorrow. And fortified by sacrificial love, thou didst visit the murderer of thy husband in prison, urging him to repent and offering up prayers to the Lord for his forgiveness. Wherefore, accept thou from us, the unworthy, these praises:

> Rejoice, thou who fulfilled the commandment of Christ to love one's enemies;
> Rejoice, thou who, following the Gospel, didst forgive the murderer of thy husband!
> Rejoice, thou who endured many sorrows and tribulations;
> Rejoice, thou who helpest us to bear the burden of sorrows and griefs!
> Rejoice, thou who guidest the lost toward the path of truth and repentance;
> Rejoice, fervent mediatress for the salvation of sinners!
> Rejoice, thou who with the light of hope dost illumine us amid the darkness of griefs;
> Rejoice, guiding star for all who hope for salvation!
> Rejoice, thou who leadest our hardened hearts toward compunction;
> Rejoice, fervent advocate for us before Christ amid our every sorrow!
> Rejoice, thou who overcamest the evil of the world by good;
> Rejoice, thou who showed true love for the Russian people!
> Rejoice, O holy and venerable martyr Elizabeth, adornment of the Church of Russia, who wast counted worthy to be the bride of Christ!

Kontakion V

Thou didst shine forth in the land of Russia like a divinely guided star, O holy Elizabeth, when, considering riches and glory to be as dust, thou didst commit thy life into the hands of God, that thou mightest serve Him in fasting and prayer; and thou didst show forth great love and lovingkindness to the suffering. Thus also do thou light the way of our life with the light of thy virtues, that we may joyously cry out to God: Alleluia!

Ikos V

Beholding thee as the wondrous foundress of the Convent of Saints Martha and Mary, the people of the divinely saved city of Moscow rejoiced, for many women and maidens of Russia found there a calm haven of salvation, emulating the holy myrrhbearers in ministering to God and neighbor. Wherefore, glorifying thee, we say thus:

> Rejoice, thou who understood the vanity of worldly life in earthly glory;
> Rejoice, thou who distributed thy property and loved the poverty of Christ!
> Rejoice, thou who adorned the city of Moscow with a wondrous convent;
> Rejoice, thou who didst take up the easy yoke of Christ!
> Rejoice, thou who brought many women and maidens into thy convent;
> Rejoice, wise guide to salvation for thy sisters!
> Rejoice, thou who emulated the ministry of the holy myrrhbearers Martha and Mary;
> Rejoice, ever-vigilant protector of thy community!
> Rejoice, thou who makest us steadfast in the struggle of the spiritual life;
> Rejoice, thou who showest us the way from earth to heaven!
> Rejoice, beacon of lovingkindness shining over the city of Moscow;
> Rejoice, protectress of all who have given their lives to serve their neighbors!
> Rejoice, O holy and venerable martyr Elizabeth, adornment of the Church of Russia, who wast counted worthy to be the bride of Christ!

Kontakion VI

In our land thou wast a preacher of the love of God and His lovingkindness, and a zealot for piety, O holy Elizabeth, enkindling in the hearts of the Russian people love for God and lovingkindness toward our brethren and sisters and all the unfortunate, that, following thy precepts, we may chant unto God: Alleluia!

Ikos VI

Thou didst shine forth with the light of thy virtuous life in the land of Russia, O our venerable mother Elizabeth; and in the monastic habit, in fasting and abstinence, thou didst live thy life in the keeping of all-night vigils and hymns of supplications, teaching the nuns of thy convent piety and humility. Wherefore, guided by thee to the straight path of spiritual struggle, we bless thee thus:

> Rejoice, thou who didst choose the path of the monastic life equal to that of the angels;
> Rejoice, thou who by the vow of chastity didst show forth the purity of thy heart!
> Rejoice, thou who by the vow of poverty didst show forth the eminence of thy spirit;
> Rejoice, thou who by the vow of obedience didst serve God and thy neighbor!
> Rejoice, wise princess and all-honorable nun;
> Rejoice, thou who wast appointed from on high to be a model for Christian women!
> Rejoice, thou who by fasting, vigil and unceasing prayer didst please God;
> Rejoice, thou who hast roused our souls from the sleep of sin!
> Rejoice, thou who guidest all to the fulfillment of the commandment to love God and neighbor;
> Rejoice, thou who teachest us heartfelt prayer!
> Rejoice, instructress of nuns and conversor with the angels;
> Rejoice, thou who in heaven art glorious among the company of venerable women!
> Rejoice, O holy and venerable martyr Elizabeth, adornment of the Church of Russia, who wast counted worthy to be the bride of Christ!

Kontakion VII

Desiring to understand the will of the Lord, O holy Elizabeth, in obedience thou didst wholly entrust thyself to the elders Gabriel of the Holy Saviour-Saint Eleazar Monastery and Alexis of the Saint Zosima Monastery, and didst also question other divinely wise elders, doing nought without their blessing and cutting off thine own will; wherefore, thou didst arrange all things in thy convent for the better, unceasingly crying out to God: Alleluia!

Ikos VII

A new wonder did the Lord reveal, O holy Elizabeth, when He gave thee the grace and power to heal sicknesses, strengthen the paralyzed, help those in trouble, and defend the oppressed. And giving ease and comfort to the suffering, with humility and love thou didst minister to the poor who were abandoned by all, and the maimed. Wherefore, by thy supplication heal also us sinners, and be thou for us a guide to salvation, that we may sing unto thee in thanksgiving:

> Rejoice, thou who didst live in obedience to thy spiritual fathers, the great elders;
> Rejoice, thou whom the Russian people called their great mother!
> Rejoice, thou who didst acquire from God the gift to heal ailing souls;
> Rejoice, thou who didst raise up the hopelessly sick from the bed of illness!
> Rejoice, thou who with a kind heart didst care for widows and orphans;
> Rejoice, feeder of the hungry and speedy helper of the unfortunate!
> Rejoice, thou who didst not reject those who were spurned and rejected by all;
> Rejoice, thou who didst save many souls from the darkness of sin and destruction!
> Rejoice, wise comforter of those despondent amid sorrows and evil circumstances;

Rejoice, thou who dost strengthen us also who are overcome by sicknesses and tribulations!
Rejoice, intercessor before God for repentant sinners;
Rejoice, merciful helper given by God to the Russian people!
Rejoice, O holy and venerable martyr Elizabeth, adornment of the Church of Russia, who wast counted worthy to be the bride of Christ!

Kontakion VIII

A strange and awesome vision did the Lord reveal to Father Metrophanes, the confessor of thy convent. And thou, O holy mother, interpreting this vision, didst prophesy that a great and threatening trial would come upon the Church of Russia and our realm: the profanation of the holy places, fratricidal strife, great tribulation, and the martyrdom of the Royal Family. Yet God hath mercy upon Russia through the supplications of its saints, with whom thou dost now chant unto God: Alleluia!

Ikos VIII

Wholly illumined by divine grace, O holy Elizabeth, with noetic eyes thou didst behold the visitation of God's wrath upon our land, and as a prophet thou didst proclaim that many martyrs and confessors would shine forth in the land of Russia. Wherefore, thou didst call upon the Russian people to place all their hope in the Mother of God, that through her supplications our land might be put in order and blessed. And, knowing the fulfillment of thy prophecy concerning the fate of our homeland, we bless thee thus:

Rejoice, thou who raised up the Church of the Protection of the All-holy Theotokos in thy convent;
Rejoice, thou who didst thus commit thy convent into the hands of all-pure Mother of the Lord!
Rejoice, thou who didst build temples of God;
Rejoice, our tireless supplicant before the Theotokos!
Rejoice, thou who didst benefit the churches of God;

Rejoice, thou who didst labor without rest for the sake of life eternal!

Rejoice, thou who by thy life didst faithfully serve God and the All-Holy Virgin Theotokos;

Rejoice, thou who dost teach us to set all our hope on God!

Rejoice, thou who impartest meekness, tranquillity and peace to our hearts;

Rejoice, thou who wast adorned with the gracious gifts of the Holy Spirit!

Rejoice, for thou didst with clear foresight predict the great tribulations of our land;

Rejoice, for the Lord hath had mercy upon it!

Rejoice, O holy and venerable martyr Elizabeth, adornment of the Church of Russia, who wast counted worthy to be the bride of Christ!

Kontakion IX

Wholly afire with love for God, O holy Elizabeth, thou wast not afraid when to the convent thou hadst founded came mindless men, who desired to execute an unjust judgment upon thee. But, preserved by the Lord, thou didst then elude death, praying for the correction and enlightenment of the foolish and errant, and chanting to God in thanksgiving: Alleluia!

Ikos IX

The mouths of human rhetors are unable worthily to praise the strength of thy love during those days of tribulations and the great perils which beset our native land, when thou didst not desire to leave Russian and the convent thou hadst founded, urging its nuns to stand fast for the Orthodox Faith even unto death. And we praise thee thus with love:

Rejoice, thou who didst love our land;

Rejoice, thou who with love art glorified by the Russian people!

Rejoice, thou who teachest us to protect ourselves in battle with the shield of faith;
Rejoice, thou who dost strengthen in us the resolve to follow the Lord by the way of the cross!
Rejoice, thou who didst make the nuns of thy convent steadfast in faith and hope;
Rejoice, thou who didst instruct them to undertake the feat of martyrdom for Christ!
Rejoice, thou who wast counted worthy to acquire the sufferings of Christ!
Rejoice, thou who dost confirm the Russian people in the struggle of confession!
Rejoice, thou who didst save man from the pit of destruction;
Rejoice, helper, protection and defender of thy convent and the city of Moscow!
Rejoice, thou who teachest us sacrificial, eternal love;
Rejoice, thou who hast entered into the joy of thy Lord!
Rejoice, O holy and venerable martyr Elizabeth, adornment of the Church of Russia, who wast counted worthy to be the bride of Christ!

Kontakion X

Seeking the struggle of salvation, O holy Elizabeth, with joy thou didst give thanks unto God, for He vouchsafed thee to bear His Cross. Wherefore, thy faith shone forth in victory when, ascending thine own Golgotha, thou didst proclaim unceasingly: "Glory to God for all things!" Pray thou, O our mother, that the Lord may grant that we may acquire the wisdom and power to stand firm for the right Faith even unto death, and to chant unto Him with one mouth and one heart: Alleluia!

Ikos X

An unassailable bulwark and help was given to the Russian land in the holy Reigning Icon of the Mother of God, which the saintly

Elizabeth received in her convent as a sign of victory over the princes of darkness of this world. Wherefore, having placed all our hope in the reigning Mistress of our land, we praise thee as a true and obedient servant of the All-Pure Mother of the Lord, saying:

> Rejoice, thou who wast full of the grace and power of God;
> Rejoice, thou who didst choose the good part, which shall not be taken from thee!
> Rejoice, thou who didst emulate the Mother of God in meekness;
> Rejoice, wise virgin of the Gospel, who obtained the oil of grace!
> Rejoice, thou who didst reverently honor the All-Holy Virgin Theotokos;
> Rejoice, thou who prayest for us unceasingly at Her throne!
> Rejoice, thou who hast provided us with a model of self-denial;
> Rejoice, thou who teachest us to bear one another's burdens!
> Rejoice, thou who through earthly sorrows and sufferings hast entered the kingdom of heaven;
> Rejoice, thou who teachest all to have love and patience amid sufferings endured for the Lord's sake!
> Rejoice, thou who lived on earth like an angel;
> Rejoice, thou who hast inherited a crown of glory in heaven!
> Rejoice, O holy and venerable martyr Elizabeth, adornment of the Church of Russia, who wast counted worthy to be the bride of Christ!

Kontakion XI

Hymnody of supplication to the Mother of God didst thou offer up on the feastday of the Her Iveron Icon, O holy Elizabeth, when the ungodly arrested thee and cast thee into prison. But thou gavest thanks unto Christ our God, Who had not only granted thee to believe in Him, but also to suffer for Him, chanting to Him in thy prison bonds: Alleluia!

Ikos XI

Divine light illumined thee, O holy passion-bearer Princess Elizabeth, with the venerable martyr Barbara, thy sister in Christ, and the other noble passion-bearers, when, cast down a deep mine-shaft, thou didst bind up the wounds of the Grand Duke John, didst ease the sufferings of the dying by chanting sacred hymns, and didst pray for your murderers, saying: "Father, forgive them, for they know not what they do!" Treat thou also the wounds of our souls, O our mother, that we may chant unto thee with love:

> Rejoice, thou who hadst foreknowledge of thy martyric end;
> Rejoice, royal passion-bearer!
> Rejoice, thou who acquired the sufferings of Christ on the day of the commemoration of the venerable Sergius;
> Rejoice, thou who wast strengthened by divine power amid thy sufferings!
> Rejoice, thou who, emulating Christ, didst pray for thy tormentors;
> Rejoice, thou who didst chant hymnody unto God until thy very end!
> Rejoice, thou who didst bedew our land with thy blood;
> Rejoice, thou who hast been numbered among the legion of the new martyrs of Russia!
> Rejoice, for thou hast joined the choir of venerable and righteous women;
> Rejoice, thou who wast a worthy co-heir of the holy and right-believing princesses of the Russian land!
> Rejoice, thou who wast offered unto God as a spotless and right pleasing sacrifice;

> Rejoice, thou who with all the saints of our land art triumphant!
> Rejoice, O holy and venerable martyr Elizabeth, adornment of the Church of Russia, who wast counted worthy to be the bride of Christ!

Kontakion XII

Your holy relics were shown to be vessels full of grace, O holy and venerable martyrs Elizabeth and Barbara, and desiring to save them from profanation and mockery, pious men carried them from Russia to the Holy City of Jerusalem and buried them in the Garden of Gethsemane, on the Mount of Olives; and those who come to venerate them call you blessed, chanting unto God Who is wondrous in His saints: Alleluia!

Ikos XII

The Church of the Holy Myrrhbearer Mary Magdalene was filled with heavenly light and a wondrous sweet fragrance when they opened the coffin which held the body of the Grand Duchess Elizabeth. Wherefore, all the children of the Orthodox Church rejoice and join chorus in the Lord, hastening to the shrine of thy relics, O venerable martyr Elizabeth, which pour forth miracles upon all the faithful; and giving thanks to the Lord Who hath glorified thee, they chant thus:

> Rejoice, for thy relics, borne to the Holy City of Jerusalem, blossomed forth with incorruption;
> Rejoice, thou who by thy relics hast spiritually joined the Holy Land to the land of Russia!
> Rejoice, thou who by the appearance of thy relics hast gladdened the Russian Church;
> Rejoice, thou who hast thereby spiritually strengthened the Russian people of the diaspora!
> Rejoice, thou who wast buried near the Tomb of the Lord;
> Rejoice, thou who wast laid to rest in the Church of the Holy Myrrhbearer Mary Magdalene!

Rejoice, for thy relics heal all sorrows and sicknesses;
Rejoice, witness to eternity in this transitory life!
Rejoice, thou who united the crown of the virtues within thyself;
Rejoice, thou who wast glorified by the inscrutable judgments of God!
Rejoice, blessed inhabitant of the Jerusalem on high;
Rejoice, guide to the heavenly Jerusalem for us all!
Rejoice, O holy and venerable martyr Elizabeth, adornment of the Church of Russia, who wast counted worthy to be the bride of Christ!

Kontakion XIII

O great passion-bearer, adornment of the women of Russia, our joy, merciful Princess Elizabeth: Accept the sighing of our hearts, which is offered unto thee with love, and by thine intercession before the Lord strengthen within us the spirit of right faith and piety, establish us in virtue and lovingkindness, help us to bear the cross of sorrows with patience and hope, and preserve our people in love and concord, that we may be vouchsafed to enter into the joy of the Lord, chanting unto Him with the angels and all the saints: Alleluia! Alleluia! Alleluia!

This Kontakion is recited thrice, whereupon Ikos I and Kontakion I are repeated.

Prayer to the Holy and Venerable Martyrs, Grand Duchess Elizabeth and the Nun Barbara

O holy new-martyrs of Russia, Grand Duchess Elizabeth, and thou, O most honored nun Barbara, her sister in Christ: ye who finished your path amid many torments, who observed the commandments in deed at your convent, who struggled for the Orthodox Faith even unto death in these latter times, and in the endurance of sufferings offered goodly fruit unto Christ! Entreat Him, as the Conqueror of death, that He establish in our homeland the Russian Orthodox Church, which hath been redeemed by the blood and sufferings of the new-martyrs, and that He not give our inheritance over to be plundered by the enemies of Russia. For, lo! the evil foe hath armed himself against us, desiring to destroy us amid civil strife, tribulations, unbearable griefs, sickness, want and cruel misfortunes. Beseech the Lord, that He set at nought all their feeble audacity. Make faith strong in the hearts of the Russian people, that when the hour of trial shall find us, we may receive the gift of courage through your supplications, and may deny ourselves and take up our cross, and follow Christ, crucifying our flesh with the passions and lusts. Preserve us from all evil; sanctify the ways of our life; grant unfeigned repentance, tranquillity and peace to our souls; beg the Lord to deliver us all from the bitter toll-houses and from everlasting torment, and to make us heirs to the heavenly kingdom with all the saints who have pleased God from ages past: that, rejoicing, we may give praise, honor and worship to the Father, and to the Son, and to the Holy Spirit, unto the ages of ages. Amen.

Akathist Hymn
to the Holy Martyrs Faith, Hope and Love, and Their Mother, Sophia

The Holy Martyrs Faith, Hope and Love,
And Their Mother, Sophia

Akathist Hymn
to the Holy Martyrs Faith, Hope and Love, And Their Mother, Sophia
Whose Memory the Holy Church Celebrates on September 17th

Kontakion I

To you, the chosen handmaids of the Lord Almighty—Faith, Hope and Love, and the wise Sophia, their mother—do we offer up hymns of praise with compunction. As ye have boldness before Christ God, pray for us, that we may be delivered from sins and tribulations, that in thanksgiving we may cry out to you:

>Rejoice, O Faith, Hope and Love, with your all-wise
>   mother, Sophia!

Ikos I

The angels rejoiced in heaven, beholding the virtuous life which ye spent in the reading of the divine Scriptures, in labors, fasting, praying and the giving of alms, unceasingly taught by your mother, that ye might be shown to be living images of the three theological virtues for which ye were named. And marvelling at the wisdom of your mother and at your perfect good understanding, with reverence we say to you:

>Rejoice, sisters one in mind, namesakes of the three
>   virtues;
>Rejoice, ye who in obedience to your divinely wise
>   mother didst enter the stages of perfection!

Rejoice, ye who like three branches of paradise did spring forth in pagan Rome;

Rejoice, O Sophia who, having given thy daughters the names of the virtues, didst teach them to fulfil their names in deed!

Rejoice, O Faith, who through faith helpest us to see what is invisible as though it were visible;

Rejoice, thou who wast clothed in incorruption!

Rejoice, O Hope, who through hope dost ease our sufferings in this vale of sorrow, and with thy right hand dost point the way to the highest;

Rejoice, thou who hast inherited the kingdom of heaven!

Rejoice, O Love, who through divine love dost open unto us the blessedness of life immortal;

Rejoice, thou who wast illumined by the grace of the Holy Spirit!

Rejoice, O Sophia, whose name doth signify wisdom, and who raised thy daughters all-wisely;

Rejoice, thou who makest us steadfast in the virtues of faith, hope and love!

Rejoice, O Faith, Hope and Love, with your all-wise mother, Sophia!

Kontakion II

Beholding the servants who had come to summon her and her daughters before the Emperor Hadrian, and knowing the reason for this summons, the wise Sophia stood in prayer with her children, asking the help of God; and after praying, they joined hands like a plaited wreath, and went forth together, chanting unto Christ God: Alleluia!

Ikos II

Ye were possessed of unwavering resolve, O saints; for when ye were brought into the imperial palace, ye stood before the Emperor

Hadrian with a radiant countenance, your eyes full of gladness and your heart full of courage. And the emperor, seeing that your honorable faces were unmarred by fear and perceiving the wisdom of Sophia, postponed your trial for a time, and sent you to a certain noblewoman, with whom ye abode for three days, your all-wise mother instructing you with divinely inspired words day and night. Wherefore, blessing you, we cry out thus:

> Rejoice, ye three unblemished ewe-lambs, who combined within you the crown of the virtues;
>
> Rejoice, ye three virtuous sisters, who showed forth firm faith, unwavering hope and unfeigned love for the Lord God!
>
> Rejoice, ye who spared not your beauty and youth for the sake of Him Who in beauty surpasseth all the children of man;
>
> Rejoice, O Sophia, who guided your beloved children to the struggle of martyrdom for Christ!
>
> Rejoice, O Faith, who by martyrdom for Christ didst confess thy faith;
>
> Rejoice, thou who with thy mighty faith didst uplift thy sisters!
>
> Rejoice, O Hope, who set a firm hope in Christ;
>
> Rejoice, thou who with unfailing hope didst strengthen thy sisters!
>
> Rejoice, O Love, who through torments endured for Christ didst show forth thy real love;
>
> Rejoice, thou who didst encircle thy sisters with the fire of love!
>
> Rejoice, O Sophia, who didst exhort thy sweet children to spurn glory, riches and all the delights of this corrupt world;
>
> Rejoice, thou who didst fervently teach thy good daughters to stand up for Christ and to die for Him!
>
> Rejoice, O Faith, Hope and Love, with your all-wise mother, Sophia!

Kontakion III

Overshadowed by divine power in the struggles of martyrdom were the martyrs, who in deed manifested the virtues for which they were named; and they chant unto God: Alleluia!

Ikos III

Possessing within themselves a pillar of faith, wings of hope and the fire of love, heeding the words of their mother to their delight, the holy martyrs made each other steadfast in longsuffering and went forth with joy, desiring honorable martyrdom for Christ. And worshiping Him as our God, we honor them with such exclamations as these:

> Rejoice, ye who did not in the least regret being deprived of this transitory life for the sake of life eternal;
> Rejoice, ye who to honor Christ gave your flesh over to torture!
> Rejoice, ye who offered three priceless vessels, of faith, hope and love, as a gift to God;
> Rejoice, O Sophia, for in your surpassing love for thy daughters didst desire with all thy heart that they inherit the kingdom of God!
> Rejoice, O Faith, who illuminest our souls with faith;
> Rejoice, thou who dost bear us up to the calm haven!
> Rejoice, O Hope, who dost enliven our hearts with the sweetness of hope;
> Rejoice, thou who dost draw us forth from the depths of despair!
> Rejoice, O Love, who turnest our sufferings and sorrows into joy;
> Rejoice, thou who bringest our hardened hearts to compunction!
> Rejoice, O Sophia, thou with wisdom dost guide us to the good;
> Rejoice, thou who enlightenest the darkened eyes of our souls!

Rejoice, O Faith, Hope and Love, with your all-wise
 mother, Sophia!

Kontakion IV

The tempest of the tyrant's ire smote thee, O holy Faith, yet did not shake thee; for who can can move the invincible faith, harder than diamonds, wherewith thou hast taught the faithful to chant with thee unto God: "Alleluia!"?

Ikos IV

Hearing her daughters confess Christ fearlessly before the emperor, and say that they desire Him alone, that they might suffer and endure bitter torments for the sake of Jesus Christ most sweet, the wise mother rejoiced exceedingly and prayed to God, that He strengthen them in the tortures which lay before them. Wherefore, praising their resolve, we chant thus to the eldest daughter of this wise mother:

Rejoice, O Faith, who sweetly accepted unmerciful beatings for the sake of Jesus most sweet;
Rejoice, thou who didst offer unto the Lord as a sacrifice thy severed breasts, as though they were two pure lilies!
Rejoice, for instead of blood milk flowed from thy wounds;
Rejoice, for thou wast set upon a forked iron rod!
Rejoice, for cast into a boiling cauldron thou wast in nowise burned, nor didst thou suffer any harm;
Rejoice, thou who stillest the flame of our passions with heavenly coolness!
Rejoice, thou who dost quench the fire of our torments amid our ailments;
Rejoice, thou who amid perils dost sign us with the sign of faith!
Rejoice, thou who coverest us with the shield of faith amid battle with the enemy;

Rejoice, thou who didst joyfully bow thy precious head beneath the sword for Christ God, the Head of the Church!

Rejoice, for arrayed in the stains of thy blood, as in purple vesture, thou didst appear before the eyes of thine immortal Bridegroom;

Rejoice, thou who didst reach the desired end and hast beheld thy beloved Saviour and Lord!

Rejoice, O Faith, Hope and Love, with your all-wise mother, Sophia!

Kontakion V

Ye were like unto the God-given stars, O Faith, Hope and Love; for, cleaving with all your heart to Jesus Christ, the only eternal Life and ineffable Beauty, ye hastened to die for Him, and to delight in the divine vision of Him, chanting unto Him: Alleluia!

Ikos V

Her right-victorious sisters, seeing the holy Faith joyfully suffering for Christ, themselves desired to lay down their life for Him. And when the emperor began to examine the holy Hope and perceived that she was of like mind with her sister, he gave her over to tortures; yet did this avail him nought. But we, blessing the holy Hope for her understanding, hymn and glorify her thus:

Rejoice, O Hope, who wast cruelly beaten, yet didst not lose thine all-radiant hope in the Lord;

Rejoice, thou who in silence didst endure thy torments without complaint!

Rejoice, thou who givest us mighty endurance;

Rejoice, for, unconsumed in the burning furnace, thou didst send up praise unto God!

Rejoice, for thou teachest us also to praise God amid sufferings;

Rejoice, for thou wast lacerated with iron claws!

Rejoice, thou who with rays of hope dost illumine us amid our tribulations;

Rejoice, for a wondrous fragrance issued forth from thy wounds!

Rejoice, thou who didst immutably preserve unshaken hope in the Lord Jesus;

Rejoice, thou who destroyest hopelessness and powerlessness in our hearts!

Rejoice, thou who for Christ joyfully accepted beheading by the sword;

Rejoice, bright daystar who revealest everlasting peace to us who are oppressed by the earthly griefs!

Rejoice, O Faith, Hope and Love, with your all-wise mother, Sophia!

Kontakion VI

Ye were like unto the God-bearing preachers and apostles, O divinely wise sisters; for by your virtues to all the faithful ye preached faith, hope and love for the Lord, the Master of all, chanting unto Him: Alleluia!

Ikos VI

Thou didst shine forth like the sun, O holy Love; for who could stand up thus for his Lord like love, for it is written: Love is strong as death; many waters cannot quench love, neither can rivers drown it. And we now beseech thee, O holy Love, who burnest with the flame of seraphic love for the Lord: Restore our hardened and withered hearts; enkindle within us, in whom love hath failed, the light of love, that, loving the Lord and all our neighbors, we may praise thee as our intercessor thus:

Rejoice, O Love, for the many waters of the deceptions of the world did not extinguish thy love for Christ;

Rejoice, for having rejected all the blandishments and gifts of the emperor thou didst lay down thy life for the Lord!

Rejoice, for rivers of misfortunes and sufferings did not drown thy love;

Rejoice, thou who wast stretched out on the wheel, beaten with staves, pierced with awls and cast into a fiery furnace!

Rejoice, for amid thy cruel tortures thou wast strengthened by the power of God;

Rejoice, thou who instillest love in our cold hearts by thy blood, which was shed out of love for Christ, thine immortal Bridegroom!

Rejoice, thou who hast manifestly shown us that all torments may be sweetly endured for the sake of love;

Rejoice, thou who hast revealed to us that divine love leadeth to life everlasting!

Rejoice, thou who in thy case itself hast assured us that divine love is a revelation of immortality;

Rejoice, for no manner of torture could separate Love from the love of Christ;

Rejoice, thou who amid torments didst like the Apostle declare that neither tribulation, nor distress, nor persecution, nor famine, nor nakedness, nor peril, nor the sword, could separate thee from the love of God;

Rejoice, thou who wast beheaded by the sword for the sake of Christ's love!

Rejoice, O Faith, Hope and Love, with your all-wise mother, Sophia!

Kontakion VII

Desiring to depart the body with all speed and to be with Christ, the holy virgins, when they went forth to be beheaded, kissed one another, embracing each other and Sophia, their mother, teaching us the love of friendship, that we may all chant unto God together: Alleluia!

Ikos VII

A new wonder did the Lord show forth when He sent His help upon the young virgins who were suffering so greatly in confessing His name; for, strengthened and uplifted by faith, hope and love, they finished their struggle with courage. And we beseech them, who remained in oneness of mind and oneness of soul until the end of their lives, that they send down oneness of mind in the doing of good works upon us who magnify them with compunction:

> Rejoice, O Faith, Hope and Love, who trod the one path of torments to the gates of heaven;
> Rejoice, ye who entered the all-radiant bridal-chamber of your all-beloved Bridegroom with a voice of rejoicing!
> Rejoice, for Jesus Christ made the wounds on your bodies shine like stars in the heavens;
> Rejoice, O Sophia, who courageously watched the torture of your children!
> Rejoice, for with heavenly beauty, such as eye hath not seen, hath the Lord adorned your beauty, which tortures had destroyed;
> Rejoice, ye who have received crowns as your reward!
> Rejoice, ye who like three stars were illumined by the Sun of righteousness;
> Rejoice, O Sophia, who found great consolation in thy daughters' valiant confession of the name of Christ!
> Rejoice, ye who dispel the gloom of our doubts;
> Rejoice, ye who strengthen us, who have become subject to passions of body and soul!
> Rejoice, ye who adorn our hearts with the beauty of love;
> Rejoice, O Sophia, thou might and consolation of those who languish in misfortunes and need!
> Rejoice, O Faith, Hope and Love, with your all-wise mother, Sophia!

Kontakion VIII

Strange and incomprehensible is it for us who are weak and bemired in worldly pleasures to envision how the holy Sophia, watching the cruel and bitter torments and death of her beloved children, was not in anywise distressed, but rejoiced exceedingly in spirit, chanting unto God: Alleluia!

Ikos VIII

Wholly in the highest was the wise Sophia, when with sweet discourse and wise admonitions she spurred her daughters on to martyrdom. And even though by nature she was straightway inclined toward tears, they were transformed by the love of Christ into joy, for the love of God overcame within her the grief of heart and maternal pain she felt for her children. Wherefore, loving her children with great love, she desired for them the kingdom of heaven above all. Therefore, marvelling at her wisdom and her great love for her daughters, and glorifying Thee, we cry aloud:

Rejoice, O Sophia, for thy soul exulted in the blessed end of thy daughters, who boldly confessed the holy name of the Lord;

Rejoice, thou who received honor and glory when thy children received the crown of martyrdom!

Rejoice, thou who wast vouchsafed the portion of the martyrs and to dwell with thy daughters in the glory of heaven;

Rejoice, thou who with tears of joy didst bury the precious bodies of thine offspring!

Rejoice, thou who didst sit by their graves for three days and didst repose in the Lord in the sleep of death;

Rejoice, thou who didst suffer in thy heart for Christ, if not in the flesh!

Rejoice, for thou didst offer as a gift to the all-holy Trinity thy three virtuous daughters, revealing faith, hope and love through them;

Rejoice, for thou wast saved through the children thou
    didst bear!
Rejoice, O wondrous mother, worthy of goodly
    remembrance;
Rejoice, thou who didst entreat thy daughters to shed
    their blood for Christ!
Rejoice, thou who givest us wisdom, that we may preserve immutable the virtues of faith, hope and
    love;
Rejoice, thou who prayest for us to the life-creating
    Trinity!
Rejoice, O Faith, Hope and Love, with your all-wise
    mother, Sophia!

Kontakion IX

All the angels marvelled at your sufferings, O holy martyrs, and celebrating your victory over the devil, and escorting your souls to heaven, they chanted unto Christ God: Alleluia!

Ikos IX

Even the most eloquent of orators are unable to describe the sufferings ye endured for Christ, and marvelling at the many great struggles ye underwent as children, they are utterly at a loss. But we, glorifying God for your honorable end, magnify you thus:

Rejoice, O Faith, Hope and Love, who sing praise unto
    God Who hath raised you up to the heaven of
    heavens;
Rejoice, O shield of faith, breastplate of hope and beacon of love!
Rejoice, ye who enjoy the sight of the all-radiant countenance of God;
Rejoice, O Sophia, who guidest pious mothers in the
    wise upbringing of their children!
Rejoice, ye who instruct us to seek the Lord, that our
    souls may live;

Rejoice, fervent intercessors for those who with faith, hope and love have recourse unto you!

Rejoice, ye who teach us that all the pleasures and deceptions of this world will vanish like smoke, will be scattered like dust before the wind, and will return to the earth;

Rejoice, O Sophia, who loved the Lord with all thy heart!

Rejoice, for ye who entered into the one Source of life like three radiant keys;

Rejoice, ye who sprang forth on a single fruitful branch like three fragrant blossoms!

Rejoice, ye who reflect in yourselves the infinite beauty of God like three mirrors;

Rejoice, O Sophia, who like an olive tree didst put forth three branches laden with the abundant fruits of the gifts of God!

Rejoice, O Faith, Hope and Love, with your all-wise mother, Sophia!

Kontakion X

Desiring to save their souls, the holy martyrs, for the love of Christ, spurned the blandishments of the emperor and the riches of this corrupt world, and joyfully accepted martyrdom for Christ, chanting to Him: Alleluia!

Ikos X

The holy martyrs are revealed as bulwarks of faith, hope and love unto all who have recourse to them with fervent and earnest supplication, and who cry out to them thus amid griefs and perils:

Rejoice, good healers of the wounds of sin;

Rejoice, ye who with the light of hope illumine us in the darkness of our grief!

Rejoice, ye who send wondrous rest upon us amid dangers and tribulations;

Rejoice, O Sophia, who showest wise care for us who are
    cast into evil sufferings!
Rejoice, O Faith, who dost raise up the Cross of salva-
    tion before us;
Rejoice, thou who healest our infirmities in accordance
    with our prayers!
Rejoice, O Hope, who givest us the anchor of
    deliverance;
Rejoice, thou who dost piously remove the despondency
    of our hearts!
Rejoice, O Love, who by thy mediation before the Lord
    dost protect us from sudden death amid dire
    peril;
Rejoice, thou who dost raise our weakening strength to
    vigilance!
Rejoice, O Sophia, ardent intercessor for us before God;
Rejoice, O our wise instructor in good deeds!
Rejoice, O Faith, Hope and Love, with your all-wise
    mother, Sophia!

Kontakion XI

Even if we were to offer you this hymn of praise ten thousand times, O holy martyrs, it would not suffice to glorify your virtues and struggles; yet sending up praise unto God for all that He revealeth unto us in His saints, we chant unto Him: Alleluia!

Ikos XI

Faith, Hope and Love, with their mother, Sophia, are shown to be like lamps burning before the Lord with heavenly light. Before them we fall down, praying that they forgive us who are benighted by griefs and who cry out from the depths of our hearts:

Rejoice, ye who on earth made your robes white in the
    blood of the Lamb;
Rejoice, mediators of life everlasting for us!

Rejoice, confirmation and preservation of souls seeking rest in the lovingkindness of God;

Rejoice, O Sophia, who protectest us from the vanity of the world!

Rejoice, O Faith, thou priceless censer offering up the incense of praise unto God;

Rejoice, thou who dost enlighten us sinners with faith!

Rejoice, O Hope, our consolation and refuge amid tribulation;

Rejoice, radiant herald of deliverance amid our griefs!

Rejoice, O Love, who pourest innocence and meekness into our hearts;

Rejoice, O mystic star bearing us up from earthly oppression!

Rejoice, O Sophia, thou wise and all-honorable rearer of children;

Rejoice, thou who dost set in order a divinely wise life for those who pray to thee!

Rejoice, O Faith, Hope and Love, with your all-wise mother, Sophia!

Kontakion XII

O holy martyrs, who were vouchsafed to receive the grace of God, entreat Christ the Master for us, that He be merciful to us sinners, who humbly, and with faith, hope and love, sing to Him alone, our Lord and Saviour: Alleluia!

Ikos XII

We hymn your mighty struggles, which were suffused with faith, hope and love; we honor your surpassing sufferings; we praise your wondrous endurance; we bless the end which ye joyously embraced for the sake of Christ; and we magnify your invincible courage, O holy martyrs Faith, Hope and Love, and Sophia, your wise mother; and glorifying you, we cry out thus:

Rejoice, ye who in your virtues were like three bolts of lightning streaking from the East even unto the West;

Rejoice, phials of faith, hope and love, nurturing our souls with life-giving sustenance!

Rejoice, ye three luminous paths which lead us to the throne of the Lord of glory;

Rejoice, O Sophia, who art praised by the choir of the saints for the sake of thy children!

Rejoice, O Faith, thou flower of faith whiter than snow;

Rejoice, ease of those who are suffering!

Rejoice, O Hope, uplifting of downtrodden hearts;

Rejoice, thou who like a torrent of healing dost slake the thirst of suffering souls!

Rejoice, O wreath of Love, woven of peace, joy and goodness;

Rejoice, noetic ray of eternity!

Rejoice, O Sophia, thou rod of strength who with meekness and wisdom trained thy children;

Rejoice, all-radiant beam of the divine knowledge shining upon our hearts!

Rejoice, O Faith, Hope and Love, with your all-wise mother, Sophia!

Kontakion XIII

O holy and right laudable martyrs Faith, Hope and Love, and thou, O Sophia, their mother! Accepting now this our entreaty, by your supplications deliver us from all misfortune, sickness and tribulation, that counted worthy to behold the immortal Lord Jesus in the kingdom of heaven, with you we may chant unto Him: Alleluia! Alleluia! Alleluia!

This Kontakion is recited thrice, whereupon Ikos I and Kontakion I are repeated.

Prayers to the Holy Martyrs Faith, Hope and Love, and Their Mother Sophia

Prayer I

O holy and right laudable martyrs Faith, Hope and Love, and thou, O Sophia, wise mother of valiant daughters! Unto you do we now hasten with earnest entreaty, for what more can intercede for us before the Lord if not faith, hope and love, the three cardinal virtues, whose namesakes ye are, and which ye demonstrated in deed. Beseech the Lord, that in His ineffable goodness He protect us amid tribulations and perils, and that He save and preserve us, in that He is good and loveth mankind. And now, beholding His holy glory like a never-waning sun, aid us in our humble supplications, that the Lord God may forgive our sins and iniquities, and may have mercy upon us, His sinful and unworthy servants. O holy martyrs, in our behalf entreat ye therefore our Lord Jesus Christ, unto Whom we send up glory, with His unoriginate Father and His All-Holy, Good and Life-Creating Spirit, now and ever, and unto the ages of ages. Amen.

Prayer II

We glorify, magnify and bless you, O holy martyrs Faith, Hope and Love, with your wise mother Sophia, whom we venerate as a model of divinely wise care. O holy Faith, entreat the Creator of all that is visible and invisible, that He grant us faith which is mighty, pure and indissoluble. O holy Hope, intercede before the Lord Jesus for us sinners, that He drive not from us our hope for good things, and that He deliver us from all tribulation and need. O holy Love, recount unto the Spirit of truth, the Comforter, our perils and griefs, that He send down heavenly glory upon our souls from on high. Help us amid our misfortunes, O holy martyrs, and with your wise mother, Sophia, beseech the King of kings and Lord of lords, that He keep all Orthodox Christians safe under His protection. With compunction falling down before you in tears, we earnestly beg your fervent intercession before God, that with you and all the saints we may supremely exalt and glorify the All-Holy and great name of the Father, and the Son, and the Holy Spirit, the preëternal Master and Benefactor, now and ever, and unto the ages of ages. Amen.

Akathist Hymn
to the Holy Hierarch John,
Archbishop of Shanghai and San Francisco,
The Wonderworker

St. John of Shanghai and San Francisco

Akathist Hymn
to the Holy Hierarch John,
Archbishop of Shanghai and San Francisco,
The Wonderworker

*Whose Memory the Holy Church Doth Celebrate
On the Saturday Following the 19th of June*

Kontakion I

O chosen wonderworker and most excellent favorite of Christ, who pourest forth upon the whole world abundant streams of instruction and a multitude of wondrous miracles! We praise thee with love, and cry out to thee:

>Rejoice, O holy hierarch, father John, speedy helper amid misfortunes!

Ikos I

In these latter times, the Author of all creation revealed thee as the image of an angel, that by God's mercy thou mightest care for those on earth. And perceiving thy virtues, O all-blessed John, we cry out to thee thus:

>Rejoice, thou who from early childhood wast adorned with piety;
>Rejoice, thou who didst do the will of God with fear and trembling!
>Rejoice, thou who didst show forth the grace of God in good deeds done in secret;

Rejoice, thou who dost speedily hearken to those suffering afar off!
Rejoice, thou who didst hasten, full of love, to save thy neighbors;
Rejoice, joy of all who fall down before thee with faith!
Rejoice, O holy hierarch, father John, speedy helper amid misfortunes!

Kontakion II

Beholding the abundant outpouring of thy virtues, O glorious and holy hierarch John, we are enlightened in spirit; for as a life-bearing fountain of divine miracles thou givest drink unto us who cry out to God with faith: Alleluia!

Ikos II

Possessed of an intellect replete with love and theology, O divinely wise John, made wise by the knowledge of God and adorned with love for suffering man, thou hast taught us to know the true God; wherefore, we cry out to thee in compunction:

Rejoice, unshakable stronghold of true Orthodoxy;
Rejoice, precious vessel of the Holy Spirit!
Rejoice, honored one who didst denounce unbelief and false doctrine;
Rejoice, zealous fulfiller of the commandments of God!
Rejoice, ascetic who didst not allow thyself to rest upon a bed;
Rejoice, beloved shepherd of the flock of Christ!
Rejoice, O holy hierarch, father John, speedy helper amid misfortunes!

Kontakion III

By the power of the grace of God thou wast shown to be a nurturer of orphans and an instructor of the young, rearing them in the fear of God and preparing them for the service of God. Wherefore, thy children look to thee and in gratitude cry out to God: Alleluia!

Ikos III

Thou shouldst truly be praised with hymns from heaven, and not from earth, O father John; for how can any man proclaim the greatness of thy works? But, offering unto God what we have, we cry out to thee thus:

    Rejoice, thou who dost shelter thy children beneath
        unceasing prayer;
    Rejoice, thou who dost protect thy flock with the sign of
        the Cross!
    Rejoice, receptacle of great love, without regard for dif-
        ferences of nationality;
    Rejoice, most radiant lamp full of love!
    Rejoice, model of unceasing prayer and loving-kindness;
    Rejoice, bestower of spiritual consolations upon those in
        need!
    Rejoice, O holy hierarch, father John, speedy helper
        amid misfortunes!

Kontakion IV

Overwhelmed by the tempest of perils, how can we worthily praise thy wonders, O blessed John? For thou didst go to the ends of the world for the sake of thy flock's salvation and to proclaim the glad tidings of the Gospel to those in darkness. And giving thanks unto God for thine angelic labors, we chant unto Him: Alleluia!

Ikos IV

Those near and far have heard of the greatness of thy miracles, which are made manifest by the mercy of God even to our times; wherefore, marveling at God Who is glorified in thee, they have cried out in fear:

    Rejoice, enlightener of those in the darkness of unbelief;
    Rejoice, thou who art most great among thy people,
        from the Far East even unto the West!
    Rejoice, well-spring of miracles poured forth by God;
    Rejoice, thou who with love dost correct those in error!
    Rejoice, swift consoler of those who repent of their sins;

Rejoice, guide for those who walk the straight path!
Rejoice, O holy hierarch, father John, speedy helper
    amid misfortunes!

Kontakion V

Thou wast shown to be a divinely bestowed light, O holy hierarch John, driving away the storm of all evils, by thy supplications preserving from deadly whirlwinds those upon the island [of Tubabao], and protecting them with the sign of the Cross. Teach us who call upon thee for help, O holy wonderworker, that we also may cry out to God with boldness: Alleluia!

Ikos V

We see thy great aid amid perils and evil circumstances, O all-blessed father John; for thou art a bold mediator before the throne of God and a speedy helper amid tribulations. Wherefore, we trust in thine intercession before God, and cry out to thee:

Rejoice, thou who dost avert the dangers of the
    elements;
Rejoice, thou who by thy prayer deliverest from need!
Rejoice, faithful giver of bread to the hungry;
Rejoice, thou who preparest an abundance for those who
    ask!
Rejoice, comforter of the sorrowful;
Rejoice, thou who dost rescue from destruction many
    who have fallen!
Rejoice, O holy hierarch, father John, speedy helper
    amid misfortunes!

Kontakion VI

Preaching salvation though slow of speech, thou wast shown to be like a new Moses, leading thy people out of the captivity of the godless, O all-blessed John. Deliver us also from bondage to sin and the invisible foe, that, rejoicing, we may cry out to God: Alleluia!

Ikos VI

Shining forth in thy righteousness, thou didst complete what was unfulfilled, O good pastor; for thou didst incline the secular powers to take pity on thy people. Wherefore, with them we also cry out to thee in thanksgiving:

> Rejoice, good shepherd who didst prepare for thy wandering flock a peaceful haven;
> Rejoice, thou who didst show the greatest care for children and the sick!
> Rejoice, thou who helpest those who earnestly call upon thee with faith;
> Rejoice, for in the weakness of thy body was the power of God abundantly made perfect!
> Rejoice, thou who repellest the assaults of the ungodly;
> Rejoice, thou who dost cast falsehood into darkness and revealest the Truth!
> Rejoice, O holy hierarch, father John, speedy helper amid misfortunes!

Kontakion VII

Desiring to glorify as is meet the ancient saints of the West, which had fallen away from the Truth, thou didst revive their veneration in the Orthodox Church, O lover of the saints of the East and the West. With them pray thou today in heaven in behalf of us who chant on earth: Alleluia!

Ikos VII

We see thee as a new chosen one of God, who in these latter times didst appear with the holy hierarchs of ancient Gaul as one of them, inspiring thy flock to maintain the Orthodox Faith as they confessed it in the West. Preserve us, that we too may abide in this Faith, who cry out to thee:

> Rejoice, thou who in fasting, struggles and miracles wast a new Martin;

Rejoice, thou who in thy confession of the Orthodox
    Faith wast a new Germanus!
Rejoice, thou who in divine theology wast a new Hilary;
Rejoice, thou who in thy veneration and glorification of
    the saints of God wast a new Gregory!
Rejoice, thou who in zeal for monasticism wast a new
    Faustus;
Rejoice, thou who in steadfast love for the canons of the
    Church of God wast a new Cæsarius!
Rejoice, O holy hierarch, father John, speedy helper
    amid misfortunes!

Kontakion VIII

A strange sight didst thou behold in a new land: thou didst encounter thy former flock, vexed by many tribulations; but as a wondrous shepherd thou didst guide it by thine instruction, patience and righteousness, and didst erect the church of the Mother of God, the Joy of All Who Sorrow. And, marveling at thy patience and humility, in thanksgiving we cry out to God: Alleluia!

Ikos VIII

Giving thyself wholly unto Christ, thou becamest a husbandman of His vineyard, O God-bearing father; for thou knewest no rest until the end of thy much-suffering life. Help us, the unworthy, in our labors, and that we may maintain faithfulness to Christ, that, rendering glory, we may cry unto thee:

Rejoice, thou who didst endure unto the end and hast
    attained salvation;
Rejoice, thou who wast vouchsafed to die before the
    icon of the Mother of God!
Rejoice, courageous preserver of righteousness in the
    midst of unjust persecution;
Rejoice, thou who didst reach the end of thy ministry
    and didst repose, seated, as a hierarch!
Rejoice, thou who after thy death didst comfort the
    flock by thy wondrous return;

Rejoice, bestower of many miracles upon those who
    with faith and love have recourse to thy shrine!
Rejoice, O holy hierarch, father John, speedy helper
    amid misfortunes!

Kontakion IX

All of angelic nature rejoiced when thy soul ascended to the mansions of heaven; and, marveling at thy wonders on earth, which are made manifest through the activity of the Holy Spirit, we chant unto God: Alleluia!

Ikos IX

Even the most eloquent of orators cannot fittingly describe the holiness of thy manner of life, O venerable father John, for thou wast the dwelling-place of the grace of the ineffable God; yet are we unable to keep silent, marveling at the miracles revealed to our age of little faith, and we glorify thee thus:

Rejoice, palace of divine instructions;
Rejoice, for in thy humble activity thou hadst angels
    serving with thee!
Rejoice, thou who in the heavens hast found an everlasting habitation not made by men's hands;
Rejoice, infirmary wherein every ailment is treated by
    God!
Rejoice, arena of prayerful struggle;
Rejoice, sanctified temple of the Holy Spirit!
Rejoice, O holy hierarch, father John, speedy helper
    amid misfortunes!

Kontakion X

Desiring to save the world, the Saviour of all sent to us a new saint, and through him hath called us forth from the dark abyss of sin; and hearing him summoning us, we the unworthy cry out to God: Alleluia!

Ikos X

Thou art a bulwark for all who have recourse unto thy heavenly aid, O father John; wherefore, defend us against all the attacks of the demons, and help us amid the tribulations and necessities which beset us on the earth, that we may cry out to thee with faith:

Rejoice, recovery of sight for the blind;
Rejoice, thou who by the power of prayer impartest life
unto those who are on their death bed!
Rejoice, divinely revealed encouragement of those who
are troubled and in doubt;
Rejoice, moisture of salvation, bedewing those perishing
amid the burning heat of grief!
Rejoice, paternal aid for those orphaned and abandoned;
Rejoice, O holy teacher of those who seek the Truth!
Rejoice, O holy hierarch, father John, speedy helper
amid misfortunes!

Kontakion XI

In mind, word and goodly works thou didst offer unceasing hymnody to the All-Holy Trinity, O all-blessed father John; and with thy great understanding of the true Faith thou didst elucidate the commandments of God, instructing us to chant with faith, hope and love unto the one God in Trinity: Alleluia!

Ikos XI

We see thee as a radiant lamp of Orthodoxy for those in the darkness of ignorance, O good shepherd of the flock of Christ. Thus, even after thy repose thou dost reveal the Truth to those ignorant thereof, illumining the souls of the faithful, who cry out to thee such things as these:

Rejoice, thou who with divine wisdom dost enlighten
those who languish in unbelief;
Rejoice, rainbow of serene joy for the meek!
Rejoice, thunder affrighting those who are obstinate in sin;

Rejoice, lightning burning up heresies!
Rejoice, downpouring of the dogmas of Orthodoxy;
Rejoice, dew of the thought of God!
Rejoice, O holy hierarch, father John, speedy helper amid misfortunes!

Kontakion XII

Knowing the grace given thee by God, we receive it with reverence and thanksgiving, hastening to thy wondrous assistance, O most lauded father John; and, glorifying thy wonders, we cry out to God: Alleluia!

Ikos XII

Singing praise unto God, the heavenly assembly of the saints rejoiceth, for the Lord hath not forsaken the fallen and faithless world, but hath revealed His omnipotent power in thee, His meek and humble servant, O blessed father John; and, rejoicing with all the saints, we honor thee thus:

Rejoice, new star of righteousness, which hath shone forth in heaven;
Rejoice, new prophet, sent before the final reign of evil!
Rejoice, thou who like Jonah didst tell of the price to be paid for sin;
Rejoice, thou who like the Forerunner didst summon all to prayer and repentance!
Rejoice, thou who like Paul didst endure much for the sake of the Gospel and the preaching of the Faith;
Rejoice, new apostle who by thy miracles hast caused reverent trembling and faith to abide in us!
Rejoice, O holy hierarch, father John, speedy helper amid misfortunes!

Kontakion XIII

O all-radiant and all-wondrous favorite of God, holy hierarch John our father, thou consolation of all the sorrowful! Accept this, our prayerful offering, that by thy supplications we may be delivered from fiery Gehenna, and may by thy God-pleasing mediation be vouchsafed to chant forever unto God: Alleluia! Alleluia! Alleluia!

This Kontakion is recited thrice, whereupon Ikos I and Kontakion I are repeated.

Prayers to the Holy Hierarch John, Wonderworker of Shanghai and San Francisco

Prayer I

O holy hierarch John our father, good shepherd and beholder of the secrets of men's souls! Thou prayest for us now at the throne of God, as thou thyself didst say after thy death: "Even though I have died, yet am I alive." Beseech the most compassionate God, that He grant us forgiveness of sins, that we may come wakefully to our senses, and cry out to God, asking that we be given the spirit of humility, the fear of God and piety in all the ways of our life. As thou wast a merciful nurturer of orphans and a skilled instructor on earth, be thou now a guide and Christian understanding for us amid the turmoil of the Church; hearken to the groaning of the troubled youth of our corrupt times, who are tempest-tossed by most wicked demonic possession, and mercifully regard the despondency of our weak pastors, caused by the inroads of the corrupting spirit of this world, and who languish in idle indifference. Hasten thou to make supplication, we cry to thee with tears, O fervent advocate; visit us, who are orphaned, scattered over the face of all the world and in our homeland, astray in the darkness of the passions, yet who by our feeble love are drawn to the light of Christ and await thy fatherly instruction; that, having acquired piety, we may be shown to be heirs of the kingdom of heaven, where thou abidest with all the saints, glorifying our Lord Jesus Christ, to Whom be honor and dominion, now and ever, and unto the ages of ages. Amen.

Prayer II

O wondrous and holy hierarch John, thou didst throw open thy heart so wide that the multitude of those who venerate thee, from among divers nations and peoples, easily find a place therein. Look upon the poverty of our words, which are yet offered unto thee with love, and help us, O favored one of God, that henceforth we may purify ourselves of all defilement of flesh and spirit, laboring for the Lord with fear, and rejoicing in Him with trembling. What shall we render unto thee for that joy which we have felt, beholding thy sacred relics in the holy church, and glorifying thy memory? Truly, we have nought to offer thee: only what beginning we can make in correcting ourselves, becoming new men instead of old. Mediate for us of this grace of renewal, O holy John; help us in our weaknesses; heal our sicknesses; cure our passions by thy supplications. O thou who didst depart this transitory life for that which is everlasting, to which the All-Pure Mistress, the Directress of the Russian diaspora, guided thee by Her wonder-working Kursk-Root Icon, whose companion thou wast on the day of thy repose, thou dost now rejoice in the choir of the saints who glorify the one God, Who is worshiped in Trinity—the Father, the Son and the Holy Spirit—now and ever, and unto the ages of ages. Amen.

Akathist Hymn
to the Holy and Righteous Juliana the Merciful, of the Village of Lazarevo, near Murom

St. Juliana of Lazarevo

Akathist Hymn
to the Holy and Righteous Juliana the Merciful, of the Village of Lazarevo, near Murom

*Whose Memory the Holy Church Doth Celebrate
on the 2nd of January*

Kontakion I

O righteous and merciful Juliana, who wast chosen by God, and amidst worldly cares didst in thy soul live in Christ, as in heaven; and who didst abide in great stillness, loving silence within thy heart! Glorifying the Lord Who hath glorified thee, with compunction we sing to thee a hymn of praise. Do thou, who endured grievous sorrows in thy life, pray for us, who are tempest-tossed by perils and sins, and entreat the merciful Saviour to grant us salvation of soul and deliverance from misfortunes, that, giving thanks unto God, we may glorify thee, saying:

> Rejoice, O merciful Juliana, boast of Murom and adornment of women!

Ikos I

A pure angel, from earliest childhood thou didst love the angelic monastic life; but the Creator of all, Who arrangeth all things in the depths of His wisdom, ordained a different path of salvation for thee—that thou please Him with a holy life within honorable matrimony. Wherefore, from childhood He led thee to the kingdom of God through many trials: for when thou wast a maiden six years of age, thou hadst already become a grieving orphan; and as a young bride thou didst soon take up the cross of motherhood. And we, though stricken with awe at this wondrous providence, yet compunctionately praise thee with faith:

> Rejoice, thou who wast born into wealth, to parents who loved the poor—Justin and Stephanida;
> Rejoice, thou who, deprived of thy mother, wast raised an orphan outside thy father's house!
> Rejoice, right fragrant lily who blossomed within the tranquility of the forests of Murom;
> Rejoice, radiant star set alight by God in the village of Lazarevo!
> Rejoice, thou who in thy heart acquired love for Christ and His All-Pure Mother;
> Rejoice, pure ewe-lamb who from childhood sought the monastic order!
> Rejoice, meek and obedient one, who by the will of God wast entrusted to a husband;
> Rejoice, righteous mother who, having lived in the world, hast been numbered among the saints!
> Rejoice, O merciful Juliana, boast of Murom and adornment of women!

Kontakion II

Seeing thee standing in vigil all night, the enemy of the Christian race assailed thee with vile terrors. But thou, O blessed heifer, didst cry out with tearful entreaty to thy guide, the all-wondrous Nicholas; and the wonder-worker straightway appeared to thee, and the demons vanished like smoke. Then the holy hierarch blessed thee, saying: "O my daughter, be thou of steadfast good cheer, for Christ the Lord hath commanded me to preserve thee from all evil. And do thou chant to Him without fear, ever crying aloud like the angels: Alleluia!

Ikos II

The human mind is at a loss how, while living in this vain world, O blessed mother, thou didst in soul abide untroubled in the mansions of heaven; how, living amid abundant wealth, thou didst regard it dispassionately as something belonging to others and entrusted to orphans; how, bearing thy cross in honorable matrimony, though thou wast like a nun amid the world, thou didst raise many holy children. And we, knowing what is impossible for men, and praising God Who can accomplish all things, with undoubting faith honor thee thus:

> Rejoice, quiet dove who unceasingly conversed with God in prayer;
> Rejoice, obedient disciple who knewest how to live in both abundance and in want!
> Rejoice, faithful spouse who saved thy husband by being a model of meekness;
> Rejoice, much suffering mother who entrusted thy pure children to the Lord!
> Rejoice, chaste woman who pleased God by childbearing and holiness;
> Rejoice, merciful lady who, following the Gospel, didst meekly minister to thine own servants!
> Rejoice, handmaid of Christ, who kept His commandments throughout thy life;
> Rejoice, thou who wast obedient to Paul, doing all things for the glory of God!
> Rejoice, O merciful Juliana, boast of Murom and adornment of women!

Kontakion III

The power of the Most High gave thee the strength to bear thy heavy cross without complaint, when the pure souls of four of thy sons and two of thy daughters flew aloft in blessedness like quick-winged birds, departing this life while yet in childhood. And thou thyself, O divinely wise mother, like a turtledove soaring up in soul to the mansions of paradise, gavest thanks unto God for all things, and wast comforted by thy remaining children. And concerning the departed, with the righteous Job thou didst say with compunction: "The Lord gave, and the Lord hath taken away. And now my little children glorify

God with the angels most sweetly, and fervently entreat Him in behalf of their parents, offering up, with their pure mouths, the seraphic hymn: Alleluia!"

Ikos III

Possessed of a heart which hath pity for all, and which is overflowing with grace-filled love, O Juliana, thou didst truly show thyself to be a merciful mother when God visited thy land with a terrible famine; for, though thou didst thyself experience want, thou wast sustenance for those who hungered and thirsted, a guide for the blind and the halt, protection and vesture for the unsheltered, and comfort for all. And thy least, hungering brethren, rending praise unto God, earnestly blessed thee thus:

> Rejoice, thou who illumined the dark time of famine with the light of love;
> Rejoice, thou who rendered mercy unto Christ in the guise of thy least brethren!
> Rejoice, thou who like the warm sun shinest forth earthly good things;
> Rejoice, thou whose left hand knew not what thy right hand was doing!
> Rejoice, thou who, feeding the starving with bread, didst deliver them from death and torment;
> Rejoice, thou who, warming the desperate with a word of welcome, didst greatly console them!
> Rejoice, thou who, seeking the kingdom of God, didst distribute things good for the body;
> Rejoice, thou who having acquired friends through riches, didst find the dwellings of heaven!
> Rejoice, O merciful Juliana, boast of Murom and adornment of women!

Kontakion IV

Amid the tempest of misfortune which beset the whole land, when for their sins the people were punished with a deadly plague, with great diligence, O loving soul, thou didst fulfil the word of Christ concerning the sick, secretly helping them without the knowledge of thy household; and offering up fervent prayers for them, thou didst receive from God the gift of healings, and requesting services for the departed in church, thou didst accompany them to their everlasting rest. And now thou hast received from God the blessed kingdom, where sickness and grief are unknown; and joining chorus there, thou chantest unto God: Alleluia!

Ikos IV

Hearing on one of those bitter days that thine eldest son had been cruelly slain by a servant, thou wast wounded in thy maternal heart, O cross-bearing woman. Yet thou wast not so much saddened by his death as thou wast grieved by the suddenness of the end of his life; and thou wast all the more distraught over the criminal murderer. But remembering the Lord Himself, Who shed drops of blood in Gethsemane, thou didst strengthen thyself in prayers to Him, immersing thy maternal sorrow in His will. And we, marvelling at thy humble faith, chant these praises as is meet:

> Rejoice, thou who didst look upon this earthly life as a sorrowful sojourn;
> Rejoice, thou who didst regard the repose of thy family as a brief separation!
> Rejoice, thou who allayed worldly griefs with trust in the will of God;
> Rejoice, thou who, unlike the wife of Job, strengthened thy despondent husband in the faith!
> Rejoice, thou who forgave the senseless murderer as Christ forgave those who crucified Him;
> Rejoice, thou who asked the Redeemer of the world that He give the kingdom of heaven to thy son!
> Rejoice, thou who by sorrows didst detach thy heart from the earthly world;
> Rejoice, thou who by suffering thy cross didst warm thy love even more greatly for God!

Rejoice, O merciful Juliana, boast of Murom and adornment of women!

Kontakion V

By the will of God thy second beloved son also met an untimely death on the field of battle; yet accepting this cross also without complaint, thou didst splendidly honor thy younger offspring with many prayers, forty memorial liturgies, and generous alms. And having consoled thy husband with good words, that he not again lose hope in God, with tears of compunction, like a wounded dove, thou didst thyself spend many nights quietly in prayer, considering a departure from the world, and transforming funeral lamentations into the hymn of praise to the Almighty: Alleluia!

Ikos V

Seeing thee yearning to hide thyself from the world in a convent, thy spouse besought thee not to leave him bereft with five children. And thou, O meek ewe-lamb, having learned humbly to cut off thine own will for the sake of others, obediently said: "Let the will of the Lord be done!" And again taking upon thy shoulder, which had been wounded by cruel sorrows, the cross given thee by God, of struggle in this world's life, thou didst increase all the more thy vigils, fasting and prayers, living in matrimony like an unmarried desert-dweller. And we, marvelling at thine obedience and ascetic feats, humbly offer thee these praises:

Rejoice, thou who didst enter into the mystery of matrimony, which thou didst solemnly preserve;

Rejoice, spouse faithful to thy husband, whom thou didst serve with humility!

Rejoice, ascetic mighty in this world, who didst bear thy cross with patience;

Rejoice, victor over the carnal passions, who vanquished the enemy in battle!

Rejoice, thou who kept the vesture of thy soul white in this benighted world;

Rejoice, star of quiet brilliance, shining amid the tumult
of life!
Rejoice, thou who didst pray fervently in the married
state, a model of ardor for monks;
Rejoice, sufferer, meek mother, who emulated the saints
in the torments thou didst endure!
Rejoice, O merciful Juliana, boast of Murom and adornment of women!

Kontakion VI

Thy son Callistratus showed himself to be the proclaimer of thy life of suffering, for he recounted to the world thy secret and wondrous struggle: thy prayers continued throughout the night; thou didst set sharp-edged planks as a bed for thy body; thy hands became calloused through thy many prostrations; thy flesh became desiccated by intense fasting; thine eyes were bathed with rivers of tears; and thy pure tongue continually chanted the hymn: Alleluia!

Ikos VI

Grace shone forth in thy heart, O holy mother, and gave thy prayer wings to soar far above all things. Ablaze with divine fire, and drawn to God like a bird of paradise, thou didst desire to visit the temple of God; for thy spirit was borne thither, casting off all the grief of life; and thou wast sweetly consoled amid thy sorrows, receiving the gift of grace from the Father. And we, the slothful, beholding the zeal for God which was in thy soul, are able only to glorify thee with our tongue, crying out thus:

Rejoice, thou who, receiving the fire of grace, didst soar
aloft from earth to heaven;
Rejoice, thou who, having tasted the sweetness of paradise, didst make thine abode in Christ Jesus!
Rejoice, thou who, burning with love for God, didst
receive from Him the gift of tears;
Rejoice, thou who, though praying in secret, didst love
church more than thy home.

Rejoice, thou who, contemplating the redemption wrought by the Lord, didst spend Fridays alone and without food;

Rejoice, thou who, emulating the incorporeal angels, didst refuse to sleep, that thou mightest pray!

Rejoice, thou who, having acquired grace in thy heart, created a temple of God within thyself;

Rejoice, thou who, receiving the Holy Mysteries, didst provide an abode for the Holy Trinity in thy soul!

Rejoice, O merciful Juliana, boast of Murom and adornment of women!

Kontakion VII

Desiring, after the repose of thy friend, to cleave unto heaven with all thy soul, thou didst add struggles unto struggles, O righteous one; and emulating Christ above all, thou didst struggle ascetically in humility and love. Wherefore, thou didst receive from Him the gift of tears of compunction and a heart full of mercy for all; and living while yet on earth as though in heaven, thou didst offer praise unto God, chanting: Alleluia!

Ikos VII

A new sign did the Lord reveal in thee: for, distributing warm garments unto all, it then being a cruel winter, thou didst cease to go to the church of God. Yet one morning, when the priest of God went to the Church of the Righteous Lazarus, he heard a voice issue forth from the icon of the All-Pure Mother of God, saying: "Go and say to the merciful widow Juliana: Wherefore dost thou not come to the church of God to pray? Prayer at home is pleasing unto God, but not as is prayer in church!" And then the voice spake further, saying: "And do thou honor her, for she is not less than sixty years of age, and the Holy Spirit resteth in her!" And when thou didst with fear learn of this wondrous miracle, thou didst beseech all who heard of it to keep silence, and didst make all haste to the All-Pure Mistress at the church of God, and kissing Her icon with fervent tears, didst humbly offer up hymns of supplication. And the faithful people, rejoicing radiantly that the Queen of heaven, the joy of all joys, loved thee so, thus glorified thee with gladness:

> Rejoice, thou who loved Christ with all thy heart;
> Rejoice, thou who offered him fervent tears!
> Rejoice, thou who considered love to be greater than prayer and fasting;
> Rejoice, thou who ever attended all the services of the Church!
> Rejoice, thou who wast called merciful by the Mother of God;
> Rejoice, thou who within thyself wast wholly overshadowed by the Holy Spirit!
> Rejoice, thou who received glory, not from men, but from the Holy Theotokos;
> Rejoice, tranquil radiance illumining the region of Murom!
> Rejoice, O merciful Juliana, boast of Murom and adornment of women!

Kontakion VIII

Strange and wondrous is it to see how on earth God giveth the greatest sorrows to His beloved children, as a surety of His love for them. Wherefore, unto thee, O blessed one, who received great mercy from the Mother of God in His church, it was also fitting to receive a greater measure of griefs, that thou mightest show forth grateful love for God and thyself be glorified, and that thou mightest teach sorrowing people to have patience, that all may sing the praise: Alleluia!

Ikos VIII

When by God's incomprehensible providence a great famine again befell thy land, all experienced want, and even thou, the merciful widow, didst fall into dire poverty. Yet entrusting thyself and thy children to the oversight of God, thou didst command them to endure all things unto death; and thus also didst thou earnestly beseech thy servants, that they dare not to touch anything belonging to anyone else. And obedient, though they were afraid, they kept this commandment and said to thee:

> Rejoice, thou only consolation in that grievous time of great famine;
> Rejoice, thou who suffered in the flesh, seeking all the more the heavenly city!
> Rejoice, thou who amid dread manifestations didst consider the precepts and wrath of God;
> Rejoice, thou who as a mother didst have compassion for children who were tormented with hunger!
> Rejoice, thou who by the power of faith didst endure sorrows without measure;
> Rejoice, thou who didst instruct thy children and thy servants, who were of one mind with thee, to be obedient to the Cross!
> Rejoice, thou who prayed to God, shedding tears with those who wept, and suffering with the people;
> Rejoice, thou who with ardent heart didst grieve in soul for sinful Russia!
> Rejoice, O merciful Juliana, boast of Murom and adornment of women!

Kontakion IX

Every living creature, receiving food for itself in due season, praiseth Thee, the good God, who openest Thine all-generous hand unto all, even before Thou art asked. But Thy mighty favorite, seeking the kingdom of heaven even when deprived of the good things of Thine earth, never ceased to cry out to Thee in praise: Alleluia!

Kontakion IX

Earthly rhetors are at a loss to describe with their tongues the pangs of mothers' souls when they are crushed by the sufferings of their beloved children; and thou, o steadfast sufferer, while pouring forth thy mercy upon all, yet unable to find bread for thine own children, didst feed them pig-weed, comforting them by saying repeatedly: "Glory to God for all things!" And we, learning the power of patience from thee, honor thee fervently with voices of praise:

> Rejoice, sojourner strange to the earthly world, who didst bitterly wander throughout the world;
> Rejoice, thou who, seeking the heavenly city, didst remain in this world a homeless orphan!
> Rejoice, thou who, having been possessed of great wealth, wast shown to be a pauper, hungry and poorly clad;
> Rejoice, thou who before gavest alms, but later wast among the children bereft of bread!
> Rejoice, thou who, looking to the joy which is to come, didst take up thy present cross with hope;
> Rejoice, thou who, having surrendered thyself to the will of the Lord, didst accept the path of poverty and wandering!
> Rejoice, thou who looking to the sufferings of Christ, didst without murmuring endure thy cross in this life;
> Rejoice, thou who, strengthened in weakness by the Spirit, didst in the midst of sorrows sing, "Glory to God for all things!"
> Rejoice, O merciful Juliana, boast of Murom and adornment of women!

Kontakion X

Desiring from childhood to save thy soul, thou didst think upon God in silence with all thy heart; and diligently caring for thy kinfolk like Martha, thou didst in spirit love the portion of Mary. And ever desiring the blessed life, thou didst keep the memory of death continually in the mind, praying the Jesus Prayer in thy heart, thereby sweetening thy bitter life, until thou didst reach the vault of heaven, the uttermost desire, O venerable one, crying unto God: Alleluia!

Ikos X

Thou didst show forth the power of courage in thy weak body to be a rampart which the waves of life could not demolish; and submitting to the law of nature and subjected to many sorrows, thou didst reach the end of thy life at a goodly old age. And the good God, Who alone is holy, desiring to see thee as a pure pearl, sent thee sickness on the second day of His Nativity, that when beholding the Saviour of the world, like Symeon thou mightest say to Him in parting: "Let thy handmaid depart this life in peace, O Master, that I may behold Thee, mine only Glory and the Saviour of my sinful soul." And thy kinfolk compassionately comforted thee well, saying:

> Rejoice, thou who traversed the sea, reaching the calm haven;
> Rejoice, thou who didst leave this world, awaiting the heavenly bridal-chamber!
> Rejoice, thou who never condemned anyone and art thyself not condemned by the Judge;
> Rejoice, thou who, having wrought deeds of mercy, dost enter the ranks of the all-wise virgins!
> Rejoice, thou who hast flown aloft to the mansions on high, on wings of dove-like meekness;
> Rejoice, thou who before didst contemplate Christ, the gentle Light of life everlasting!
> Rejoice, thou who like an all-radiant beam didst flow into the bridal-chamber of the Father;
> Rejoice, thou who hast thine abode with the choir of the saints in the Holy Spirit!
> Rejoice, O merciful Juliana, boast of Murom and adornment of women!

Kontakion XI

Yearning to hear the chanting of the angels in the mansions on high, thou didst not cease to utter tearful prayers even on thy death bed; for, though suffering greatly in body and lying abed during the day, at night thou didst secretly rise up to pray, and like a sputtering candle didst give off thy last flame. And when others learned of thy nocturnal struggle, O dove of God, thou didst meekly say to them: "God examineth the spiritual prayers even of one who is sick." For even the angels praise Him unceasingly, crying ever: Alleluia!

Ikos XI

Though greatly sanctified by the holy light, the grace of the Spirit, thou didst ever consider thyself to be a wretched sinner. Wherefore, trusting only in the mercy of the Saviour, thou didst tearfully receive the most Holy Mysteries after a fervent confession, O honored one. And thus, united in heart with thy Redeemer, and receiving the surety of the eternal kingdom without doubting, thou didst leave unto thy children and and to all a testament of love, prayer and almsgiving. And then, lying down, taking up thy prayer-rope, and making the sign of the Cross, thou didst utter thy last words: "Glory to God for all things! Into Thy hands do I commit my spirit. Amen." And thus, like a lamp flickering out, thou didst quietly fly away from the earth to the dwellings of incorruption, in a dream commanding that thy body be buried next to thy husband and friend. And we, compunctionately rejoicing with thy close kinfolk at thine unashamed and peaceful repose, following thine ascent, sing glorious praise with the angels, chanting:

> Rejoice, thou who at thy final and grievous hour didst provide a model of humility;
> Rejoice, thou who wast for us an image of prayer until thy reflection disappeared!
> Rejoice, bride of Christ, whose head the Bridegroom adorned with a crown;
> Rejoice, pure and holy temple who before thine end wast covered by God with a white kerchief!
> Rejoice, thou whose holy body was more fragrant than the lilies of the field even after death;
> Rejoice, thou who wast illumined at night by candles lighted by an invisible power!

Rejoice, thou who easily passed through the aërial way-stations because of thy mercy toward the poor;

Rejoice, thou who endured many crosses and hast reached the kingdom of God!

Rejoice, O merciful Juliana, boast of Murom and adornment of women!

Kontakion XII

Having received the grace to offer up prayers for the world from which thou hast departed, in thy love thou hast not forsaken those who love thee and are beloved of thee on earth; and having splendidly attained unto the mansions of heaven, thou hast been vouchsafed blessed joy with those who passed on before thee. And thy sons, guided by thy spirit, led a pious life, teaching one another to preserve Holy Orthodoxy. And thy one daughter, Theodosia, receiving the monastic rank in thy stead, reposed in holiness in the great schema, soaring aloft unto thee, like a chick under thy wings. And we today, composing heartfelt hymns to thee with love, do earnestly pray: Entreat Christ God in our behalf, that with thee we may all ever offer up to Him, unto the ages of ages, the hymn: Alleluia!

Ikos XII

O holy woman, the all-glorious Church of Christ singeth funeral hymns of gladness unto thee, having wondrous and beautifully found thy relics to be fragrant; and having reckoned among the choir of the saints thee who before wast blessed exceedingly by the Mother of God herself, it now rejoiceth all-radiantly: for it is meet to glorify those whom God hath glorified; for the honor rendered the saints redoundeth divinely unto God Who resteth in the saints. Wherefore, leaping up in heart and joining chorus in the Spirit, O ye Orthodox people, with the angels let us today all chant together:

Rejoice, adornment of the land of Murom;

Rejoice, ornament of the nation of Russia!

Rejoice, beauty of Christian women;

Rejoice, summit of holy mothers!

Rejoice, thou who wast upborne to paradise by the angels;
Rejoice, thou who hast been blessed by the Lord!
Rejoice, boast of thy kinsmen;
Rejoice, consolation of all who honor thee!
Rejoice, O merciful Juliana, boast of Murom and adornment of women!

Kontakion XIII

O merciful and pure turtledove, blessed and righteous Juliana! With thy usual love accept these fervent praises, and as a mother full of pity, who carest for thy children, beseech the All-Merciful Saviour, that He grant us a single blessing—the divine grace of the Holy Spirit, wherein all the good things of earth and of heaven are hid; that having been enriched thereby, we may pass through this sorrowful life untroubled, and with thee may receive the blessed kingdom of the all-holy Trinity, gloriously crying out thereto: Alleluia! Alleluia! Alleluia!

This Kontakion is chanted thrice, whereupon Ikos I and Kontakion I are repeated.

Prayers to Saint Juliana of Lazarevo

Prayer I

O blessed and righteous Juliana, who wast wondrously called the merciful widow by the All-Holy Theotokos! Unto thee, a mother full of pity, do we earnestly have recourse, praying that we also may be granted mercy. For, having endured many crosses in thy life, and been thyself tried by all things, in thy supplications thou art able to help us in our bitter trials; for, beset by many sins and weighed down by great sorrows, we are assailed by cruel enemies. Wherefore, O mother who bore thy crosses, ask for us the spirit of meekness and patience, sincere repentance of our sins, the power to oppose the invisible foe and to defeat them, and firm trust in the will of God amid all misfortunes and perils, that we may take up our cross without murmuring, unto the salvation of our souls, and may proceed with faith for Christ our Saviour. Moreover, beseech the All-Merciful Lord, O merciful favorite of God, that He cause to dwell in us, as it did in thee, the grace of a heart which hath mercy upon all, which blesseth even one's enemies, which accuseth itself only of sins, as thou didst: for love hath grown exceeding scarce because of our iniquities; and in name only can we show ourselves to be disciples of Christ, while in heart and deed we are as pagans, caring only for ourselves with love of self. O blessed one, intercede also for the Russian land, and for all who are in dispersion, that they may receive peace and prosperity, and all the more a return to thine ancient piety, a quenching of malice and envy, and increase in brotherly love and reconciliation, repentance for our passions, and cleansing and sanctification through grace. That with one mouth and one heart we may all again confess the consubstantial and indivisible Trinity unto the ages of ages. Amen.

Prayer II

O merciful Juliana, helper of orphans, mother who bore thy cross! With thy generous right hand make bestowal upon us who now pray to thee, and ask the All-Merciful God, Whose very name is love, that He grant us rich mercies. Be thou a good helper unto mothers who have given birth unto children; a holy preserver of purity and love within marriage; a wise nurturer of little children and youths; a compassionate comforter of the orphaned and sorrowful; a sympathetic healer of those who are tempest-tossed by sins; a mighty defender of those subjected to trials by their enemies; and a merciful mediator before God and the All-Pure Theotokos for all who ask thine aid. And pray thou all the more, O holy favorite of God, that we be given the grace of the all-holy Spirit, that preserved thereby and saved unceasingly in this life, with thee we may glorify the All-Merciful Redeemer, our Lord and Saviour Jesus Christ, to Whom is due glory, with His All-Good Father and His Holy and All-Compassionate Spirit, unto the ages of ages. Amen.

Akathist Hymn
to the Holy Apostle and Evangelist Luke

The Holy Apostle and Evangelist Luke

Akathist Hymn
to the Holy Apostle and Evangelist Luke
Whose Memory the Holy Church Celebrates on the 18th of October

Kontakion I

O chosen apostle, holy Evangelist Luke, who with the net of thy preaching didst draw forth the souls of many men to salvation and lead them to Christ! Accept these hymns, which are offered to thee with love; and as thou hast boldness before the Lord, free us from all manner of misfortunes, that we may cry to thee:

Rejoice, O holy Apostle and Evangelist Luke, twofold adornment of the Church of Christ!

Ikos I

Likening thyself to a wingèd angel, thou didst soar aloft in the virtues and didst attain unto the depths of the mystery of heaven; wherefore, we praise thee with hymns, crying out to thee such things as these:

Rejoice, thou who didst travel from Antioch to Jerusalem and didst come to know the Messiah;
Rejoice, thou who didst convert many to Christ!
Rejoice, divinely inscribed book of mystic treasures;
Rejoice, godly tablet and heavenly mirror!
Rejoice, thou who didst show great zeal in the proclamation of the Gospel of Christ;
Rejoice, thou who didst love the Lord Jesus most sweet with all thy heart!

Rejoice, O holy Apostle and Evangelist Luke, twofold
adornment of the Church of Christ!

Kontakion II

Beholding the miracles of Christ, O all-glorious Luke, with faith thou didst follow Him Who had revealed Himself in the flesh, and as a lover of His glory thou wast beloved of Him, and wast reckoned among the choir of the seventy elect apostles. Ask that such zeal for the glory of God also be given us, that with thee we may cry out to Christ God: Alleluia!

Ikos II

Illumining thy soul with the understanding of the true knowledge of God, O divinely wise Luke, thou didst follow after thy good Teacher, and didst lay up in thy heart the wisdom which issued forth from His mouth. Wherefore, bringing forth fruit an hundredfold like good soil, thou didst enlighten the whole world with the preaching of the Gospel, that thou mightest hear from us such things as these:

Rejoice, heaven declaring to us the glory of God;
Rejoice, day-star announcing to us the Sun of righteousness!
Rejoice, cloud bedewing arid hearts with the water of grace;
Rejoice, well-spring giving drink to thirsty souls with a stream of life!
Rejoice, wondrous guide for those seeking salvation;
Rejoice, thou who dost divinely move the penitent to understanding!
Rejoice, O holy Apostle and Evangelist Luke, twofold adornment of the Church of Christ!

Kontakion III

The power of God overshadowed thee, O holy Apostle Luke, when thou didst follow after Christ the Lord, traveling with Him through

Judæa and Galilee, listening to His divine teaching and pondering on His all-glorious miracles. Wherefore, Christ gave to thee, as to His faithful disciple, the power to heal diseases and to expel unclean spirits, that, glorifying His power, all may chant unto Him the hymn of praise: Alleluia!

Ikos III

Having grace on thy lips, O blessed Luke, with a tongue of fire thou didst proclaim the honored Gospel unto us; and we, receiving it with a compunctionate heart, cry out to thee thus:

> Rejoice, thou who alone didst record for us the angel's announcement to the all-pure one;
> Rejoice, thou who madest known to us the mystery of the nativity of John the Baptist!
> Rejoice, thou who hast glorified the tears of the harlot for all the ages;
> Rejoice, thou who hast revealed to us the lovingkindness of the heavenly Father in the forgiving of the prodigal son!
> Rejoice, thou who by the parable of the publican and the Pharisee hast magnified humility and denounced pride;
> Rejoice, thou who hast opened paradise to us through the repentance of the noble thief!
> Rejoice, O holy Apostle and Evangelist Luke, twofold adornment of the Church of Christ!

Kontakion IV

The storm of Jewish rage nailed Christ God to the Cross and smote thee with great grief. But after His resurrection the Lord appeared unto thee when thou wast traveling to Emmaus with Cleopas; and straightway thou didst recognize thy Saviour in the breaking of the bread, and with heart afire didst chant unto Him: Alleluia!

Ikos IV

Having heard of thee, the disciple of grace and faithful companion of the Apostle Paul, we praise thee as the most excellent recorder and most wise narrator of the acts of the apostles of the Saviour, blessing thee thus:

> Rejoice, thou who beheldest the ascension of the Lord.
> Rejoice, thou who didst share in the Holy Spirit's dread descent in tongues of fire!
> Rejoice, thou who didst leave to the Church of Christ an account of the suffering of the Protomartyr;
> Rejoice, thou who hast described God's overtaking the persecutor Saul on the road to Damascus!
> Rejoice, thou who hast related the Apostle Paul's fiery preaching of love for the Lord unto all nations;
> Rejoice, thou who with Paul didst bear the labors and tribulations of the apostolic struggle!
> Rejoice, O holy Apostle and Evangelist Luke, twofold adornment of the Church of Christ!

Kontakion V

Chosen as a companion by the divinely traveling Paul, O most blessed Luke, thou didst journey through the East and the West, and did reach Rome, teaching all nations, tribes and peoples to cry out to Christ God: Alleluia!

Ikos V

Seeing the first icon thou didst paint of the Mother of God and the preëternal Infant, and mindful of the words of the All-Pure one—"May the grace of Him Who was born of Me, and Mine own grace, be with these icons!"—we kiss them with love and cry out to thee:

> Rejoice, thou who didst confirm the veneration of icons by the lips of the All-Pure One;
> Rejoice, thou who by this means didst set iconoclasm at nought!

Rejoice, thou who hast adorned the Orthodox Church
    with holy icons;
Rejoice, thou who hast taught us the art of iconography!
Rejoice, thou who hast left us the image of the All-Pure
    One;
Rejoice, thou who thereby hast glorified the Mother of
    God!
Rejoice, O holy Apostle and Evangelist Luke, twofold
    adornment of the Church of Christ!

Kontakion VI

Thou wast shown to be a divinely eloquent preacher, O Luke, apostle of Christ; and casting for reason-endowed fish in the deep of ignorance with the net of thy glad tidings, thou didst pull them in to the knowledge of God; and offering them to Christ God like goodly food, thou didst teach them to chant unto Him: Alleluia!

Ikos VI

O disciple of the Saviour, like a brilliant beacon thou didst shine forth in heathen lands, where, having abolished the falsehood of idolatry, thou didst bring those sitting in darkness into the light of life, and didst teach them to believe in the Trinity. And praising thy labors, we cry out to thee thus:

Rejoice, thou who dost draw the souls of the faithful
    forth from the abyss of death;
Rejoice, thou who with showers of divine knowledge
    dost water a world dried up by the burning heat
    of godlessness!
Rejoice, thou who with divine salt dost dispel the foul
    stench of unbelief;
Rejoice, thou who, having drained the cup of wisdom,
    dost teach us to recognize Christ the Saviour!
Rejoice, for thou who in the font of Christ didst heal
    the sickness of ungodliness;

Rejoice, for with the brilliant rays of thy words thou
 didst dispel the darkness of delusion!
Rejoice, O holy Apostle and Evangelist Luke, twofold
 adornment of the Church of Christ!

Kontakion VII

Desiring to reveal the great mystery of our salvation, which the Holy Spirit revealed to thee because of thy fiery love for thy divine Teacher, thou didst make the precious Gospel like a well-spring of grace for the whole world, so that, reading it, men might find salvation for their souls until the end of the world, chanting to the all-wondrous Lord the hymn: Alleluia!

Ikos VII

Giving thyself over to a new struggle as an apostle of Christ, thou didst spurn all the joys of this world, that thou mightest obtain Christ, O most wondrous Luke. For, filled with the Holy Spirit, thou didst work great wonders: healing the diseases of men, expelling demons, and illumining the whole world with the light of divine dogmas. Wherefore, honoring these thy labors, with the angels we cry out to thee thus:

Rejoice, thou who didst love Christ more than all else;
Rejoice, thou who throughout the whole world didst
 glorify His name!
Rejoice, thou who wast a witness to the wondrous
 miracles of Christ;
Rejoice, thou who hast lovingly related them to us!
Rejoice, thou who didst endure reproach for the sake of
 the Lord;
Rejoice, thou who didst receive from him the power to
 heal!
Rejoice, O holy Apostle and Evangelist Luke, twofold
 adornment of the Church of Christ!

Kontakion VIII

Looking upon thy tireless journeys, we see that, traversing Thebes, Libya, Egypt and the Upper Thebaïd, thou didst preach Christ everywhere, causing the Christian Church to grow and teaching repentance unto all. And having recognized Christ, those enlightened by thee chant unto Him: Alleluia!

Ikos VIII

All the tribes of the earth praise thee, O Apostle Luke, for thou wast one of the four pillars of the Gospel whereon Christ founded His Church and established it so that the gates of hades would not prevail against it. And now all the children of the Christian Church glorify thee together, crying out:

    Rejoice, thou who by thy Holy Gospel hast taught us to love the Lord;
    Rejoice, thou who hast adorned the Christian Church with thy words!
    Rejoice, thou who didst plant the seed of Orthodoxy among us;
    Rejoice, thou who hast gladdened the Lord with these fruits!
    Rejoice, thou who hast strengthened us in virtue;
    Rejoice, thou who hast taught us to endure for Christ!
    Rejoice, O holy Apostle and Evangelist Luke, twofold adornment of the Church of Christ!

Kontakion IX

All mortals await with trembling the dread Second Coming of Christ to earth. And when thou also shalt sit with the Master on a high throne to judge the whole world, O saint, entreat His goodness, that He have mercy on us, and not condemn us to everlasting damnation, but that we be vouchsafed to chant to Him with all the saints: Alleluia!

Ikos IX

Human orators are at a loss how to hymn thy struggles and miracles, O most praised Luke; yet mercifully accept these our meager and crudely crafted hymns which are offered as praise unto thee, that with faith and love we may cry out to thee such things as these:

> Rejoice, thou who art praised and glorified from the East even unto the West;
> Rejoice, thou who wast greatly beloved of the Apostle Paul!
> Rejoice, thou who didst share in the labors of Paul;
> Rejoice, wondrous receptacle of the mysteries of Christ!
> Rejoice, companion of the choirs of the angels;
> Rejoice, thou who didst heal the infirmities of men!
> Rejoice, O holy Apostle and Evangelist Luke, twofold adornment of the Church of Christ!

Kontakion X

We have inherited from thee the pledge of salvation, the Orthodox Faith, O Luke, apostle of Christ; wherefore, we beseech thee: Preserve us, thy children, from all heresies and ecclesial divisions by thy prayerful intercession before God, and help us to abide unshaken in Orthodoxy unto the end of our days, that we may chant to God with faith: Alleluia!

Ikos X

Thou hast been set in the habitations of paradise by the King of heaven, O blessed Luke, that thy zeal for the keeping of the law of God might be imparted also unto us, His unworthy servants, that we may ready ourselves for the struggles of doing good Christian works and for the confession of our Orthodox Faith. For this we entreat thee and cry:

> Rejoice, all-radiant star, pointing all to the Sun of righteousness;
> Rejoice, inextinguishable lamp, unceasingly burning in prayer before the throne of the Lord of glory!
> Rejoice, beauty of the Church of Christ;

Rejoice, fragrant myrrh pouring forth streams of healing upon us!
Rejoice, thou who didst receive from Christ gifts of the grace of the Holy Spirit;
Rejoice, thou who didst receive from Him the authority to loose and to bind!
Rejoice, O holy Apostle and Evangelist Luke, twofold adornment of the Church of Christ!

Kontakion XI

Offering hymnody to the All-Holy Trinity on high with all the saints, O all-praised Luke, thou bendest down to the earth, to look upon the place of thy struggles and journeys, and by thy supplications helpest all who honor thy holy memory with faith, and who for thy sake chant unto God the hymn: Alleluia!

Ikos XI

Thou hast been revealed to the faithful as a light-giving beacon of the three-Sunned Light, O holy Apostle Luke, invisibly illumining us all on the path of our earthly sojourn, that we not fall into the snares of our enemy, the devil, but may remain unharmed by all his wiles, and that we may with a pure heart be vouchsafed to cry out to thee:

Rejoice, good shepherd of the reason-endowed flock of Christ;
Rejoice, thou who dost not permit the soul-destroying wolf to ravage thy rational flock!
Rejoice, thou who in the net of thy preaching didst catch all the ends of the earth;
Rejoice, thou who by thy supplications dost further our salvation!
Rejoice, fire-breathing mouth of the Holy Spirit;
Rejoice, dove of the ark of Noah, who hast brought us the glad tidings of Christ as a branch!
Rejoice, O holy Apostle and Evangelist Luke, twofold adornment of the Church of Christ!

Kontakion XII

Great grace and healing poured forth from thy tomb, and it imparted cures to the faithful who had recourse to it. And the Emperor Constantius, son of Constantine the Great, learning of thy healing relics, transferred thy beloved remains to the Imperial City, where a eunuch of the imperial chamber, having received healing, together with others chanted to God the hymn: Alleluia!

Ikos XII

Hymning thy pangs and labors, O apostle of the Saviour, we honor thy holy and ever-glorious memory which, perfuming us spiritually, delighteth and gladdeneth our souls; for the sweat and toils wherein thou didst labor in spreading the glad tidings of Christ were truly shown to be fragrant myrrh in the sight of God. And crafting our praises, we cry out to thee with joy:

>Rejoice, inexhaustible fountain of the wisdom of God;
>Rejoice, all-wise fisher and husbandman of the Saviour!
>Rejoice, sword cutting down the blasphemies of the heretics;
>Rejoice, thou who didst plumb the depths of the mysteries of God!
>Rejoice, thou who wast informed of the Second Coming by the angels of God;
>Rejoice, unashamed mediator before our all-pure Mistress!
>Rejoice, O holy Apostle and Evangelist Luke, twofold adornment of the Church of Christ!

Kontakion XIII

O holy and most lauded Luke, apostle and evangelist of Christ! Accept this, our meager hymn of supplication offered in praise of thee, and entreat our Saviour, the Lord Jesus Christ, that He deliver us from everlasting torment and vouchsafe us the ineffable joy of the saints, that with them we may unceasingly chant to God in three Hypostases: Alleluia! Alleluia! Alleluia!

This Kontakion is recited thrice, whereupon Ikos I and Kontakion I are repeated.

Prayer to the Holy Apostle and Evangelist Luke

O all-holy and most lauded Apostle and Evangelist Luke, earthly angel and heavenly man! With faith and love we fall down before thy holy icon and thy precious relics, and we beseech thee with tears: Forget not us, thy children, whom thou hast gathered together, O divinely wise one. Depart from us never, but with thy tireless intercession protect us from the evil wiles of the enemy. Put down the uprising of our passions, and strengthen our weakness amid spiritual warfare and struggles. Dispel from our hearts all despondency and sinful grief, and beseech the Lord to grant us consolation amid our sorrows. Preserve, O divinely wise one, this holy city [town/village/monastery] from all want, from fire and the sword, from deadly contagion and from all evil. Hearken, O merciful apostle, to everyone who approacheth thee with faith and imploreth thy gracious aid. Be thou a defender for orphans, consolation for the sorrowful, a healer for the sick, strengthening for the weak, a guardian for travelers, a pilot for those at sea; and at the dread hour of our death stand before us as one who fendeth off the dark visages of the demons and strengtheneth our hope of salvation: that having finished our earthly course in peace and repentance, we may attain unto the havens of everlasting joy, that with thee we may glorify the most holy name of the Father, the Son and the Holy Spirit, now and ever, and unto the ages of ages. Amen.

Akathist Hymn
to the Venerable Mary of Egypt

The Venerable Mary of Egypt

Akathist Hymn
to the Venerable Mary of Egypt
*Whose Memory the Holy Orthodox Church Doth Celebrate
On the Fifth Sunday of the Great Fast and on April 1st*

Kontakion I

Unto thee who wast chosen by God from our fallen race and through thine onerous struggle hast acquired great glory in heaven, do we cry out, O holy Mary: Entreat the Lord God in our behalf, that He rescue from the pit of the passions us who chant hymns of praise to thee:

> Rejoice, O venerable mother Mary, who by thy struggles
> didst amaze the angels!

Ikos I

The angels were astonished by the sudden change in thee, O venerable mother: how within the space of a single hour thou didst forsake the broad path which leadeth to destruction and didst begin to tread the narrow path of salvation. O favorite of Christ, accept from us this hymnody:

> Rejoice, thou who didst pray to the Mother of God, that
> thou mightest be deemed worthy to venerate
> the Cross;
> Rejoice, thou who didst beseech the pure Virgin to en‐
> treat forgiveness of Christ!
> Rejoice, thou who didst promise the holy Virgin not to
> turn back to the path of destruction;

Rejoice, O venerable one, who didst shed bitter tears upon thy pain-wracked breast!

Rejoice, for thy helper quickly hearkened to thy supplication;

Rejoice, for that very hour thou wast able to approach the Cross without hindrance!

Rejoice, for with compunction thou didst kiss the Tree upon which Christ was crucified;

Rejoice, thou whose whole being was shaken, so that thou didst pour forth torrents of tears!

Rejoice, for then thou didst resolve not to turn back;

Rejoice, thou who didst choose to shoulder the yoke of Christ and His burden!

Rejoice, thou who with this steadfast decision didst smite the head of Satan;

Rejoice, for over this one decision there was great joy in heaven!

Rejoice, O venerable mother Mary, who by thy struggles didst amaze the angels!

Kontakion II

Seeing the ineffable love of the Mother of God for thee, O venerable one, in that at the very hour of thy tearful prayer She gave thee unimpeded access to the all-pure tree of the Cross on the feast of its honorable exaltation; and vouchsafed to kiss it, joyfully moved to tremble by the power of God thou didst cry out to Him: Alleluia!

Ikos II

With thy whole heart and reason, O holy Mary, thou didst resolve firmly never again to return to the way of the passions; and in compunction of heart thou didst beseech the All-Holy Virgin Theotokos to show thee a place where thou couldst work out thy salvation. And suddenly thou didst hear a mysterious voice naming the wilderness of the Jordan as just such a place. Wherefore, O venerable one, accept from us such laudations as these:

Rejoice, thou who for unhindered access to the Cross didst thank her who helpeth the world;

Rejoice, thou who didst choose the Virgin as a witness that thou wouldst thenceforth serve Christ alone!

Rejoice, thou who didst entreat the pure Virgin to show thee the path of salvation;

Rejoice, thou who through Her icon didst receive the counsel to choose the wilderness as the site of thy struggle!

Rejoice, thou who that very hour didst renounce the vanity of this world;

Rejoice, thou who in a boat didst sail over to the far bank of the Jordan!

Rejoice, thou who wast preserved by the Mother of God in a desert land;

Rejoice, thou who, unseen by this sinful world, didst escape the vainglory thereof!

Rejoice, thou who by the Cross didst fend off the assaults of the devil;

Rejoice, O chosen one who rejoiced with Christ amid thine onerous struggle!

Rejoice, thou who didst endure fear and hunger for His sake;

Rejoice, thou who didst spurn the allurements of the world for the sake of Christ alone!

Rejoice, O venerable mother Mary, who by thy struggles didst amaze the angels!

Kontakion III

Strengthened by power from on high, thou madest thine abode in the wilderness, O venerable mother; and preserved by the help of the Lord, thou didst continually chant unto Him: Alleluia!

Ikos III

The venerable Zosimas, having a truly great desire to see the chosen one who in the divine sublimity of her life surpassed his own, withdrew into the wilderness beyond the Jordan when the holy days of the Great Fast arrived; and, as God willed, he encountered thee there, O venerable one. Yet, in thy humility desiring not to be seen by men, thou didst at first flee from him; but later, persuaded by the saint, thou didst count him worthy to converse with thee. Disdain not even our lowly discourse, O favored one of God, but accept from us such praises as these:

> Rejoice, thou who didst offer up repentance in the desert;
> Rejoice, thou who didst weep therein day and night!
> Rejoice, thou who didst bedew all the ground with thy tears;
> Rejoice, thou who didst attain unto the heights of heaven!
> Rejoice, thou who didst flee the stench of the life of sin;
> Rejoice, thou who didst hasten to the tranquility of the wilderness!
> Rejoice, thou who didst suffer, bearing thy cross;
> Rejoice, for the Lord is ever with thee!
> Rejoice, thou who hast been magnified by Christ for thine ascetic feats;
> Rejoice, thou who was glorified while yet on the earth!
> Rejoice, thou who wast made excellent by the Lord in clairvoyance;
> Rejoice, for thou didst call Zosimas by name!
> Rejoice, O venerable mother Mary, who by thy struggles didst amaze the angels!

Kontakion IV

A tempest of sacred awe smote the venerable Zosimas, for thou, who hadst never known him by name, didst prevail upon him to listen to the tale of thy wondrous life. And thou, O humble saint, didst not hide from him thy former sinful way of life, that the Lord, Who abundantly rewardeth the penitents, might be glorified in thee. Wherefore, we give thanks to the Creator, entreating Him not to spurn the repentance even of us, that in joyful hope we may chant unto Him: Alleluia!

Ikos IV

The venerable Zosimas heard how thou didst bravely endure all the difficulties of the desert life, waging war against temptations and the devil; and he was amazed, and cried out to thee with compunction:

Rejoice, thou who in the wilderness didst nourish thy body only with roots;
Rejoice, thou who didst lay upon the Lord all thy fear that He might forsake His creature!
Rejoice, thou who in thine onerous struggle didst surpass many;
Rejoice, thou who therefore didst ascend into paradise and wast crowned with a diadem of light!
Rejoice, thou who wast taught the Scriptures in the wilderness by the Spirit of God;
Rejoice, for the All-Good One bestowed gifts of holy beauty upon thee!
Rejoice, O Mary, for thou wast vouchsafed to become a vessel of the Holy Spirit;
Rejoice, for on thy difficult path thou didst strive to live thy life for the Lord!
Rejoice, thou who didst set thy hand to the plough without turning back;
Rejoice, thou who didst love Christ with all thy being, and didst receive His grace!
Rejoice, thou who didst cause thy whole life to blossom like a most beautiful lily in the desert;
Rejoice, for thou wast humble, emitting thy sweet fragrance for the Lord God!
Rejoice, O venerable mother Mary, who by thy struggles didst amaze the angels!

Kontakion V

O Lord, Who by Thy Blood divinely shed didst redeem us, Thou hast not called the righteous, but sinners to repentance. Vouchsafe that we also may imitate the life of Mary, Thy favored one, and with thankful heart may forever glorify Thee with the hymn of paradise: Alleluia!

Ikos V

Seeing thee standing in the air and praying, O venerable one, Zosimas was seized with trembling, at a loss how a woman who before had reveled in her fall was now vouchsafed so much grace; and giving thanks to the Lord with compunction, he chanted thus:

> Rejoice, thou who by the holiness of thy life attained the gift of foresight;
> Rejoice, thou who with thine own mouth didst relate to Zosimas things known only within his monastery!
> Rejoice, for thou wast like the angels in the radiance of thy purity;
> Rejoice, O blessed one, for thou wast vouchsafed to stand in the air!
> Rejoice, for thou didst hide thine ascetic feats from Zosimas;
> Rejoice, for thou didst conceal the many revelations thou didst receive from heaven!
> Rejoice, for thou didst preserve them solely in thy heart for the sake of holy salvation;
> Rejoice, thou who didst command Zosimas to keep silence concerning thee until thine end!
> Rejoice, thou who didst not wish to be glorified by men on earth;
> Rejoice, for, unknown to all, thou didst spend forty-seven years of thy life in the desert!
> Rejoice, thou who didst thus desire to depart, known by none, from the path of thy cross;

Rejoice, for by the ways of God's providence thou hast
    become known to the pious!
Rejoice, O venerable mother Mary, who by thy struggles
    didst amaze the angels!

Kontakion VI

In heaven, the angels proclaim thy wondrous life, O blessed desert-dweller, for in thy feeble body thou didst acquire great power of spirit and didst destroy the snares of Satan. And with the angels we glorify the Lord Who by His grace gave thee might, and we chant unto Him: Alleluia!

Ikos VI

Experiencing a great hunger for the taste of the all-pure Mysteries of Christ, O favorite of God, thou didst ask Zosimas to come the following year, on the holy feast of Great Thursday, bearing the Holy Gifts to the bank of the River Jordan, that thou mightest be vouchsafed to partake thereof. And, glorifying in thee thy zeal for the closest unity with our Lord Jesus Christ, we utter these words of praise unto thee:

Rejoice, thou who wast tormented by a holy thirst for
    the communion of the Holy Gifts;
Rejoice, for in thy heart was love for the Lord God
    preserved!
Rejoice, O venerable one, for thou didst wed thyself
    wholly to Christ the Saviour;
Rejoice, thou who didst acquired meekness, humility
    and angelic purity!
Rejoice, for thou didst soon bid farewell to Zosimas, O
    woman of holy beauty;
Rejoice, O Mary, for thou didst straightway conceal
    thyself from his gaze in the depths of the
    wilderness!
Rejoice, for in the heart of Zosimas thou didst leave
    behind the ecstasy of compunction;
Rejoice, for thou didst guide the mind of that elder to a
    torrent of reasonings!

Rejoice, for he carried away the thought of thee like a precious pearl;

Rejoice, for all the way back to his monastery he was bedewed with tears of joy!

Rejoice, for thy wondrous image remained in the elder's eyes;

Rejoice, for only after a year was the elder consoled over your parting!

Rejoice, O venerable mother Mary, who by thy struggles didst amaze the angels!

Kontakion VII

Desiring to keep the rule of the holy monastery, the abbot sent the monks forth to struggle in stillness and greater prayer in the remote deserts. But the venerable Zosimas was unable to leave because of the illness thou hadst foretold unto him, O holy Mary; and having awaited Great Thursday with joyful trepidation, on which day thou hadst promised to receive Communion, surrendering to the incomprehensible judgments of God, he chanted unto Him: Alleluia!

Ikos VII

A new and sacred trembling seized the soul of the venerable elder when the great day of the our Lord's institution of the Mystical Supper arrived; and taking with him the most Holy Gifts, he set out for the riverbank, O holy and blessed mother, to give thee Communion. And with the elder we make obeisance before the Lord Who came to thee in His All-Pure Mysteries; and unto thee, the worthy bride of the Bridegroom most sweet, who goest with love to the wedding of the Lamb, do we cry out with compunction:

Rejoice, for thy request was fulfilled by the holy priest;

Rejoice, for, trembling, he arrived at the riverside with the Holy Gifts!

Rejoice, for thou didst desire to receive Communion on the night of Christ's suffering;

Rejoice, for, having shared in those sufferings, thou
    dwellest with Him in heaven!
Rejoice, for thou didst cause the venerable one anxiety
    by thy long delay;
Rejoice, for thy traversing of the river was likewise a
    source of perplexity to him!
Rejoice, for in the light of the moon thou didst show
    thyself afar off;
Rejoice, thou who didst approach the far bank of the
    river on foot!
Rejoice, for thou didst make the saving sign of the Cross
    over the Jordan;
Rejoice, for thou didst easily walk upon the river as
    upon dry land!
Rejoice, for the priest was filled with awe when he beheld this sight;
Rejoice, for thou didst calm him with thy holy
    discourse!
Rejoice, O venerable mother Mary, who by thy struggles
    didst amaze the angels!

Kontakion VIII

We are all strangers, sojourners upon the earth, as the Apostle saith; and thou didst abide as a sojourner in the wilderness until the day of thy repose, O Mary, ewe-lamb of Christ, that having passed from the earthly Jerusalem to the Jerusalem on high, thou mayest glorify the Creator with the song of paradise: Alleluia!

Ikos VIII

Jesus Christ was all thy delight, all thy desire, and it was Him Whom thou didst receive with trembling in the All-Pure Mysteries at the hands of the blessed elder. And, gazing upon thee, as upon a truly worthy partaker of these most holy Gifts, we cry out to thee with love:

Rejoice, thou who in the Holy Mysteries wast betrothed
    to thine immortal Bridegroom;

Rejoice, thou who for this wast adorned by Him with the imperishable crown of paradise!

Rejoice, thou who after receiving the divine Gifts wast surrounded by a wondrous light;

Rejoice, for Zosimas was unable to gaze upon thee unafraid!

Rejoice, thou who didst recite the prayer of Symeon with serene gladness;

Rejoice, thou who didst straightway lift up thy compunctionate eyes and hands to heaven!

Rejoice, thou who, having spurned earthly food, didst taste of the food of heaven;

Rejoice, thou who didst deign to accept three grains of wheat from Zosimas as a gift of love!

Rejoice, for after receiving Communion thou didst not tarry long by the riverside;

Rejoice, thou who in partaking of the Holy Gifts wast united to thy Master!

Rejoice, thou who as His good and faithful handmaid didst enter into the joy of thy Lord;

Rejoice, thou whose sins were burned away in His supernal light!

Rejoice, O venerable mother Mary, who by thy struggles didst amaze the angels!

Kontakion IX

Men and every angelic rank bless the Lord for perfecting His power in the weak. Thus did He also strengthen thee, His greatly victorious favorite; for in thy struggle in the wilderness thou didst in thy naked body endure cold and unbearable, burning heat, fear, hunger and the manifold wickedly devised temptations of the devil. Yet for the help thou didst receive from the Lord thou didst chant unto Him continually: Alleluia!

Ikos IX

The orator's tongue is unable to describe what took place in the soul of the righteous Zosimas after thy departure, O secret desert-dweller; for by thine image, full of the grace of the most Holy Spirit, thou didst raise the spiritual gaze of the elder to the heavenly contemplation that God in His omnipotence hath raised up man, who is made of dust, to the heights of the angels. With Zosimas accept our humble laudation:

Rejoice, thou who didst mortify thy flesh in the wilderness;
Rejoice, thou who therein didst rid thy mind of the temptations sown by the passions!
Rejoice, for thou wast downcast at the thought of encountering wordly people;
Rejoice, for thou didst hasten quickly to the desert to converse with the angels!
Rejoice, for there, day and night, thou didst pray in stillness, unseen by the world;
Rejoice, for thou didst withdraw from all into the depths of the wilderness for the sake of thy salvation!
Rejoice, for only the stars of the sky witnessed thy tears;
Rejoice, for in those wondrous moments Christ Himself gazed upon thee with love!
Rejoice, for thou didst gladden thyself by choosing the Theotokos as a wondrous surety;
Rejoice, for by her mighty aid thou didst attain unto everlasting rest!
Rejoice, thou who didst ask Zosimas to come again to the desert in a year's time;
Rejoice, thou who with hope didst await him again!
Rejoice, O venerable mother Mary, who by thy struggles didst amaze the angels!

Kontakion X

For us who desire to be saved be thou an advocate before the throne of the Most High, O venerable mother, that, having eluded all manner of temptations, with thee we also may be vouchsafed to glorify the Lord continually, and to chant unto Him: Alleluia!

Ikos X

For all ascetics Thou art a bulwark against the malicious wiles of the devil, O All-Holy Theotokos, and didst save Her who chose Thee as Her surety before thy Son most sweet. Nor didst Thou put her hope to shame, O All-Pure one, but didst lead her to the desired gates of paradise. Vouchsafe also that we sinners may worthily praise Thy holy favorite, Mary, with these hymns:

> Rejoice, thou whom Zosimas awaited with joyful trembling;
> Rejoice, for he comforted himself with thoughts all full of joy!
> Rejoice, for during the days of the Great Fast he departed with love into the wilderness;
> Rejoice, for he traveled twenty days in all to reach the place whereat he was to meet thee!
> Rejoice, for the elder sought thee in bitter anxiety;
> Rejoice, for, full of turmoil, the elder was beside himself!
> Rejoice, for he discovered thee lying on the sands, radiant with the light of heaven;
> Rejoice, for having parted from him in peace, thou hadst passed into everlasting rest!
> Rejoice, for with bitter lamentation the elder fell upon thy body;
> Rejoice, for Zosimas did not believe his agèd eyes!
> Rejoice, for thou hadst long since passed over to the wondrous bridal-chamber of heaven;
> Rejoice, for now thou dost rejoice eternally, having left sorrows and vexations behind!
> Rejoice, O venerable mother Mary, who by thy struggles didst amaze the angels!

Kontakion XI

Praised with the hymnody of the angels, and surrounded by their company, thy righteous soul ascended to the throne of the Most High, to hymn the Lord with divinely beauteous melody, chanting amid the sound of rejoicing: Alleluia!

Ikos XI

Thy venerable countenance was illumined by the Holy Spirit of God; but the elder Zosimas was in great turmoil, for he knew not thy name, O blessed one. Then he beheld the inscription graven in the ground by thy head. Wherefore, we say with joy:

Rejoice, for to Zosimas was revealed the day of thy passing;
Rejoice, for thou wast named "the humble Mary" in those miraculous words!
Rejoice, for thou hadst departed to the Lord a year before;
Rejoice, for thou hadst been counted worthy to depart on the very day of thy Holy Communion!
Rejoice, for suddenly a fearsome lion emerged from that burning desert;
Rejoice, for, having scraped out a grave with his mighty paws, he then departed!
Rejoice, for with ardent prayer the elder committed thy remains to the earth;
Rejoice, for he stood long over the grave, shedding tears of compunction!
Rejoice, for the priestmonk uttered his prayers quietly, with trembling lips;
Rejoice, for with love he glorified Him Who is incomprehensible in His judgments!
Rejoice, for he magnified the Lord Who is wondrous in His saints;
Rejoice, for he gave thanks to the Saviour for the ineffable ways of His dispensation!

Rejoice, O venerable mother Mary, who by thy struggles
    didst amaze the angels!

Kontakion XII

Ask God to grant us grace, O pure Mary, bride of Christ, that He have mercy on us on the day of His dread judgment, and number us among His chosen flock; and vouchsafe that we may continually chant unto Him: Alleluia!

Ikos XII

Hymning thy repentance, at which the angels in heaven marveled, and all thy sufferings, which no human tongue can describe, we cry out to thee with love and joy:

Rejoice, for though thy flesh was naked, yet now thou
    art covered with wondrous vesture in paradise;
Rejoice, for though scorched by the burning heat of the
    desert, in heaven thou dost drink from a torrent
    of coolness!
Rejoice, for though thou didst constantly endure hunger,
    in heaven thou now sharest in Christ our Bread;
Rejoice, for though thou didst bear all manner of tribulations, thy mouth now uttereth a cry of joy!
Rejoice, for thou didst spend seventeen years in heavy
    battle against the devil;
Rejoice, for thou wast glorious in victory, and a wondrous light surrounded thee!
Rejoice, for like an all-wise virgin thou didst not permit
    thy lamp to flicker out;
Rejoice, for thy struggle led straight from the Tree of
    the Cross to salvation!
Rejoice, for having made thy vow to the holy Virgin, with
    her help thou didst never stray from the path;
Rejoice, for though thou didst suffer much in the wilderness, thou didst not permit thyself to go
    astray!

Rejoice, for by the sign of the Cross thou didst destroy
   the wiles of the enemy;
Rejoice, for thou dost now taste of the compassions and
   gifts of God!
Rejoice, O venerable mother Mary, who by thy struggles
   didst amaze the angels!

Kontakion XIII

O holy, much lauded and all-victorious Mary, favorite of Christ, most excellent model of repentance, we entreat thee: Beseech the Lord God, that He grant us His grace, that we also may rid ourselves of the darkness of our sins through tears of contrition, and that we may be vouchsafed to receive everlasting consolation in the abode of the penitent according to God's true promise, and with the choirs of the angels may chant to the All-Holy Trinity the angelic hymn: Alleluia! Alleluia! Alleluia!

This Kontakion is recited thrice, whereupon Ikos I and Kontakion I are repeated.

Prayer to Our Venerable Mother Mary of Egypt

O holy Mary, great favorite of Christ, who didst astonish the angels with thine incomparable struggle! We pray thee, O blessed one: As thou standest now before the throne of the most Holy Trinity, entreat the Lord, since thou hast acquired great boldness before Him, that He vouchsafe us, as He did thee, to repent of our myriad offenses, and that, having in His love for mankind chastised us here, He not destroy us in the age to come. O holy Mary, beseech thine all-holy surety, who strengthened you amid thine onerous struggle, that she fortify us also with her omnipotent aid for this earthly path beset by thorns; and as thou didst kiss the most precious Cross of Christ with faith and love, didst receive His almighty grace to do battle with the devil, the world and the flesh, and didst bravely destroy all the snares of Satan, so may we also, with the aid of the life-creating Tree of the Cross of the Lord, be vouchsafed to destroy all the ramparts of sin, that we may gain access to the heavenly kingdom and, having been counted worthy of life everlasting, may with thee continually hymn the All-Holy Trinity in a single Essence—the Father, the Son and the Holy Spirit—unto the ages of ages. Amen.

Akathist Hymn
to the Holy Apostle and Evangelist Matthew

The Holy Apostle and Evangelist Matthew

Akathist Hymn
to the Holy Apostle and Evangelist Matthew
Whose Memory the Holy Church Celebrates on the 16th of November

Kontakion I

Of thee, O great apostle and evangelist, doth the Holy Church chant today in Orthodox manner, inspired and nourished by the immortal words of thy Gospel. And uplifted thereby in spirit, we cry out to thee in thanksgiving:

>Rejoice, O holy Matthew, who hast given us the words of salvation!

Ikos I

Having forsaken thy customs house when summoned by the Lord, thou didst labor tirelessly for Him as an apostle, O Matthew, and didst describe in writing His mighty works. Wherefore, with compunction we cry out to thee:

>Rejoice, O divinely wise disciple of the Lord, who didst record His descent from David the King;
>Rejoice, thou who didst proclaim His nativity in the flesh!
>Rejoice, thou who bearest witness concerning the ministry of His honorable Forerunner;
>Rejoice, thou who didst describe the Spirit, Who at His baptism in the Jordan descended on Him!
>Rejoice, thou who didst recount His forty-day fast in the wilderness;

Rejoice, thou who didst tell how He prevailed over Satan the tempter!

Rejoice, thou who didst describe the summoning of His disciples;

Rejoice, thou who didst set forth the Beatitudes!

Rejoice, thou who didst faithfully record His parables and teachings;

Rejoice, thou who didst tell of the manifold wondrous cures He wrought!

Rejoice, thou who dost bear witness that the power of the Lord rested upon His followers;

Rejoice, for Christ sent thee forth as a sheep among wolves!

Rejoice, O holy Matthew, who hast given us the words of salvation!

Kontakion II

O the transformation of thy life and ways! For when the Saviour called thee to His ministry, O holy Matthew, thou didst straightway rise up, forsake thy former greed and avarice, and follow after Him, to Whom we all cry out in praise: Alleluia!

Ikos II

Levying the taxes of brutal overlords upon thine oppressed and downtrodden people, thou didst corruptly enrich thyself by extortion and bribery; but when the Light of the world shone upon thee, thy soul was transfixed, and thou didst rise forthwith to join the band of the Lord's disciples. Wherefore, in gladness we cry out to thee such things as these:

Rejoice, for with the other apostles thou wast wise as a serpent and harmless as a dove;

Rejoice, for as the Lord foretold ye were delivered up to the councils of men!

Rejoice, for they scourged you in their synagogues;

Rejoice, for ye were brought before kings and governors for His sake!

Rejoice, for the Spirit of God the Father spake within thee;

Rejoice, for thou didst endure to the end!

Rejoice, for what Jesus told thee in darkness thou hast spoken in the light;

Rejoice, for thou hadst no fear of those who destroy the body!

Rejoice, for thou didst take up thy cross and follow thy Master;

Rejoice, for in losing thy life for His sake thou didst find it in paradise!

Rejoice, for, having labored and been heavy laden, thou hast received rest;

Rejoice, for thou didst shoulder the easy yoke of the Lord!

Rejoice, O holy Matthew, who hast given us the words of salvation!

Kontakion III

Ye Orthodox Christians, come and chant in jubilation to the Lord Who, when He visited the house of Matthew His disciple, rebuked those who reproached Him for dining with sinners and tax collectors, saying: "I am come not to call the righteous, but sinners to repentance." And ever mindful of our own sins and His infinite compassion, with compunction let us all cry out to Christ: Alleluia!

Ikos III

Most highly favored by Christ our God was Matthew, for the Lord deigned to number him among His twelve closest followers—with Peter and Andrew, James and John, Philip and Bartholemew, Thomas and Simon, Thaddæus, James son of Alphæus, and Judas the betrayer—and gave him power to cast out demons and to heal every sickness and disease. Wherefore, marveling at the power of the divine grace which abode within him, we cry:

Rejoice, thou who didst go forth to minister to the lost sheep of the house of Israel;
Rejoice, thou who didst preach that the kingdom of heaven is at hand!
Rejoice, thou who by the power of God didst heal the sick;
Rejoice, thou who by His grace didst cleanse the lepers!
Rejoice, thou who by His name didst restore the dead to life;
Rejoice, thou who didst expel unclean spirits from the possessed!
Rejoice, for as thou hadst freely received, so didst thou freely give;
Rejoice, for with no provision save the Lord's command thou didst set forth to do His will!
Rejoice, for as a true disciple thou wast like thy Teacher;
Rejoice, for as a faithful servant thou wast like thy Lord!
Rejoice, for through thee hath the Lord revealed unto us, as to babes, what He hath hidden from the wise and prudent;
Rejoice, for thou camest to know the Father as the Son revealed Him to thee!
Rejoice, O holy Matthew, who hast given us the words of salvation!

Kontakion IV

All throughout Galilee and Judæa thou didst follow thy Master as He imparted unto the people His immortal teachings, that they might live righteously and treat all men as brethren, and thus, by His grace and lovingkindness, might be brought to life everlasting. Wherefore, mindful of the hardships thou didst endure in the service of the Lord, we chant unto Him: Alleluia!

Ikos IV

Thou didst traverse the lands of Israel with the Saviour, and didst lay up in thy heart all that He said and did for the salvation of mankind, O holy apostle; and thou wast with Him when He journeyed to Jerusalem, there to be arrested, scourged and mocked, brought to trial, and condemned to die on the Cross. Wherefore, filled with awe by thine account of the saving death and glorious resurrection of our Lord, we cry to thee:

> Rejoice, for the people who sat in darkness saw a great Light;
> Rejoice, for Light sprang forth for those who languished in the shadow of death!
> Rejoice, for thou didst not hide the lamp of our Saviour under a bushel;
> Rejoice, for in thy Gospel thou didst set it forth like a candle upon a candlestand, to give light unto all!
> Rejoice, for thy light hath so shone before men that they have seen thy good works;
> Rejoice, for they glorify the heavenly Father for thee!
> Rejoice, for thou didst do and teach the commandments of the Lord;
> Rejoice, for thou art now called great in the kingdom of heaven!
> Rejoice, for thou didst truly love thine enemies;
> Rejoice, for thou didst bless those who cursed thee!
> Rejoice, for thou didst do good to those who hated thee;
> Rejoice, for thou didst pray for those who despitefully used thee!
> Rejoice, O holy Matthew, who hast given us the words of salvation!

Kontakion V

The Lord's disciples, among them the holy Matthew, in fear of the Jews concealed themselves in the Upper Room where Christ had performed the Eucharist; but in manner past understanding He appeared in their midst, even though the doors were locked, assuring them that He was not a specter, but the living God. Wherefore, giving thanks to the divine Logos for assuming our humanity and deifying it, we cry unto Him: Alleluia!

Ikos V

Having opened your minds that ye might understand the Scriptures, the Lord Jesus commanded thee, O holy Matthew, and thy fellow apostles to go forth and teach all nations, baptizing them in the name of the Father, and of the Son, and of the Holy Spirit. And as He blessed you, He departed from you and ascended into heaven, where He sitteth at the right hand of the unoriginate Father. Wherefore, we offer unto thee these praises:

> Rejoice, for thou didst ask, and it was given unto thee;
> Rejoice, for, seeking, thou didst find that for which thou didst search!
> Rejoice, for thou didst knock, and it was opened unto thee;
> Rejoice, for what thou didst desire that men do, thou didst teach them by thine example!
> Rejoice, for thou didst enter in by the narrow gate, which leadeth to life;
> Rejoice, for thou didst avoid the wide gate that leadeth to destruction!
> Rejoice, for thou didst take the hard way, which brought thee to salvation;
> Rejoice, for thou didst spurn the broad path whose end is damnation!
> Rejoice, for as a fertile tree planted by the Lord thou didst yield good fruit;
> Rejoice, for by thy fruits do we know thee!
> Rejoice, for as thou didst do the will of the heavenly Father, thou hast entered into paradise;

Rejoice, for like the Son of Man, thou hadst nowhere to
    lay thy head!
Rejoice, O holy Matthew, who hast given us the words
    of salvation!

Kontakion VI

Eternal life and the things of the kingdom did the risen Saviour teach thee, O honorable Matthew, and His other followers during the forty days after His resurrection, before He ascended from the Mount of Olives and was concealed from his disciples by a cloud. But heeding His words, thou didst tarry in Jerusalem with the rest, until, as the Son had promised, the Father sent down upon them the Holy Spirit, to Whom we chant: Alleluia!

Ikos VI

While waiting in the Upper Room, as thou didst continue in prayer with the other followers of Christ, His All-Pure Mother, and His kinfolk, the feast of Pentecost arrived. Then a sound from heaven, like unto a rushing, mighty wind, filled the chamber, and tongues as of fire appeared and rested upon you all; and ye were filled with the Holy Spirit, Who taught you every human tongue, that ye might bear witness to the salvation wrought by God, even unto the uttermost parts of the earth. Wherefore, in joy and gladness we say to thee:

Rejoice, for like the sower in the parable thou didst go
    forth to cast the Gospel of Christ like seed
    upon a fertile field;
Rejoice, for thy glad tidings fell like seed upon rich soil,
    and produced a bountiful harvest!
Rejoice, for thy preaching was like unto a grain of mus-
    tard, which grew into a plant of great height;
Rejoice, for thy writings were like unto leaven which,
    when added to the flour of humanity, hath
    increased the Church of Christ!

Rejoice, for thou wast like the merchant who, when he found a pearl of great price, sold all he had, and bought it;

Rejoice, for thou didst lay up the teachings of the Lord in the treasury of thy heart, like costly pearls and jewels in a coffer!

Rejoice, for when the Lord calmed the raging sea, thou and the others in the ship cried out: "Of a truth, Thou art the Son of God!"

Rejoice, for thou didst embrace the confession of the holy Apostle Peter, who cried out: "Thou art the Christ, the Son of the living God!"

Rejoice, for, obedient to the Saviour, thou didst deny thyself, and take up thy cross, and follow Him;

Rejoice, for in losing thy life for His sake thou didst save it!

Rejoice, for thou didst turn away from thy former sinful ways;

Rejoice, for, having become as a little child, thou hast entered into the kingdom of heaven!

Rejoice, O holy Matthew, who hast given us the words of salvation!

Kontakion VII

Perceiving the ignorance of men, and desiring that, for their instruction and edification, all might come to know of the Messiah and His great sacrifice for the redemption of men, inspired by the Holy Spirit thou didst relate in thy Gospel the mighty works of the Lord our God, to Whom all Christians cry: Alleluia!

Ikos VII

Receiving Ethiopia as thy portion when the apostles and the Mother of God cast lots for the parts of the world they were to evangelize, thou didst straightway arise and, with thy companion Plato, didst set forth to undertake the conversions of that benighted land to belief in

Christ, which holy task the Lord assisted by giving thee a miraculous staff which, when planted in the ground, grew straightway into a lofty tree laden with goodly fruits, pouring forth at its root a healing spring of pure water. Wherefore, we cry out to thee:

> Rejoice, for as thou becamest like an innocent child, thine angel ever beheld the countenance of God;
> Rejoice, for through thee the Son of Man hath saved those who were lost!
> Rejoice, for whatsoever thou didst bind on earth was bound in heaven;
> Rejoice, for whatsoever thou didst loose on earth was loosed in paradise!
> Rejoice, for thou didst sell what thou hadst, give to the poor, and win treasure on high;
> Rejoice, for by thy words and writings thou didst teach that what is not possible for men is possible with God!
> Rejoice, for, according to the Lord's saying, thou shalt be seated on a throne at the end of time;
> Rejoice, for with the other apostles thou shalt sit in judgment over the twelve tribes of Israel when He shall come in glory!
> Rejoice, for as thou didst not exalt thyself among men, thou wast not abased;
> Rejoice, for as thou didst humble thyself before others, thou wast exalted!
> Rejoice, for Christ foretold that thou wouldst be delivered up to be afflicted and slain;
> Rejoice, for even amid tortures thou didst preach the Gospel of the kingdom to the gentiles!
> Rejoice, O holy Matthew, who hast given us the words of salvation!

Kontakion VIII

Although thou didst heal his wife and son, who were possessed by evil spirits, Fulvian, who ruled in Ethiopia, grew wroth in jealousy against thee, O Matthew, for all the people followed thee and were baptized. But of the soldiers he dispatched to arrest thee some were covered with darkness, and others were dazzled by divine light, casting away their weapons as they fled. Wherefore, unto Christ, the Dispeller of darkness and Bestower of light, we cry: Alleluia!

Ikos VIII

Yet more wroth did Fulvian grow when his minions failed to carry out his will; and raging, he set forth with a multitude of servants, to arrest the holy one himself; but when he approached the man of God, he was struck blind, so that someone had to guide him; yet, merciful and compassionate, Matthew took pity on him and restored his sight. Wherefore, marveling at his loving-kindness, we cry unto him:

>Rejoice, for in thy Gospel hath the Lord's saying been fulfilled: "Heaven and earth shall pass away, but My words shall not";
>Rejoice, thou who like the wise virgins filled the lamp of thy soul with the oil of good works!
>Rejoice, thou who with the wedding guests hast entered into the marriage-chamber of Christ, the Bridegroom;
>Rejoice, thou whose wedding vesture was dyed in the blood of thy martyrdom!
>Rejoice, for thou didst increase the talents which the Saviour entrusted to you;
>Rejoice, for having been given grace from on high, thou didst have the gifts of the Spirit in abundance!
>Rejoice, for in that thou wast blessed by the heavenly Father, thou hast inherited His kingdom;
>Rejoice, for with the righteous thou hast entered into life everlasting!

Rejoice, for with the rest of the apostles thou didst sit with Christ at the Last Supper;

Rejoice, for thou didst receive from His hand His precious Body!

Rejoice, for thou didst drain the cup of His precious Blood;

Rejoice, for thou hast taught all nations that this Eucharist is a sacrifice made for many, for the remission of men's sins!

Rejoice, O holy Matthew, who hast given us the words of salvation!

Kontakion IX

Fulvian regained his sight through the supplications of the holy apostle, but the prince's malice against him in nowise abated, and he brought the saint to the place of execution, where he committed him to the fire as a sorcerer; but though the flames rose up to a great height, and all thought that the apostle must surely have perished, he was seen standing, alive and unharmed, in the midst of the ashes, praying and glorifying God, to Whom we all cry: Alleluia!

Ikos IX

O the long-suffering of the holy apostle! For when the prince commanded that a second fire be kindled over the saint, and set round about the pyre his idols of gold, praying for them to destroy Matthew, the flames of the fire reached out at the entreaty of the holy one, and surrounded the graven images, and they melted in the heat thereof. Wherefore, as thou didst reveal to the pagans the impotence of their false gods, we cry unto thee:

Rejoice, for in Gethsemane Christ admonished thee to watch and to pray;

Rejoice, for thou didst record all that Christ said and endured, that the Scriptures might be fulfilled!

Rejoice, for though thou didst flee with the others at His arrest, the Lord appeared to thee also after His resurrection;

Rejoice, for Christ, Who was crucified, died and was buried, gave thee the power to bind and loose the sins of men!

Rejoice, for God sent His All-Holy Spirit upon thee;

Rejoice, for thou didst show justice to the nations!

Rejoice, for thou didst deliver countless souls from damnation;

Rejoice, for thou didst cast out of men the demons who afflicted them!

Rejoice, for in papyrus and ink thou didst contain the immaterial fire of the Word;

Rejoice, for with great labor thou didst set forth the words of salvation!

Rejoice, O deft-handed scribe inspired from on high;

Rejoice, O thou who in binding thy book didst bind the heretics!

Rejoice, O holy Matthew, who hast given us the words of salvation!

Kontakion X

Repenting sorely of his error, Fulvian sought to entice thee from the ashes of the fire, that he might render honor unto thee; but, using the words that the Lord uttered on the Cross, thou didst cry out with a loud voice: "O Lord, into Thy hands do I commit my soul!", and thus didst surrender thy life unto Him. Wherefore, marveling at the glory thou hast attained among the choirs of saints and angels, we all cry out to God: Alleluia!

Ikos X

Still uncertain was Fulvian of the sanctity and power of the holy evangelist, and he commanded that a coffin of iron be made ready, and the precious body of the saint be sealed therein, and cast into the depths of the sea. But the apostle appeared in a dream to Bishop Plato, his disciple, and commanded him to take up the sacred relics, which had miraculously floated to the shore of the sea in their iron coffin. Wherefore, unto him do we address these hymns:

Rejoice, O thou for whom the kingdom of heaven was like a treasure;
Rejoice, O thou who hast shone forth like the sun in the realm of the Father!
Rejoice, O thou who like a fisherman didst cast thy net into the sea of humanity;
Rejoice, O thou who therein didst gather a great draught of men's souls!
Rejoice, O thou who didst declare unto all the glad tidings of the coming of the Messiah;
Rejoice, O thou who didst write down thy Gospel that all men might understand!
Rejoice, for the words of our redemption proceed from thy mouth;
Rejoice, for thy teachings wash away the defilements of men!
Rejoice, for thy doctrines are the foundation of our Faith;
Rejoice, for in thy Scriptures thou didst record what Christ said and did!
Rejoice, for the Lord's miracles, which thou didst relate, are past understanding;
Rejoice, for His parables, recorded by thee, are full of edification!
Rejoice, O holy Matthew, who hast given us the words of salvation!

Kontakion XI

All the people, and with them their ruler, approached the sacred body of the Evangelist with fear and trembling, loudly proclaiming that Christ our God is the one true God, Who brought His faithful servant through trials of fire and water. Then Fulvian, full of remorse, fell down before the coffin of the saint and besought his forgiveness, and was converted and baptized, and given the new name Matthew; whereupon he destroyed all the idols of that land, and taught his nation to sing in worship to the Trinity: Alleluia!

Ikos XI

The blessed Bishop Plato again received a vision of the holy Matthew, wherein the saint foretold that hierarch's end and ordered him to ordain the newly baptized Matthew and his son as priest and deacon. And before the bishop's repose in three years' time, again at the saint's command, Matthew was also ordained to the episcopate, wherein he labored well in the vineyard of Christ. Wherefore, the apostle heareth from us such things as these:

>Rejoice, O initiate of supernal mysteries divine;
>Rejoice, thou who didst teach the people to praise the Lord!
>Rejoice, thou who didst offer unto Him the bloodess Sacrifice!
>Rejoice, thou who didst unite them with the Godhead through the All-Pure Body and Blood of Christ!
>Rejoice, thou who didst convert the unbelieving to piety;
>Rejoice, thou who, guided by the Spirit, didst bring all Ethiopia to the Faith!
>Rejoice, for the stream of thy teachings was like the mighty Nile;
>Rejoice, for they have filled the whole world, like the flooding of a great river!
>Rejoice, for thy words carry life unto the dry and barren wastes of our souls;
>Rejoice, for enriched by the grace which is in thy Gospel, men's souls blossom forth for their Creator!
>Rejoice, for they bear fruit a hundredfold for the heavenly Husbandman;
>Rejoice, for when they are harvested, they are laid up in the granaries of heaven!
>Rejoice, O holy Matthew, who hast given us the words of salvation!

Kontakion XII

Throughout the rest of his life, guided by thee from on high, O apostle of Christ, the holy Bishop Matthew strove to spread the marvelous tidings of the coming of our Saviour—His wondrous advent, sublime teachings, miraculous works, salvific sufferings, and glorious death and resurrection—and the Lord blessed his apostolic labors, so that they bore fruit, and the holy Orthodox Faith was established throughout that land, among all the people. Wherefore, we cry out to God: Alleluia!

Ikos XII

Having passed from this transitory life to that which is everlasting in heaven, O saint of Christ, thou didst watch over the Church of Ethiopia, which thou hadst founded by the grace of the all-holy Spirit; and thou likewise regardest all faithful Orthodox Christians with thy compassionate eye, healing their sicknesses and heeding the entreaties they offer unto thee in time of tribulation and misfortune. Wherefore, thou hearest from us such praises as these:

Rejoice, O glorious apostle, chosen apostle of Christ;
Rejoice, O marvelous healer of all manner of diseases;
Rejoice, O wondrous apostle who in obedience to God didst forsake thy native land;
Rejoice, O marvelous disciple of the Lord, made perfect by the power of the Spirit divine!
Rejoice, O thou who didst betake thyself to a land beset by spiritual darkness;
Rejoice, O thou who didst bring light to a people that languished in the shadow of death!
Rejoice, for by thee were they illumined with the uncreated light of God!
Rejoice, for through thee did they come into fellowship with Christ!
Rejoice, O thou whom the Saviour sent to bring His salvation to the ends of the earth;
Rejoice, O thou who didst declare His glory to the multitudes!

Rejoice, for in thine apostolic labors thou didst reap a great harvest for thy Master;
Rejoice, O thou who wast a true and faithful steward of His inheritance!
Rejoice, O holy Matthew, who hast given us the words of salvation!

Kontakion XIII

Every true Christian is filled with joy and gladness on hearing the words which the All-holy Spirit of God inspired thee to record, O holy Apostle and Evangelist Matthew; and, moved to jubilation by the glad tidings of thy Gospel, we all cry out in praise and thanksgiving unto the One God in three Persons: Alleluia! Alleluia! Alleluia!

This Kontakion is recited thrice, whereupon Ikos I and Kontakion I are repeated.

PRAYER TO THE HOLY APOSTLE AND EVANGELIST MATTHEW

With compunction of heart let us all entreat the holy Apostle and Evangelist Matthew who, when called by the Lord to His service, cast away all covetousness and avarice and forsook all that he possessed, that he might sit at the Saviour's feet and imbibe His ineffable teachings. And let us offer to him supplications when we are beset by affliction and distress, crying out to him amid the pain of our souls and bodies: O holy one, look down from heaven, and see how we are oppressed by the demonic powers and the wicked men who do their bidding, for they seek our death and damnation. Wherefore, come thou quickly to our aid as a mighty ally, repelling their crafty assaults and putting them utterly to flight, that preserved by thee in peace and tranquility of heart, we all may adore the one true God Who is worshipped in Trinity—the Father, and the Son, and the Holy Spirit—to Whom be glory, honor and worship, now and for endless ages. Amen.

Akathist Hymn to the Holy New-Hieromartyr Maximus Sandovich, Protomartyr of the Lemko People

St. Maximus Sandovich

Akathist Hymn
to the Holy New-Hieromartyr
Maximus Sandovich, Protomartyr of the Lemko People
*Whose Memory the Holy Church Celebrates on
the 24th of July and the 24th of August*

Kontakion I

To Maximus, the martyred priest, do we sinners offer up hymns of victory and thanksgiving; for, unlike the hirelings, he laid down his life for his flock, and hath therefore acquired invincible might, and received from the hand of Christ, the Chief Shepherd, the imperishable crown of victory. Wherefore, with love we chant unto him: Rejoice, O Maximus most great, intercessor for the afflicted and the oppressed!

Ikos I

How deep was thy faith, which was rooted in thee by thy pious parents, Timothy and Christina, who reared thee well in love for God and neighbor, and in reverence for things divine! Wherefore, let the land of Lemkovina, the land of thy birth, O saint, be glad, and with us let it cry out to its offspring, saying:

> Rejoice, child of devout parents, who wast born into a pious family;
> Rejoice, for like a fruitful olive tree didst thou grow up round about thy father's table!
> Rejoice, O Zhdynya, who, like Bethlehem of old, art not the least among the habitations of thy land;
> Rejoice, for from thee arose a new-hieromartyr, a valiant champion of the Orthodox Faith!

Rejoice, O Lemkovina, for after ages of persecution and enslavement thine offspring hath delivered thee by his sacrifice;

Rejoice, for he established Holy Orthodoxy firmly within thee, that thou mightest worship God in spirit and truth!

Rejoice, O ye mountains of Carpathia, from whence cometh Maximus, the help of the Lemko people;

Rejoice, for with his martyr's blood he hath sanctified and hallowed you all!

Rejoice, for by his confession he made his people steadfast in the Holy Faith;

Rejoice, fervent intercessor of our times, entreating the mercy of God for us sinners!

Rejoice, thou whose pleas for those who honor thee are heard at the throne of the Most High;

Rejoice, thou who dost mediate salvation for thy kinsmen and compatriots!

Rejoice, O Maximus most great, intercessor for the afflicted and the oppressed!

Kontakion II

Entering a Roman Catholic monastery to receive religious instruction, thou was repelled by the ungodliness of the monks and their contempt for thy people; wherefore, thou didst flee unto Mount Pochaev, to the safe haven of the Holy Lavra, where in purity and chastity thou didst study the truths of the Holy Orthodox Faith, that thou mightest pray aright unto God: Alleluia!

Ikos II

How can we praise thy courage and struggle as is meet, O holy Maximus? How can our sullied lips of clay form words of pure laudation? Yet accept this, our poor offering, as Christ accepted the widow's mite, and reject us not who cry unto thee with faith:

Rejoice, thou who helpest us to vanquish Satan;

Rejoice, thou who drivest away from us the soul-destroying demons, like as they were carrion fowl!

Rejoice, thou who teachest us to recognize the wiles of heretics, who are like jackals in the night;
Rejoice, thou who repellest their bestial ravages upon our minds and hearts!
Rejoice, thou who overcamest all temptations;
Rejoice, thou who with the wings of thy spirit dost noetically shelter and protect us!
Rejoice, thou who, as our champion and defender, dost aid us in our every need;
Rejoice, thou who art a mighty ally against the prince of evil who assaileth this world!
Rejoice, sword of the Spirit honed to sharpness to smite false belief;
Rejoice, dispeller of ungodliness!
Rejoice, thou who disdained all temporal things as of no account;
Rejoice, thou who madest thy flesh subject to thy spirit!
Rejoice, O Maximus most great, intercessor for the afflicted and the oppressed!

Kontakion III

O the power of the Most High, which overshadowed thee in thy pastoral ministry and thy cruel imprisonment, O holy hieromartyr Maximus! For thou didst cleave to the Holy Orthodox Faith without wavering and didst meet thine end with valor; and in thanksgiving to God thy people ever chant unto Him: Alleluia!

Ikos III

Love for thy long-suffering people induced thee to accept ordination to the holy priesthood at the hands of the most blessed hierarch Anthony; and thou wast sent to thy native land to shepherd the flock of Christ, which was beset by all manner of predatory beasts. And, dwelling now with the incorporeal hosts in the heavens, thou hearest from us such things as these:

Rejoice, thou who openest the portals of God's loving-kindness to the sinful;

Rejoice, thou who from God impartest forgiveness to repentant sinners!

Rejoice, for thou didst receive the grace of the Spirit of truth with a purified heart;

Rejoice, for having made thyself steadfast by thy manner of life and patient mind, thou didst trample the falsehood of the noetic foe underfoot!

Rejoice, shield of faith who protectest us amid battle with the enemy;

Rejoice, thou whose precious body was felled by the weapons of the ungodly!

Rejoice, for, clad in a robe empurpled with the dye of thine own blood, thou hast presented thyself to Christ;

Rejoice, thou who attained thy desired goal and now lookest upon thy beloved Saviour and Lord!

Rejoice, thou who dost quench the flame of our passions with heavenly coolness;

Rejoice, thou who dost extinguish the fire of fever amid our illnesses!

Rejoice, for thou didst stain the earth with thy blood;

Rejoice, for thou didst trample the devil underfoot!

Rejoice, O Maximus most great, intercessor for the afflicted and the oppressed!

Kontakion IV

Ye pious people of Lemkovina, let no storm of doubts and adverse thoughts affright you and keep you from holding firm to the right Faith! For the holy Maximus perished valiantly, that by his sacrifice he might confirm within your souls the Holy Orthodox Faith. Wherefore, giving thanks for his right acceptable witness, we cry out to God: Alleluia

Ikos IV

Hearing of thy piety, the Orthodox people of Graba came to thee and besought thee to become the pastor of their right-believing flock; and taking up this ministry, thou didst not show thyself to be a hireling, but a true shepherd who laid down his life for his sheep. Wherefore, we rightly chant these praises unto thee, saying:

> Rejoice, for the merciful Christ gave thee the grace to endure to the end;
> Rejoice, for He strengthened thee to undergo most grievous torments!
> Rejoice, thou who instructest those in tribulations and sorrows to flee to the intercession of the saints;
> Rejoice, thou who teachest us to turn to God in all our needs!
> Rejoice, thou who valiantly endured the wounding of thy body;
> Rejoice, thou whose courage and patience moved the tormentor to rage!
> Rejoice, thou who didst show his force to be impotent;
> Rejoice, for with love for God and thy people thou didst depart unto the Lord!
> Rejoice, thou who showed the power of faith in God;
> Rejoice, thou who movest the faithful to glorify our Redeemer!
> Rejoice, thou who by the example of thy life and death hast turned many to the Lord;
> Rejoice, for a crown of righteousness hath been bestowed upon thee in heaven for thy patient endurance!
> Rejoice, O Maximus most great, intercessor for the afflicted and the oppressed!

Kontakion V

In the slaying of thy body, thy soul soared aloft to join the saints and angels on high, forming with them a wondrous constellation in the firmament of the Church, each, like a star, shedding the light of grace upon the faithful, who chant unto God: Alleluia!

Ikos V

Even those who are weak in faith and love are astonished by thy martyrdom, O hieromartyr, for as the holy children cast into the furnace of Babylon did not waver in their confession of the true God, so thou didst not waver in thy confession of Holy Orthodoxy, and for thy courage and endurance thou dost hear from us these hymns:

> Rejoice, thou who settest at nought the machinations of the devil and his angels;
> Rejoice thou who castest down all their power!
> Rejoice, thou who showest them to be devoid of strength;
> Rejoice, thou who strikest them with fear and trembling!
> Rejoice, thou who leadest the faithful to salvation;
> Rejoice, forthright reprover of those in error!
> Rejoice, thou who didst manifest complete self-denial when thou didst move Uniates to return to the Church of Christ;
> Rejoice, thou who fulfilled the words of Christ, that he who endureth to the end shall be saved!
> Rejoice, thou who by pleasing God hast received as an inheritance the kingdom of heaven;
> Rejoice, morning-star who art for us the harbinger of the never-setting Sun!
> Rejoice, model of a life of righteousness;
> Rejoice, thou who showest the heretics the paths of true repentance!
> Rejoice, O Maximus most great, intercessor for the afflicted and the oppressed!

Kontakion VI

Right justly doth the Pope of Rome bear the blame for thine undeserved incarceration and martyrdom, O Maximus most great, for in the arrogance of his power he sought to enslave the Lemko people to his errors; but, led by thee to the true light of Orthodoxy, they eluded his wiles and machinations, and cleaved anew to the Faith of their fathers, crying out in joy: Alleluia!

Ikos VI

O the light which is poured forth upon the oppressed through thy brave sacrifice, O new martyr! For armed with the fiery sword of God's grace, thou didst dispel the darkness of falsehood from those who for long centuries had languished disconsolate in the shadow of the Latins' errors. Wherefore, praising God Who is wondrous in His saints, we cry out to thee:

> Rejoice, most radiant beacon of Gorlitsa;
> Rejoice, thou who shinest as a light therein, guiding all to safe haven!
> Rejoice, thou who put Satan to shame;
> Rejoice, thou by whom Christ hath been glorified!
> Rejoice, radiant glory of all the passion-bearers;
> Rejoice, for the report of thy martyrdom filleth the faithful with joy!
> Rejoice, treasury of the great gifts of the Spirit;
> Rejoice, thou who by thy manner of life wast well-pleasing unto the Lord!
> Rejoice, uprooting of the tares sown in the field of the Church by the ancient foe of mankind;
> Rejoice, thou whose patience was a stern reproof to those who executed thee!
> Rejoice, thou who hast cast down the deception of the heretics;
> Rejoice, thou who puttest to flight the councils of the ungodly!
> Rejoice, O Maximus most great, intercessor for the afflicted and the oppressed!

Kontakion VII

Many of thy compatriots suffered imprisonment and an unjust death during the Great War; and though their lot was wretched, yet did they take heart from thy courageous sacrifice and lift up their hands and mouths to chant unto God in Orthodox manner: Alleluia!

Ikos VII

After thy blessed repose, the faithful of the city of Gorlitsa took up thy holy remains and interred them with honor near the place of thy murder, O righteous Maximus; and thy precious relics have become a cup ever flowing with gifts of healings for those who approach them with faith and cry out to thee:

>Rejoice, thou who lookest down from heaven upon thy brethren on earth;
>Rejoice, thou who prayest for all who invoke thine aid!
>Rejoice, thou who by thy holy example hast called all of us to follow after Christ;
>Rejoice, thou whose name signifieth the all-greatness of God!
>Rejoice, wondrous guide to the Most High for those who seek salvation;
>Rejoice, for thou didst follow the straight and narrow path to Christ!
>Rejoice, for thou hast entered the mansions of paradise;
>Rejoice, thou who didst not accept the words of heretics!
>Rejoice, for, confessing Christ's Holy Faith before men, thou hast borne witness by Him before the heavenly Father;
>Rejoice, faithful servant of Christ who for thy loyalty hast inherited the kingdom on high!
>Rejoice, thou who dwellest with the angels and art the friend of all the saints;
>Rejoice, thou who didst love the Lord Jesus most fervently!
>Rejoice, O Maximus most great, intercessor for the afflicted and the oppressed!

Kontakion VIII

Ruthless was the tyrant who dragged thee from thy narrow cell and set thee forth in the square of Gorlitsa to be executed; but his wrath and anger were to no avail, for instead of dealing a fatal blow to Orthodoxy, he created a holy martyr, who with the angelic hosts doth chant unceasingly unto the Trinity: Alleluia!

Ikos VIII

The whole land of Lemkovina rejoiceth today, but especially the towns and villages of thine earthly sojourn, O Maximus—holy Zhdynya, thy birthplace; pious Graba, where thou didst administer the most holy Mysteries of Christ; and fair Gorlitsa, where thou didst shed thy precious blood for thy Lord. And we, mindful of thy might in interceding for the oppressed, cry out to thee with thanksgiving:

Rejoice, thou who hast received from the Spirit the gift of healings;
Rejoice, thou who expendest this gift to benefit thy neighbor;
Rejoice, thou who healest all manner of diseases;
Rejoice, thou who givest relief in all infirmities!
Rejoice, thou who transformest sufferings into joy;
Rejoice, thou who workest these healings unto the glory of God!
Rejoice, for thou didst make no attempt to entreat the tyrant for thine earthly life;
Rejoice, for by thy suffering and death thou hast won the kingdom of heaven!
Rejoice, thou who by thy martyrdom for Christ didst show true love for Him;
Rejoice, thou who hast earnestly taught us to stand firmly for the Lord, even unto the shedding of our blood!
Rejoice, for in heaven thou hast been invested with the purple robe of incorruption;
Rejoice, for thou didst reject the errors of the Latins!

Rejoice, O Maximus most great, intercessor for the
    afflicted and the oppressed!

Kontakion IX

Your hands and voices uplifted to the Almighty in praise and supplication, O immaterial angels of God, ye were astonished and amazed by the fortitude of the hieromartyr Maximus, who, undaunted, feared not the threats of the tyrant, since he had no power to slay his soul. Wherefore, all the ranks of heaven cry aloud to our omnipotent God: Alleluia!

Ikos IX

Rich reward hast thou received on high from Christ our God, the Judge of the contest, O Maximus most great, for thou didst run the race and keep the Faith. Wherefore, even in these evil times the most eloquent of orators are as mute as fish, at a loss how to hymn thee worthily. But we who honor thee cry aloud unto thee:

Rejoice, thou who amazed both angels and men with
    thy long-suffering;
Rejoice, thou who professed thy faith by dying for
    Christ!
Rejoice, thou who hast uplifted all Orthodox Christians
    with thy mighty confession;
Rejoice, thou who placed steadfast trust in God!
Rejoice, for thou didst eagerly hasten to the fragrant
    myrrh of Christ;
Rejoice, thou who hast received the good pleasure of the
    Most High!
Rejoice, olive tree planted in the house of God;
Rejoice, lofty cedar of Lebanon!
Rejoice, gladness of all the noetic hosts;
Rejoice, shaming of blasphemous heretics!
Rejoice, thou who hadst great desire to care for the souls
    of thy flock;
Rejoice, for thou didst hold the glory of this world to be
    foolishness!

Rejoice, O Maximus most great, intercessor for the
   afflicted and the oppressed!

Kontakion X

Dying from the wounds inflicted upon thee, thou didst lift up thy God-pleasing voice, and didst proclaim for all to hear: "Long live Holy Orthodoxy!", whereupon the tyrant dealt thee a mortal blow, and thou didst surrender thy chaste soul into the hands of thy Master, to Whom we all cry: Alleluia!

Ikos X

O bulwark of the Orthodox, defender of the oppressed, champion of the down-trodden, intercessor and mediator for all! We give thanks to our merciful Saviour, that He hath provided us with so great an advocate before His radiant throne; for the holy Maximus standeth in glory before the King of heaven, making unceasing supplication for those who honor his memory, and crying out to him:

Rejoice, thou who strengthened thyself with earnest
   prayer to God before thy struggle;
Rejoice, thou who wast humble in spirit!
Rejoice, thou who wast simple of heart;
Rejoice, champion of the Faith, who chose to please
   God more than all!
Rejoice, fertile ground which received the seed of the
   word of God;
Rejoice, field producing fruit a hundredfold!
Rejoice, wheat ground into flour for the celestial Bread;
Rejoice, thou who art laid up in the granaries of God!
Rejoice, thou who placed all thy hope of the providence
   of God;
Rejoice, thou who didst find the pearl of great price and
   purchased it with all thou hadst!
Rejoice, thou who didst guide the ship of thy soul across
   the sea of life;

Rejoice, thou who didst safely pass through its treacherous shoals and reefs!

Rejoice, O Maximus most great, intercessor for the afflicted and the oppressed!

Kontakion XI

With psalms, hymns and spiritual songs do we laud the new-hieromartyr Maximus; for as a faithful laborer in the vineyard of Christ, his blood hath become the wine which maketh glad the heart of man, delighting all the faithful and filling all heretics with dismay, who cannot cry out to God in Orthodox manner: Alleluia!

Ikos XI

Every town and village of Lemkovina is filled with radiance, for the holy Maximus is set on high, like a splendid lamp, shining brightly with the light of grace, and guiding all along the straight and narrow path of Orthodoxy, which leadeth to the mansions of heaven. Wherefore, in compunction we cry unto him:

Rejoice, invincible ally given us by God;

Rejoice, most fervent intercessor!

Rejoice, thou who didst cleave unto Christ with all thy soul;

Rejoice, thou who hast ascended to the heights of virtue!

Rejoice, for thou didst not reject the straight and narrow path of martyrdom;

Rejoice, O wise one, who exchanged a transitory life for one that is eternal!

Rejoice, fearless preacher of the truth;

Rejoice, mighty champion of piety!

Rejoice, thou who dedicated thy whole soul unto the Lord;

Rejoice, thou who didst suppress all the uprisings of the flesh!

Rejoice, thou who hast received from the Lord the gift of healing every ailment and every sickness;

Rejoice, thou who wast far wiser than the heretics who slew thee!

Rejoice, O Maximus most great, intercessor for the afflicted and the oppressed!

Kontakion XII

Hearkening to the voice of our laudation and entreaty, O Maximus most great, entreat our merciful Redeemer, that He send down upon us sinners His radiant grace, that our hearts may be illumined and our minds given enlightenment, and with all who confess the triune God we may cry out: Alleluia!

Ikos XII

Ye who love the feasts of the Church and venerate the struggles of the martyrs of Christ, come and join chorus today in the memorial to the holy Maximus; for, lo! his precious relics have shone forth from the ground like the dawning sun, and give light to those in darkness and warmth to those whose hearts have grown cold. Wherefore, with gladness we cry to him such things as these:

Rejoice, thou who considered all the good things of this earth to be as nought;

Rejoice, elect of God!

Rejoice, pious rule of faith;

Rejoice, thou who didst faithfully and blamelessly keep all the commandments of the Lord!

Rejoice, thou who art far more glorious than kings and emperors;

Rejoice, thou who didst manfully shoulder the yoke of Christ!

Rejoice, thou who didst reject all the quickly-fading attractions of this world;

Rejoice, for thou didst offer thyself unto the Lord as a living sacrifice!

Rejoice, teacher of righteousness adorned by God;

Rejoice, for because of thee the all-holy name of the Lord is glorified throughout the world!
Rejoice, O our intercessor before the all-holy Trinity;
Rejoice, valiant martyr who now joinest chorus with the right glorious choir of the saints!
Rejoice, O Maximus most great, intercessor for the afflicted and the oppressed!

Kontakion XIII

Maximus, who confessed the Holy Spirit to proceed from the Father alone, who laid down his life for the Orthodox Faith, and was well-pleasing to his Lord and Master, standeth now amid the choir of the martyrs, arrayed in splendid vesture and wearing the crown which he received from Christ for his struggle; and with all the saints he joyously crieth aloud: Alleluia! Alleluia! Alleluia!

This Kontakion is recited thrice, whereupon Ikos I and Kontakion I are repeated.

PRAYER TO THE HOLY NEW-HIEROMARTYR MAXIMUS SANDOVICH

Never-ending bliss is now thy lot in the heavens, O holy hieromartyr Maximus, where, overflowing with the uncreated grace of God, thou lookest with unwavering gaze upon the face of Christ in glory. Wherefore, knowing thee to be a fervent intercessor for all who honor thee, and the protector of the oppressed and afflicted, we earnestly beseech thee: Entreat our Lord and God, Jesus Christ, that He fill the hearts of the Lemko people with love for the Holy Orthodox Church and a firm resolve to hold fast to the Faith of their ancestors, lest the wolves of heresy and indifference fall upon them and carry them away to devour them, and the wiles and machinations of the demons lead them astray in the trackless wilderness of errors. Yea, O favorite of God, lift up thy holy hands to the Most High, and beg for us peace and prosperity, that the wicked may not say, Where is their God? For through thy fearless confession thou becamest a great mediator for all who honor thy holy memory and have recourse to thy precious relics; and thou dost ever beseech the Saviour, that He grant our souls great mercy and compassion. Amen.

Akathist Hymn to Our Venerable Father Moses of the Carpathians (the Hungarian)

St. Moses of the Carpathians (the Hungarian)

Akathist Hymn
to Our Venerable Father
Moses of the Carpathians (the Hungarian)
*Whose Memory the Holy Church Celebrates
on the 26th of July*

Kontakion I

O chosen wonderworker, who art full of the Holy Spirit, venerable father Moses, wondrous ascetic and healer of infirmities of soul and body: As thou hast boldness before the Lord, free us from all tribulations, that we may cry to thee in joy of heart:

Rejoice, O venerable father Moses, wondrous worker of miracles and champion of purity!

Ikos II

The Creator of the angels and Lord of hosts revealed thee, O right wondrous one, as an angel in the flesh and an intercessor for the faithful. Wherefore, having recourse to thine assistance, we offer thee such cries of joy:

Rejoice, lover of the purity of the angels;
Rejoice, all-good instructor of monks!
Rejoice, wondrous lamp of chastity;
Rejoice, earnest observer of fasting and abstinence!
Rejoice, radiant model of meekness and humility;
Rejoice, thou who givest comfort to the faithful!
Rejoice, heavenly protector of monasteries on earth;

Rejoice, thou who didst take upon thyself the easy yoke!
Rejoice, O venerable father Moses, wondrous worker of
    miracles and champion of purity!

Kontakion II

Seeing the purity of thy heart, the Lord chose thee to look upon the glory of heaven. And when with thy two brethren thou didst move to the city of Kiev and didst labor assiduously for the holy passion-bearers Boris and Gleb, thou wast diligent in thy prayers, in so far as it was possible for a youth to emulate the saints. Wherefore, thou didst cry out to God with gladness: Alleluia!

Ikos II

Thou didst possess a divinely spiritual understanding through the wondrous providence of God, O venerable father Moses, and when on the River Alta the soldiers of Svyatopolk slew thy brother George together with the holy passion-bearers Boris and Gleb, thou alone, escaping the slaughter, didst go to Kiev, to Predislava, the sister of Yaroslav, and there didst pray earnestly to the Lord. Wherefore, praising God Who saved thee, we say to thee:

Rejoice, thou who didst choose beforehand the fear of
    God, which is the beginning of wisdom, as the
    rule of thy life;
Rejoice, for thou didst never offend thy guardian angel!
Rejoice, ray of light divine;
Rejoice, fragrant lily of virginity and incorruption!
Rejoice, for by thy piety thou didst please Christ God;
Rejoice, O our tireless advocate before the Theotokos!
Rejoice, excellent healer of our infirmities;
Rejoice, chosen vessel of the Holy Spirit!
Rejoice, O venerable father Moses, wondrous worker of
    miracles and champion of purity!

Kontakion III

Thou wast greatly adorned by the power of the Most High and thy long-suffering when they led thee, thine arms and legs weighted down with heavy chains, and held thee under close arrest. But, ever aflame with love for God, thou didst cry out: Alleluia!

Ikos III

Possessing the right-acceptable zeal which cometh from piety, thou wast tempted by a certain young woman of wealth and standing, whose husband had gone forth with Boleslav to do battle and did not return; for, entertaining fantasies in her mind, she spoiled her goodness with carnal desire for the venerable one; but he, enduring all things, did pray. Wherefore, reverently marveling at this, we cry out to thee with joy:

> Rejoice, thou who gavest thyself over to the service of the Lord from thine earliest years;
> Rejoice, thou who didst love Him alone above all else!
> Rejoice, thou who didst make thy flesh subject to thy spirit;
> Rejoice, thou who in godly manner didst will to endure all things!
> Rejoice, thou who didst vigilantly confound the wiles of the widow;
> Rejoice, thou who didst tread the narrow path of the Gospel!
> Rejoice, sacred adornment of the Lavra of the Caves of Kiev;
> Rejoice, for through thee is the Lord glorified!
> Rejoice, O venerable father Moses, wondrous worker of miracles and champion of purity!

Kontakion IV

Beset by a tempest of evil thoughts, the ungodly widow dashed herself against the temple of thy soul, O venerable one; but, seeing thee to be a faithful servant of Christ, she was confounded exceedingly. Wherefore, beholding the sea of life surging with the storm of passions and temptations, we flee to the calm haven of thy supplications, crying out to Christ God: Alleluia!

Ikos IV

Hearing and beholding thy holy life, the people marveled at the power of the grace which issued forth from thy mouth, and they glorified God. Wherefore, we also joyously bless thee, saying:

Rejoice, wondrous chosen one of God;
Rejoice, thou who didst consider the vain glory of this world to be as dung!
Rejoice, thou who didst lay down thy life for Jesus most sweet;
Rejoice, thou who standest with the heavenly hosts at the throne of God!
Rejoice, thou who didst mount to the heights of dispassion;
Rejoice, O venerable father who wast unvanquished in endurance!
Rejoice, partaker of never-waning Light;
Rejoice, thou who hast acquired great grace from the Lord!
Rejoice, O venerable father Moses, wondrous worker of miracles and champion of purity!

Kontakion V

Thy manner of life revealed thee to the world as a divinely guided star, O venerable father Moses; for thou didst love purity of body and soul above all else, and, trusting that thou wouldst be delivered from eternal torments by thy transitory tortures, thou didst chant unto God in thanksgiving: Alleluia!

Ikos V

Seeing thy pure and holy way of life, the enemy of the human race enflamed the widow all the more, and she arrayed thee in costly vesture and fed thee with sweet foods. She then shamelessly stripped herself naked for an unholy act; but thou, O holy father, didst prefer fasting and prayer. Wherefore, we chant to thee thus:

>Rejoice, valiant warrior of Christ;
>Rejoice, boast and joy of the Holy Church!
>Rejoice, thou who art replete with the gifts of grace;
>Rejoice, thou who teachest us not by word alone, but all the more by deed!
>Rejoice, thou who dost quickly come to the defense of those beset by divers perils and temptations;
>Rejoice, chosen one of Christ, whose miracles have borne witness unto thee!
>Rejoice, thou who finished thine earthly course in ascetic struggles;
>Rejoice, thou who hast been vouchsafed to behold the glory of God!
>Rejoice, O venerable father Moses, wondrous worker of miracles and champion of purity!

Kontakion VI

The valor of thy struggle is proclaimed throughout the whole world, O blessed one; for thou didst consider the life of this world to be as nought. The wicked woman thought to starve thee to death and cast thee into prison; and thy friends mocked thee, saying: "Who doth not deride thy foolishness? It would be better for thee to submit to this woman!" But thou, O blessed one, didst say: "I have overcome all these things for the sake of the heavenly kingdom!", chanting unto God: Alleluia!

Ikos VI

In the clay of thy body thou didst shine forth with heavenly light, speaking the words of the Apostle: He who hath not married careth for the things of the Lord and how to please the Lord. Wherefore, we cry out to thee:

Rejoice, O father, who hast illumined the world with the light of thy virtues;
Rejoice, thou who shone forth within thyself the fire of the love of Christ!
Rejoice, speedy helper amid misfortunes;
Rejoice, thou who dost manifest a life equal to that of the angels!
Rejoice, thou who didst not incline thy heart to earthly pleasure;
Rejoice, thou who prayest for those who honor thy holy memory!
Rejoice, thou who hast attained unto rest eternal;
Rejoice, inheritor of ineffable good things!
Rejoice, O venerable father Moses, wondrous worker of miracles and champion of purity!

Kontakion VII

Desiring to be ever well-pleasing to the Lord in life and faith, thou wast clad in the holy, angelic, monastic habit by a monk of Holy Mount Athos; wherefore, enlightened by the radiance of thy struggles, we earnestly magnify thee and cry out to Christ God Who glorified thee: Alleluia!

Ikos VII

That wicked woman committed a new evil when, in her mindlessness, she command that thou be castrated; and thou didst lie as one dead from loss of blood, barely breathing. Wherefore, mindful of thy reverent long-suffering, we bless thee with these praises:

Rejoice, for thou didst unceasingly hold the fire of love for God in thy heart;
Rejoice, most valiant teacher of vigilance and sobriety!
Rejoice, thou who guidest the faithful to salvation;
Rejoice, thou who showed thyself to be harder than a diamond in endurance!

Rejoice, for by thy blood hath the Church been adorned
    as with a purple robe;
Rejoice, thou who camest to the venerable Anthony, to
    labor for the Lord!
Rejoice, thou who hast glorified the Monastery of the
    Caves with thy miracles;
Rejoice, thou who didst submit thy will to the will of
    the heavenly Father!
Rejoice, O venerable father Moses, wondrous worker of
    miracles and champion of purity!

Kontakion VIII

A strange wonder is revealed unto those who have recourse to thee, O blessed Moses; for the Lord hath enabled thee to vanquish the passions. And emulating the first Moses, who wrought miracles with his staff, thou didst heal the passion of thy brother with a staff, O Moses. And giving thanks for this to God Who gave thee such might, we cry out with love: Alleluia!

Ikos VIII

Wholly filled with the gifts of grace, having spent ten years in stillness within the Cave, as an equal of the angels thou didst shine with heavenly light, and wast vouchsafed to behold God; for thou wast found worthy of the blessedness of the pure in heart, O venerable father Moses. Wherefore, we cry out to thee as is meet:

Rejoice, for through thee the Lord imparteth the heal-
    ing of the passions;
Rejoice, O blessed one, who with a pure heart didst
    faithfully keep the commandment of God!
Rejoice, for thou wast vouchsafed to behold the Light
    divine;
Rejoice, tireless defender of our souls!
Rejoice, thou who adopted the ways of the holy and
    God-bearing fathers of old;
Rejoice, high boast of the venerable!

Rejoice, thou who overcamest evil in humility;
Rejoice, for the Holy Church glorifieth thy dormition!
Rejoice, O venerable father Moses, wondrous worker of miracles and champion of purity!

Kontakion IX

All the angelic beings marveled at the exaltedness of thy purity, and the Church again glorifieth thee, for thou wast a great initiate of the mysteries of the grace of God, and hast been accounted worthy to gaze upon the Lord face to face, that with thee we may continually cry: Alleluia!

Ikos IX

The most eloquent of orators are unable to describe thy purity, O blessed one; but we, vanquished by love, dare to chant to thee such praises:

Rejoice, strengthening of the weak;
Rejoice, comfort of the grieving and sorrowful!
Rejoice, instiller of goodly morals;
Rejoice, thou who hast been crowned by the Lord for thy virginal purity!
Rejoice, ardent lover of the glory of God;
Rejoice, thou who didst increase the talent entrusted to thee!
Rejoice, thou who didst love Christ God with all thy heart;
Rejoice, beacon illumining the hearts of those who honor thy memory!
Rejoice, O venerable father Moses, wondrous worker of miracles and champion of purity!

Kontakion X

Desiring to save thy soul, thou didst treat thy flesh with neglect, and didst reach the end of thine earthly sojourn in the Lavra of the

Caves of the holy Anthony, attaining a righteous and holy end in the Lord; and as a victor thou didst chant unto God, not with men, but with the angels: Alleluia!

Ikos X

Girded about with a rampart of patience, thou becamest a faithful servant of Christ, the King of heaven, and didst pass through thy life following the narrow path. And, lovingly honoring the memory of thy repose and the uncovering of thy precious relics, we call thee blessed, crying out such things as these:

> Rejoice, O our all-glorious helper;
> Rejoice, thou who dost anticipate the petitions of those
> who cry out to thee amid temptations!
> Rejoice, thou who through many tribulations didst enter
> into the joy of the Lord;
> Rejoice, thou who didst wash thy soul with outpourings
> of tears!
> Rejoice, for thou didst fulfill the words of the Apostle:
> "Love suffereth long";
> Rejoice, thou who hast inherited the blessedness of
> paradise with the saints!
> Rejoice, thou who didst confirm thy faith with a God-
> pleasing life;
> Rejoice, thou who givest thy help to those near and far!
> Rejoice, O venerable father Moses, wondrous worker of
> miracles and champion of purity!

Kontakion XI

In chanting this akathist hymn we honor and magnify thee, O venerable father Moses, zealously celebrating thy holy memory. Be thou an ally, intercessor and advocate for us before the Lord, mercifully accepting our meager entreaty. And, mindful of thy God-pleasing life and most onerous struggles, we chant unto the Creator Who hath glorified thee: Alleluia!

Ikos XI

Thy precious and healing relics are like a splendid lamp, O right wondrous father Moses; for never-waning light is emitted from them through abundant miracles. Wherefore, with love in our hearts we exclaim to thee joyously:

Rejoice, thou who through a temporal death hast passed over to eternal life;
Rejoice, thou who didst miraculously heal John the Much-suffering!
Rejoice, lily planted in the earth to achieve a dwelling-place in paradise;
Rejoice, good husbandman of the vineyard of heaven!
Rejoice, most fruitful olive tree of the orchard of Christ;
Rejoice, greatness of the venerable fathers of the Caves!
Rejoice, calm harbor for those tempest-tossed by the passions;
Rejoice, thou who hast been glorified by God throughout the world!
Rejoice, O venerable father Moses, wondrous worker of miracles and champion of purity!

Kontakion XII

God gave thee the grace to preserve from unclean passions every one who with faith and love hath recourse to thine aid. And in thanksgiving we chant unto the Lord, Who hath given thee to us as a speedy and merciful healer: Alleluia!

Ikos XII

Hymning thine angelic life, we bless thee, O father Moses, as an advocate for us before the Lord, a helper and guide to salvation; and with compunction we exclaim such things as these:

Rejoice, all-excellent advocate for the world;
Rejoice, thou who illuminest the way to heaven, not only for monks, but for the laity as well!

Rejoice, thou who by love drawest the hearts of all to thee;

Rejoice, thou who hast been glorified by God with a multitude of miracles!

Rejoice, traveller who hast reached the heavenly homeland;

Rejoice, thou who by enduring tribulations didst emulate Job of old!

Rejoice, faithful helper amid temptations;

Rejoice, healing myrrh of the grace of God!

Rejoice, O venerable father Moses, wondrous worker of miracles and champion of purity!

Kontakion XIII

O all-wondrous favorite of God and holy wonder-worker, venerable father Moses! Mercifully accepting from us this meager hymnody, which is lovingly offered in thy praise, entreat the Creator and Lord of all, that He grant salvation of soul and health of body unto us who chant unto God with faith: Alleluia! Alleluia! Alleluia!

This Kontakion is recited thrice, whereupon Ikos I and Kontakion I are repeated.

**PRAYER TO OUR VENERABLE FATHER
MOSES OF THE CARPATHIANS**

O all-wondrous and God-bearing father Moses, excellent favorite of Christ and great wonder-worker! We humbly fall down before thee and pray: Grant that we may share in thy love for God and neighbor; help us to do the will of the Lord in simplicity of heart and humility, that we may fulfill the commandments of the Lord without sinning; and look with compassion upon the souls of all who faithfully honor thee, seeking mercy and help from thee. Yea, O most good favorite of God: Hearken unto us who pray to thee, and disdain not those who are in need of thine aid, and who offer fitting hymnody unto thee. We bless thee, O father Moses, and we hymn thee, O lamp of purity, glorifying the merciful God Who is worshipped in the Holy Trinity Which is without beginning—the Father, and the Son, and the Holy Spirit—now and ever, and unto the ages of ages. Amen.

Akathist Hymn
to the Venerable Fathers and Elders Who Shone forth in the Optina Hermitage

Venerable Fathers of Optina

Akathist Hymn
to the Venerable Fathers and Elders
Who Shone forth in the Optina Hermitage
Whose Memory Is Celebrated on October 10th

Kontakion I

O venerable fathers of Optina, we offer earnest entreaty now unto you who were chosen by God out of the vain world, and who reverently took up your cross and with faith followed after Christ; and as to our bold intercessors before the Lord we cry out to you with love:

>Rejoice, O venerable fathers of Optina, beacons of the grace of eldership!

Ikos I

Having searched for the angelic monastic life with all your heart, ye cast away all the passionate attachments of the world, O divinely wise ones; and having hastened with love to your Father's embrace at the Monastery of Optina, to the end of your lives ye trod the narrow and sorrowful path. Wherefore, we chant thus:

>Rejoice, ye who hastened with joy at the call of the Lord;
>Rejoice, ye who followed after Christ with all your desire!
>Rejoice, ye who took your cross upon your shoulders;
>Rejoice, ye who loved naught more than the Lord!
>Rejoice, ye who utterly denied yourselves for the sake of Christ;

Rejoice, blessed heirs to the kingdom of God!
Rejoice, O venerable fathers of Optina, beacons of the grace of eldership!

Kontakion II

Seeing the snares of the devil like a spider's web spread out in the world, and feeling in the depths of your hearts that men could be saved therefrom only through humility, ye cast yourselves down before the Lord in fervent prayer, crying out with compunction: Alleluia!

Ikos II

Understanding with heart and mind that no man living can be justified before God by his own works, and ever keeping before your eyes your own sins, ye did not cease to pour forth streams of tears, seen by the Lord alone, offering Him repentance of soul, the image whereof ye have shown to us who cry out:

Rejoice, ye who clearly perceived your own sins as unconcealed;
Rejoice, ye who received the gift of compunction and tears from the Lord!
Rejoice, ye who recognized that it is blessèd to weep over one's sins;
Rejoice, ye who acquired perpetual sorrow for them!
Rejoice, preachers of repentance on earth;
Rejoice, ye who are now comforted by the Lord in heaven!
Rejoice, O venerable fathers of Optina, beacons of the grace of eldership!

Kontakion III

Considering yourselves to be the worst of men and in nowise deserving of mercy, O saints, ye saw the power of the redemptive sufferings of Christ as the only sure hope of salvation; and therefore, with great humility and thankfulness, ye ever cried out to God: Alleluia!

Ikos III

Possessing within your hearts the divine gift of humble-mindedness, O true disciples of Christ Who humbled Himself even to death on the Cross, ye considered all your ascetic feats and labors as naught; for as your struggles increased, so did your humility grow apace. And marveling at this, we say:

> Rejoice, ye whom the Saviour taught obedience and humility;
> Rejoice, ye who for your humility have been exalted by the Lord of glory!
> Rejoice, ye who through humility attained the state of meekness and lack of anger;
> Rejoice, ye who found rest for your souls through humility and self-reproach!
> Rejoice, ye elect, who enriched yourselves by poverty of spirit;
> Rejoice, for yours is the kingdom of heaven, which hath been prepared for the poor in spirit!
> Rejoice, O venerable fathers of Optina, beacons of the grace of eldership!

Kontakion IV

Stilling the tempest of the passions, which is stirred up by the flesh and the devil, through asceticism ye made your mind the master over the pernicious passions; for manfully wreaking violence upon nature, ye strove with the grace of God to make what is baser subject to that which is higher, and to enslave the flesh to the spirit, never ceasing to chant to Christ, the Judge of the contest: Alleluia!

Ikos IV

Hearing the words of the Lord, that the kingdom of heaven suffereth violence, and only the violent take it by storm, through fasting, vigils and prayer ye unceasingly struggled, and for Christ ye crucified your flesh with its passions and lusts, faithfully observing the rules of monasticism. Wherefore, we bless you:

Rejoice, ye who, loving labor, took the light yoke of
    Christ upon your shoulders;
Rejoice, ye who with watchful hearts did not extinguish
    the Spirit!
Rejoice, ye who by your mouths set forth a mighty
    preservation;
Rejoice, ye who pitilessly afflicted your bodies!
Rejoice, ye who joined mental activity to bodily
    struggles;
Rejoice, ye who in your patience possessed your souls.
Rejoice, O venerable fathers of Optina, beacons of the
    grace of eldership!

Kontakion V

Unceasingly and faithfully bearing the radiant name of Jesus in your hearts as an invincible weapon against the demonic armies, ye discovered the ever-flowing well-spring of grace; and ascending from glory to glory, and adding fire to fire, with purified minds ye chanted to God: Alleluia!

Ikos V

Ever perceiving your own weakness and the saving and grace-filled power of the Jesus Prayer, ye never ceased to pray it, thereby beating back the assaults of the passions and burning up all the snares of the enemy. And having mystically found prayerful conversation with the Lord in stillness of heart, ye teach us to cry out to you:

Rejoice, ye who immersed your whole mind in prayer;
Rejoice, ye who kept your hearts wholly on high!
Rejoice, ye who in prayer pondered no vain thing;
Rejoice, ye who tirelessly invoked the name of Jesus!
Rejoice, excellent ascetics of the prayer of the heart;
Rejoice, men of prayer, who received all things soever ye
    asked in the name of the Lord!
Rejoice, O venerable fathers of Optina, beacons of the
    grace of eldership!

Kontakion VI

Interceding with your heart in prayer before the Cross of the Lord Who suffered for the sins of men, ye groaned in lamentation, O venerable ones, consumed with sorrow for your own sins and burning with ineffable love for our Redeemer; therefore, until the end of your lives ye cried out to Him with trembling: Alleluia!

Ikos VI

The light of divine love having shone forth in your hearts, ye hated and abominated earthly glory and praise; and with open hearts joyfully accepting dishonor and all tribulations from men, ye earnestly acquired the reproaches which Christ endured. Wherefore, a model of the endurance of evils and of patience have ye provided for us who cry out:

> Rejoice, ye who bore the wounds of the Lord Jesus Christ upon your bodies;
> Rejoice, ye who zealously swallowed reproaches like a purifying remedy!
> Rejoice, ye who with all your heart turned away from earthly honors;
> Rejoice, ye who prayed with love for those who hated you!
> Rejoice, ye who loved as benefactors those who oppressed you;
> Rejoice, ye who never ceased to thank the tender-hearted Lord!
> Rejoice, O venerable fathers of Optina, beacons of the grace of eldership!

Kontakion VII

Seeing your good volition and tireless labor in the fulfilling of His commandments, the Lord Who desireth that all men be saved and come to a knowledge of the Truth opened your mind to understand His ways and taught you by His righteousness. Wherefore, with hearts continually enlightened, ye chanted: Alleluia!

Ikos VII

Wondrous are Thy works, O Lord! For more than a scribe Thou enlightenest Thy servants who seek Thee with all their heart, and Thou openest their eyes, that they may understand Thy wonders through Thy law. Wherefore, we bless Thy venerable ones, the fathers of Optina, who ever studied Thy commandments, which they loved exceedingly; and we chant unto them:

> Rejoice, ye who concealed the words of God in your hearts like great riches;
> Rejoice, ye who loved the ways of the commandments of God with all your heart!
> Rejoice, ye who abominated every path of unrighteousness;
> Rejoice, ye who in nowise strayed from the path of the Lord!
> Rejoice, ye who trained for the good fight and were not confounded;
> Rejoice, ye who embodied the word of God, having found great peace in Christ!
> Rejoice, O venerable fathers of Optina, beacons of the grace of eldership!

Kontakion VIII

Considering yourselves to be wanderers and sojourners on the earth, ye in nowise desired to acquire for yourselves the corruptible things of this world, lest your hearts be dragged down to the earth; instead, ye cleaved unto the one God, in purity offering Him the song: Alleluia!

Ikos VIII

Every passionate attachment of the flesh which separateth one from the love of the Lord ye rejected with all your soul, seeking the one thing needful. Wherefore, ye sat at the feet of Jesus with love which brooked no parting, keeping your hearts from the good things of life and setting all your hope on the Lord. For this cause, O holy ones, we praise you, singing:

Rejoice, ye who finished your lives without any passionate attachment to the world;

Rejoice, ye who, having freed yourselves from earthly cares, came to know the sweetness of pure prayer!

Rejoice, ye who with steadfast faith set aside the concerns of life;

Rejoice, ye who mortified the pernicious passions by obedience and lack of acquisition!

Rejoice, ye who in a holy manner kept the monastic vow of poverty;

Rejoice, ye who were obedient to Christ, and cut off your own will!

Rejoice, O venerable fathers of Optina, beacons of the grace of eldership!

Kontakion IX

All your prayers and all your strength did ye apply, O venerable ones, to the acquisition of purity of soul and body, without which, in the words of Christ, no one can see God; wherefore, through your pure hearts ye have been vouchsafed in the paradise of the Lord to chant worthily the wondrous hymn of the righteous, crying out: Alleluia!

Ikos IX

Taming by fasting and prayer the carnal desires which embattle the soul, ye did not permit sinful thoughts to gain dominion over you; and from the Lord God, Who alone hath the power to overthrow the order of nature, ye received the gift of purity and chastity. Wherefore, accept from us such laudations as these:

Rejoice, ye who by humility drew down the grace of God in your war with the flesh;

Rejoice, ye who, loving labors and privations, spurned bodily repose!

Rejoice, ye who mortified carnal lust by fasting and by prayers which lasted all night;

Rejoice, ye who by the power of Christ overturned the
    laws of nature!
Rejoice, ye who offered to the Lord your pure bodies
    and souls;
Rejoice, ye who in everlasting blessedness gaze upon
    God with a pure heart!
Rejoice, O venerable fathers of Optina, beacons of the
    grace of eldership!

Kontakion X

Desiring to save your souls for everlasting life, ye repelled all thoughts of what is earthly and transitory, and in deed and truth followed after our Saviour, Who gave His disciples the great commandment of love. Wherefore, ye loved your neighbor with an ardent love, crying out to the heavenly Father of all men: Alleluia!

Ikos X

Loving your neighbor with all your soul, ye discovered the kingdom of God within you; wherefore, the consuming fire of the love of God descended into your hearts, and filled therewith incomprehensibly, by an act of love ye offered yourselves wholly as a sacrifice. And now ye hear from us this reverent hymnody:

Rejoice, ye who loved all men with a holy love;
Rejoice, ye who became all things for all men, that ye
    might save some!
Rejoice, ye who sighed tearfully over the misfortunes of
    the people;
Rejoice, ye who made room in your hearts for all who
    had recourse unto you!
Rejoice, ye who sent no one empty away;
Rejoice, ye who laid down your life for your neighbor!
Rejoice, O venerable fathers of Optina, beacons of the
    grace of eldership!

Kontakion XI

Hymnody of supplication do we offer unto you, O our venerable fathers of Optina; for following your path we have truly learned to walk aright. Blessed are ye who labored for Christ and put the power of the enemy to shame, for ye have shown the true rule of virtue unto all who cry out to the Lord: Alleluia!

Ikos XI

Praising your splendid struggles, O our venerable fathers of Optina, we bless you as glorious instructors of monks and wondrous companions of the angels, standing now in heaven before the throne of God and praying for us, who chant to you with love:

> Rejoice, earnest zealots of ceaseless vigilance;
> Rejoice, tireless keepers of the flame of the heart!
> Rejoice, unshakable towers of obedience, who endured all things;
> Rejoice, ye who through many tribulations entered into the kingdom of God!
> Rejoice, angelic ascetics of the monastic life;
> Rejoice, good and faithful servants of God!
> Rejoice, O venerable fathers of Optina, beacons of the grace of eldership!

Kontakion XII

Ask ye that the Lord bestow the gift of grace upon us who with faith praise you O blessed ones. Hearken unto our sighs, and spurn not our tears. Beseech the Lord to ease our grievous sufferings, and to grant us tears of compunction for our sins, that with a pure soul and undefiled lips we may be vouchsafed to chant with you in paradise unto the Lord: Alleluia!

Ikos XII

Though we hymn you now with voices of praise, O venerable ones, we know that ye seek not hymnody from men's lips, but rather the following of your struggles, humility of heart and correction of life. Wherefore, asking your help to achieve repentance, moved by love we say:

Rejoice, ye who protect those who lead good lives;
Rejoice, ye who strengthen the weak and orphaned!
Rejoice, ye who extend a helping hand to the fallen;
Rejoice, ye who send tears of compunction down upon the penitent!
Rejoice, speedy helpers of all who call upon you;
Rejoice, fervent mediators before God for our salvation!
Rejoice, O venerable fathers of Optina, beacons of the grace of eldership!

Kontakion XIII

O all-glorious favorites of Christ, venerable fathers and elders—Moses, Anthony, Isaacius, Hilarion, Anatolius, Joseph, Isaacius the Younger, Leo, Macarius, Ambrose, Barsonuphius, Anatolius the Younger, Nectarius and Nikon—who shone forth like seven pillars and seven lamps in the Monastery of Optina! Hearken now to this, our present supplication, and entreat the Lord, that He grant us humility and the remembrance of death, that He may deliver us from all evil and vouchsafe a Christian end unto all who cry out to Him: Alleluia! Alleluia! Alleluia!

This Kontakion is recited thrice; whereupon Ikos I and Kontakion I are repeated.

Prayer to the Holy Fathers of Optina

O ye divine company of holy fathers, God-bearing elders of Optina, who shone forth on earth in the angelic life and are now glorified in the heavenly city! We know that in the days of your earthly ministry no one departed from you empty and disappointed, for ye were all things to all men—healers for the infirm, reassurance for the perplexed and comforters for the sorrowful— for the grace of abundant healings, clairvoyance, the curing of sick souls, were shown to abide within you. And now ye are mediators for all of us as well, and tireless intercessors for the suffering Russian land: for it hath been given you to pray for us continually before the throne of God. Wherefore, look ye down from the glory of heaven and watch over your flock, which ye pastured on the grass of the teachings of Christ, for it is troubled, and brought low, and hath fallen prey to the rapacity of the soul-destroying wolves. In your pity visit us who are weak and helpless; seek out those who have gone astray; gather the dispersed; convert those who have been deceived and unite them to the one, holy, catholic and apostolic Church; instruct the young; support the elderly; maintain the married in peace and concord; and defend monastics from all the wiles of the enemy. Hearken unto us, O godly physicians of men's souls, and guide us to the path of repentance, that, following your words, we may place ourselves and all our life in the compassionate hands of God, that His will may direct our minds and senses in all our doings and words. Extend unto us a helping hand, O most blessed fathers, and teach us to pray, to believe, to hope, to be patient, to forgive, and to love: that, walking thus in the commandments of the Lord, we may through your intercessions be vouchsafed everlasting joy in the kingdom of heaven, where with you we may glorify God, Who is wondrous in His saints—the Father, the Son and the Holy Spirit—for endless ages. Amen.

Akathist Hymn to the Holy Photius, Patriarch of Constantinople, the Confessor, Great among Hierarchs and Equal of the Apostles

St. Photius the Great

Akathist Hymn
to the Holy Photius,
Patriarch of Constantinople, the Confessor,
Great among Hierarchs and Equal of the Apostles
Whose Memory the Holy Church Doth Celebrate On the 6th of February

Kontakion I

We bless thee as a right flourishing meadow of wisdom and the unshakable foundation of the Church, O divinely inspired hierarch. As one who wast filled with the enlightenment of the divine Spirit, enlighten the understanding of us who cry to thee:

Rejoice, O Photius most wise!

Ikos I

As a minister of wisdom, thou wast shown to be an angel of truth, O divinely revealed Photius, and with thine angelic voice thou proclaimest the beauties of Orthodoxy. Wherefore, marveling at thy brilliance, we cry aloud:

Rejoice, thou by whom the Trinity is hymned;
Rejoice, thou by whom the enemy is repelled!
Rejoice, great teacher of the Church;
Rejoice, most wise rhetor of piety!
Rejoice, God-proclaiming mouth of sacred doctrines;
Rejoice, lips of pious dogmas, filled with the thunder of
       the heavens!
Rejoice, for thou dost mightily refute heresies;

Rejoice, for with divine wisdom thou didst endure persecution!
Rejoice, thou who didst share in the ways of the glorious martyrs;
Rejoice, dweller with pious and saintly monastics!
Rejoice, thou by whom falsehood is abolished;
Rejoice, thou through whom the Truth shineth forth!
Rejoice, O Photius most wise!

Kontakion II

By apostolic zeal and all thy wisdom thou wast shown to be the foundation of the Church, O wondrous Photius, casting down the demonic thoughts of the heretics; for thou teachest all to chant unto the Holy Trinity: Alleluia!

Ikos II

By the will of the Lord thou didst sprout forth like a fruitful date-palm from a noble family O most sacred father Photius, and with the fruits of thy virtues thou dost nurture the multitudes of the pious who cry out to thee with faith:

Rejoice, scion of a flourishing root;
Rejoice, cultivation of valuable fruit!
Rejoice, blossom put forth by holy parents;
Rejoice, acquisition of a divine lot!
Rejoice, height of abundant understanding, hard to discern;
Rejoice, most glorious depth of manifest grace!
Rejoice, for thou shinest with rays of the virtues;
Rejoice, for thou settest all creation afire with light!
Rejoice, most radiant lamp of faith;
Rejoice, unapproachable star of Him Who hath dominion over all!
Rejoice, abundance of all-wise teachings;
Rejoice, harp of precious gifts!
Rejoice, O Photius most wise!

Kontakion III

Abiding in imperial palaces, O wise one, as one full of understanding thou didst disdain earthly glory; and in every way looking to Christ, by Whom thou wast guided by light, O father Photius, thou didst cry out: Alleluia!

Ikos III

Thou wast resplendent in wisdom and a radiant way of life, and wast shown to be a rhetor of piety, for which cause we thus cry out to thee, as to the wise chief shepherd of the Church, who wast prophesied by divine benevolence:

Rejoice, rhetor of piety;
Rejoice, mouth of the Truth!
Rejoice, shepherd of the Church, appointed by God;
Rejoice, divinely inspired hierarch of Christ!
Rejoice, most wondrous name, beacon of the Orthodox;
Rejoice, report spread far and wide, confirmation of the pious!
Rejoice, for thou dost refute the errors of the iconoclasts;
Rejoice, for thou dost away with the harm of the Manichæans!
Rejoice, thou who art wise in word and deed;
Rejoice, thou who art great in benefactions and good works!
Rejoice, thou who washest away the impurity of men's souls;
Rejoice, thou who dost manifest God's compassion toward us!
Rejoice, O Photius most wise!

Kontakion IV

Thou didst show thyself to be a zealot of the apostles of Christ in all things, O most sacred father. Wherefore, O father Photius, thou didst with faith preach the light of the Gospel among the Bulgars, whom thou didst bring to Christ, so that they chant: Alleluia!

Ikos IV

Thy radiant wisdom and the light of thy holy life have brought to Christ many who sit in the darkness of heresies, O divinely eloquent one. Wherefore, marveling at thy brilliance, we cry:

> Rejoice, lamp for the benighted;
> Rejoice, beacon for the lost!
> Rejoice, great teacher of piety;
> Rejoice, successor of the holy apostles!
> Rejoice, mouth of the doctrine of salvation, moved by God;
> Rejoice, untroubled eye of the luminous soul!
> Rejoice, for thou pourest forth the sweetness of salvation;
> Rejoice, for thou driest up the venom of evil!
> Rejoice, divinely sculpted image of shepherds;
> Rejoice, rule of holy meekness!
> Rejoice, lover and servant of Christ;
> Rejoice, gazer upon the light of heaven!
> Rejoice, O Photius most wise!

Kontakion V

With thy divinely eloquent tongue, O wise Photius, thou didst refute the error of Nicholas, the primate of Old Rome, and didst humble his pride down to the earth; for, mindless, he did not understand how rightly to cry unto the Trinity: Alleluia!

Ikos V

Directing the immaculate Church of Christ to the meadows of salvation in sacred manner, thou didst endure cruel persecutions, and wast separated from thy flock by force. Yet those faithful to thee, O holy one, did not cease to cry:

> Rejoice, thou who art great among hierarchs;
> Rejoice, thou who art divinely inspired among archpastors!

Rejoice, unshakable tower of patience;
Rejoice, thou who art unceasingly hymned by the devout!
Rejoice, sun of great splendor, illumining all the earth;
Rejoice, two-edged sword, cutting down the pride of the pope!
Rejoice, for thou didst endure persecution and afflictions;
Rejoice, for thou dost reprove the persecutors' ranks!
Rejoice, shepherd of all shepherds, chosen beforehand;
Rejoice, defender of all the faithful!
Rejoice, initiate of the mysteries of God;
Rejoice, our helper and deliverer!
Rejoice, O Photius most wise!

Kontakion VI

As a proclaimer of piety, O father, thou preachest, in Orthodox manner, that the most Holy Spirit proceedeth from the Father, and thou didst denounce the erroneous faith of the Latins; but thou didst teach the faithful, O Photius, to chant to the Trinity: Alleluia!

Ikos VI

Having shone forth in the East like the radiant morning-star, thou castest light upon the whole world and the darkness of the West, O most wondrous hierarch, and winnest victory through thy luminous dogmas, hearing from us such things as these:

Rejoice, great luminary of the East;
Rejoice, thou who art revered by all the faithful!
Rejoice, denouncer of the darkness of the West;
Rejoice, thou who partakest of the effulgence of God!
Rejoice, burning coal, consuming all the falsehood of the Latins;
Rejoice, lamp illumining all with the grace of the Trinity!
Rejoice, for thou preachest the Holy Trinity;

Rejoice, for thou cuttest off the error of the Latins!
Rejoice, thou who art filled with immaterial light;
Rejoice, thou who aboundest with great grace!
Rejoice, thou who dost manifest divine gifts;
Rejoice, wise and glorious revealer of God!
Rejoice, O Photius most wise!

Kontakion VII

As a recorder of Orthodox dogmas, thou dost refute the error of the Manichæans and the might of the iconoclasts, thundering forth in thy discourses, O Photius; and thou wast shown to be a divine revealer of sacred things, crying out: Alleluia!

Ikos VII

Wisely championing the canons of the Church and the rules of the saints, O divinely eloquent one, thou didst mightily withstand the attacks of the Latins, O Photius; wherefore, marveling at thy meekness, we cry out:

Rejoice, wounder of the Latins;
Rejoice, thou who dost lay delusion low!
Rejoice, thou who didst emulate the zeal of the apostles;
Rejoice, thou who didst repel the audacity of those whose faith is in error!
Rejoice, divinely inspired instrument of the wisdom of God;
Rejoice, two-edged sword brandished against the falsehood of the enemy!
Rejoice, phial of heavenly virtues;
Rejoice, pillar recording holy battles!
Rejoice, well-spring of the waters of grace;
Rejoice, ray of heavenly brilliance!
Rejoice, thou who knewest the sacred life beforehand;
Rejoice, true instructor of the faithful!
Rejoice, O Photius most wise!

Kontakion VIII

The richness of thy great wisdom amazeth the hearts of the faithful, O divinely eloquent one, for having passed through all that is good, thou wast shown to be a receptacle of virtues, O Photius of great renown, who guidest with light those who cry out: Alleluia!

Ikos VIII

Wholly at peace, and showing thyself to be a model of greatness of soul, O father, thou didst stand before the company of persecutors who assembled against thee, and by thy godly demeanor didst amaze the faithful, who cried out:

Rejoice, arranger of grace;
Rejoice, most excellent theologian!
Rejoice, thou who didst endure most irrational rage;
Rejoice, thou who didst show forth invincible power!
Rejoice, treasury of meekness and love;
Rejoice, holiness of the Spirit and radiant guide for men's souls!
Rejoice, for thou didst confront the unjust assembly;
Rejoice, for thou dost teach with words of grace!
Rejoice, thou who wast undaunted by thine enemies' mindlessness;
Rejoice, thou who dost illumine the understanding of the faithful!
Rejoice, shaming of unjust judges;
Rejoice, our God-given victory!
Rejoice, O Photius most wise!

Kontakion IX

Guided through life by the Holy Spirit, thou didst manfully endure persecutions, O most sacred Photius; and having conformed thyself to the sufferings of Christ, thou didst come to share in His divine glory, crying: Alleluia!

Ikos IX

Being a divinely eloquent rhetor, as a wise chief shepherd thou didst set the words of salvation before thy reason-endowed flock and the whole Church, O Photius; and unto all thou didst show thyself to be a beacon illumining those who cry:

>Rejoice, lamp of the entire Church;
>Rejoice, consuming of soul-corrupting falsehood!
>Rejoice, great and most wondrous Photius;
>Rejoice, most sacred and glorious pastor!
>Rejoice, torrent issuing forth from the mystic Eden;
>Rejoice, impregnable rampart of the honored Church!
>Rejoice, for thou shinest forth heavenly knowledge;
>Rejoice, for thou givest health unto those who entreat thee!
>Rejoice, sacred joy of the faithful;
>Rejoice, utter wounding of enemies!
>Rejoice, thou by whom the Latins are stricken mute;
>Rejoice, thou to whom the faithful cry out!
>Rejoice, O Photius most wise!

Kontakion X

In that He is good, the Saviour of all, the never-waning Effulgence, set thee again as a light for the Church, that by thy divinely wise discourse thou mightest illumine, guide and cultivate those who chant unto the Lord: Alleluia!

Ikos X

The wise men of the West, who spake against thee with blasphemous tongue, O father, were in nowise able to contradict thine all-wise words and the divine power of thy doctrines; and we cry out to thee with faith:

>Rejoice, most radiant morning-star;
>Rejoice, most magnificent and divine orator!
>Rejoice, most fragrant meadow of wisdom;

Rejoice, denouncer of the use of painful torture!
Rejoice, treasury of divine gifts;
Rejoice, sacred phial of exalted thoughts!
Rejoice, for thou dost shepherd thy people most wisely;
Rejoice, for thou dost utterly consume the tinder of heresies!
Rejoice, for thou burnest with the divine fire;
Rejoice, thou who woundest the most wicked foe!
Rejoice, most sacred glory of the wise;
Rejoice, God-given strength of the faithful!
Rejoice, O Photius most wise!

Kontakion XI

As is meet, the entire Holy Church praiseth thee with sacred hymns, O wise hierarch Photius, for by thee hath it been delivered from most evil heresies through grace divine; and it chanteth to the Chief Shepherd: Alleluia!

Ikos XI

The prince of darkness trembleth before thy light, O father, and the horde of heresies vanisheth before thy light-bearing name, driven away as by fire, O Photius; and we cry out to thee with joy:

Rejoice, divinely inspired high priest;
Rejoice, our intercessor before the Lord!
Rejoice, thou who burnest up the tares of falsehood;
Rejoice, thou who reverseth demonic possession!
Rejoice, glittering fire of the Orthodox Faith;
Rejoice, luminous star of divine traditions!
Rejoice, reprover of the mindlessness of the popes;
Rejoice, bestower of mystic joy!
Rejoice, most fervent minister of Christ;
Rejoice, most wise pastor of pastors!
Rejoice, thou who illuminest the minds of the faithful;
Rejoice, thou who dost conquer the hordes of the enemy!
Rejoice, O Photius most wise!

Kontakion XII

Rejoicing, thou didst make thine abode in the mansions of heaven, O divinely inspired one, where thou dost gaze directly upon the effulgence of the most Holy Trinity, which passeth description; and, deified by communing therewith, O Photius, thou dost unceasingly chant: Alleluia!

Ikos XII

Hymning thy struggles, O hierarch Photius, we fall down before thee with great compunction. O father, thou foundation of the fathers, grant me also a drop of thy wisdom, enlightening my heart, that I may continually cry to thee:

> Rejoice, great primate;
> Rejoice, intercessor for all the faithful!
> Rejoice, enlightenment of Orthodox Christians;
> Rejoice, adornment of the divinely eloquent fathers!
> Rejoice, might and confirmation of the Church of Christ;
> Rejoice, thou who with great power didst lay low the lies of the enemy!
> Rejoice, thou who illuminest the beauty of Orthodoxy;
> Rejoice, thou who dost cast down the errors of false religion!
> Rejoice, thou by whom I am delivered from darkness;
> Rejoice, thou through whom I am filled with light!
> Rejoice, mediator between the faithful and Christ;
> Rejoice, my deliverer, who bestowest light upon me!
> Rejoice, O Photius most wise!

Kontakion XIII

O all-wondrous father, hierarch Photius, adornment of the whole Church! Mercifully accepting our chanted supplications, ask for us the divine and heavenly light, that we may sing unto the Holy Trinity: Alleluia! Alleluia! Alleluia!

This Kontakion is recited thrice, whereupon Ikos I and Kontakion I are repeated.

Prayer to the Holy Hierarch Photius the Great, Patriarch of Constantinople, the New Rome, Confessor of the Faith and Equal of the Apostles

O all-wise and most excellent hierarch, equal of the apostles and enlightener of the land of Bulgaria, bright sounding harp of the divine Spirit, holy father Photius. Unto thee do we now hasten, and with compunction we offer thee this meager entreaty: Hearken unto us, thy lowly children, and show forth thine intercession for us to the Most High, fervently beseeching Him to forgive us, His servants, and that He open unto us the gates of His lovingkindness. For we are not worthy, neither is it meet for us to gaze upon the heights of heaven, since we are bent over by the multitude of our sins. Yet even though we have sinned grievously and have in nowise done the will of our Creator, nor kept His commandments, yet have we not turned to any other god, nor have we stretched forth our hands to such. Kneeling before our Maker with contrite and humble hearts, we again ask thy paternal help: O Photius of who art gilded with light as with gold, intercede before Him for our land and Church of Bulgaria, which were once watered by the sweat of thy labors and is now eaten up by bitter temptations. Help us, O saint of God, lest we perish in our iniquities; deliver us from all evil and every contrary thing; direct our minds, and strengthen our hearts in the Orthodox Faith wherein, by thine intercession and mediation, let us not be separated from our Creator either by wounds, threats or any anger. We beseech thee, O good shepherd: Drive far from the flock of Christ the cruel wolves of the Latins' pride, both when it clotheth itself in humility and speaketh falsely of love, and when it riseth up with strength against the Church Universal; and cut it down as thou didst of old. Preserve us well from the machinations of the heretics, and instruct us how to speak the Truth with love. Teach us to do every good work, and even more to offer tearful repentance for our sins, that covered by the omophorion of thy supplications at the time of our departure for the life to come, and protected by the maternal aid of our all-blessed Mistress, we may be delivered from the aerial way-stations and from everlasting torment, that with thee and all the saints we may ever glorify the most hymned name of the Father, and the Son, and the Holy Spirit, now and ever, and for endless ages of ages. Amen.

Akathist Hymn
to the Holy Hierarch Theophan,
Recluse of Vyshensk

St. Theophan

Akathist Hymn
to the Holy Hierarch Theophan,
Recluse of Vyshensk

Whose Memory the Holy Church Doth Celebrate On the 10th of January

Kontakion I

O luminary of the Church of Russia, chosen by the Lord, excellent ascetic and true servant of Christ, divinely wise and holy hierarch Theophan! We praise thee with love and honor the struggles and labors whereby thou didst serve well the faithful people, since, abiding in seclusion, thou didst trace the path of salvation with grace-filled teachings. As thou now standest before the throne of God, pray for us who cry to thee:

> Rejoice, O holy hierarch Theophan, all-wise teacher and instructor in the Christian life!

Ikos I

Seeking angelic purity, and possessed of great love for the Lord, thou didst take up the struggle of the monastic life, O all-wondrous hierarch. And increasing an hundredfold the gift of wisdom given thee by the Lord, thou didst advance the salvation of the people. Wherefore, we cry out to thee with love:

> Rejoice, thou who didst love the Lord more than all that is earthly;
> Rejoice, thou who didst set all thy hope on Him alone!
> Rejoice, thou who didst devote thy heart to the Lord

from childhood;
Rejoice, thou who didst nurture thy mind with the wisdom of God from thy youth!
Rejoice, imitator of the life of the angels;
Rejoice, thou who didst acquire the Holy Spirit!
Rejoice, thou who was chosen beforehand by God to fish for men;
Rejoice, thou who wast lighted by the Lord as a radiant lamp!
Rejoice, O holy hierarch Theophan, all-wise teacher and instructor in the Christian life!

Kontakion II

Seeing that no earthly pleasure is unmingled with grief, O holy Theophan, thou didst despise the vanity of vanities and reject all the beauties of this world, committing thyself wholly unto God, and chanting to Him: Alleluia!

Ikos II

Gifted by God from childhood with an understanding of the wisdom contained in books, thou didst nourish thy mind by reading holy writings, finding great power and spiritual light therein. And understanding this, we cry out to thee with compunction:

Rejoice, divinely elect child of pious parents;
Rejoice, treasury of chastity, filled with grace from on high;
Rejoice, thou who wast aflame with love for God from childhood;
Rejoice, thou who didst apply thyself to obedience from thy youth!
Rejoice, thou who didst imitate the Lord in meekness and innocence;
Rejoice, thou who didst choose the path of virginity and purity!
Rejoice, thou who didst desire the monastic life with all

thy heart;
Rejoice, thou who didst commit thyself wholly to the service of the Lord!
Rejoice, O holy hierarch Theophan, all-wise teacher and instructor in the Christian life!

Kontakion III

The power of God made of thee, a weak human vessel, a well-spring of wisdom, O holy hierarch Theophan, and gave thee to the people as a good shepherd who giveth up his life for their salvation and unceasingly crieth to the Lord: Alleluia!

Ikos III

Having the Lord alone in thy heart, O favorite of God, with great joy thou didst commit all the treasures of thy soul and mind to the service of the Church, teaching and instructing all who had recourse unto thee. And, blessing thy labors, we cry out to thee thus:

Rejoice, thou whose thirst the Lord quenched with great wisdom;
Rejoice, thou who wast nourished amid ascetic labors!
Rejoice, hierarch chosen by God;
Rejoice, untiring advocate for us before the Lord!
Rejoice, humble bearer of the rank of bishop;
Rejoice, faithful teacher of the knowledge of God!
Rejoice, uprooter of schisms harmful to the soul;
Rejoice, zealot of the Orthodox Faith!
Rejoice, O holy hierarch Theophan, all-wise teacher and instructor in the Christian life!

Kontakion IV

A tempest of dismay filled the children of thy flock when thou didst desire to dedicate thyself to the feat of reclusion, O holy hierarch Theophan; but they later rejoiced, seeing thee taking even greater care for their salvation; and they chanted unto God: Alleluia!

Ikos IV

When the people heard that thou hadst made thine abode in the Hermitage of Vyshensk, they hastened to thee and, honoring thee, their good shepherd, asked thee to pray for them and guide them to salvation. And we, knowing this, offer thee such praises as these:

> Rejoice, for thou who wast as a solicitous father to thy flock;
> Rejoice, thou who didst unceasingly make it thy concern!
> Rejoice, shepherd who didst lay down thy life for the sheep;
> Rejoice, thou who didst unceasingly work for their salvation!
> Rejoice, thou who didst love stillness and divine contemplation above all;
> Rejoice, thou who didst wall thyself off from the world with goodly intent!
> Rejoice, abundantly loving instructor of monks;
> Rejoice, ever-burning lamp of the Monastery of Vyshensk!
> Rejoice, O holy hierarch Theophan, all-wise teacher and instructor in the Christian life!

Kontakion V

Thou wast shown to be a divinely guided star, O right wondrous and holy hierarch; for, abiding in the Monastery of Vyshensk amid spiritual and bodily struggles, thou wast a goodly model for the Christ-loving brethren who looked upon thee, teaching all to chant unceasingly to the Lord: Alleluia!

Ikos V

Seeing thee waging the monastic struggle in humility and meekness, the brethren approached thee and were edified. And, honoring thee, who art truly chosen of God, we cry out to thee such things as these:

Rejoice, ever-flowing fountain of love;
Rejoice, well of humility and meekness, which giveth
   drink to those who thirst!
Rejoice, storehouse feeding all with spiritual food;
Rejoice, lamp shining with the light of faith!
Rejoice, good lover of abstinence;
Rejoice, thou who earnestly carest for the salvation of
   men's souls!
Rejoice, tireless preacher of Orthodoxy;
Rejoice, lily of paradise sprung forth in the wilderness!
Rejoice, O holy hierarch Theophan, all-wise teacher and
   instructor in the Christian life!

Kontakion VI

In thy hierarchal ministry thou wast a constant preacher and proclaimer of the truths of God, enlightening and instructing thy flock, O right wondrous Theophan; and even in reclusion thou didst not deprive all who had recourse unto thee of thy grace-filled words, moving them to chant unto God: Alleluia!

Ikos VI

Thy wisdom shone forth like an all-radiant star, O marvelous servant of Christ; for, as God permitted, the torrents of thy living words poured forth from thy place of reclusion and disclosed a healing spring of grace-filled teachings, slaking the thirst of everyone who falleth down before it with faith. And we cry out to thee thus:

Rejoice, thou who didst declare the word of God with
   thy lips;
Rejoice, thou who didst therewith give drink to those
   who thirst;
Rejoice, thou who wast unflagging in the struggles of
   the monastic life;
Rejoice, unshakable pillar of Orthodoxy;
Rejoice, wise uprooter of sinful habits;
Rejoice, tireless guide to virtues!

Rejoice, healer of our souls;
Rejoice, thou who steerest us to piety!
Rejoice, O holy hierarch Theophan, all-wise teacher and
　　　instructor in the Christian life!

Kontakion VII

Desiring to attain unto the kingdom of God, O holy father, thou didst spurn the world and find the grace of the Holy Spirit; and thou didst serve the people with love, imitating Christ, the Chief Shepherd, and chanting unto Him: Alleluia!

Ikos VII

Perceiving thee to be a new ascetic and favorite of Christ, full of humility and meekness, the people hastened with hope to the Hermitage of Vyshensk, trusting in thy gracious aid. And we likewise, asking help of thee, cry out such things as these:

Rejoice, thou who by the meekness of thy spirit didst
　　　turn many to God;
Rejoice, thou who enlightenest benighted souls!
Rejoice, thou who didst acquire angelic purity on earth;
Rejoice, thou who with thy love didst treat the suffering!
Rejoice, wondrous instructor of innocence;
Rejoice, most radiant lamp of piety!
Rejoice, thou who callest all to repentance;
Rejoice, thou who dost not forsake those who ask for
　　　thy help!
Rejoice, O holy hierarch Theophan, all-wise teacher and
　　　instructor in the Christian life!

Kontakion VIII

A strange and wondrous struggle didst thou reveal in thy life, O holy hierarch: thou who didst abide in labors and constant thought of God, didst acquire a treasure of spiritual understanding and by thy writings didst fervently serve the Church. And seeing this, with thanksgiving we chant to God in the compunction of our hearts: Alleluia!

Ikos VIII

Thou showest thyself to be all things for all men, O holy hierarch of God: a pastor and father, a teacher, instructor and true preacher; for even to this day, in every city and village, thy writings constantly proclaim the glad tidings of the Gospel. Wherefore, we, thy spiritual children, say unto thee with love:

Rejoice, thou who wast watered by the dew of the Holy Spirit;
Rejoice, thou who wast covered by the light of grace divine!
Rejoice, thou who hast acquired an incorruptible treasure;
Rejoice, thou who didst imitate the acts of the apostles!
Rejoice, thou who showest the way to the knowledge of God;
Rejoice, thou who seekest gracious wisdom!
Rejoice, thou who didst blossom forth in the Church of Russia;
Rejoice, adornment of the holy fathers!
Rejoice, O holy hierarch Theophan, all-wise teacher and instructor in the Christian life!

Kontakion IX

Every hour of thy transitory life thou didst labor for the one thing needful, O holy hierarch, and didst make thy soul a pure habitation for the Holy Spirit, warming thy heart with the constant recitation of the Jesus Prayer, and chanting unto the Lord: Alleluia!

Ikos IX

Meek and wise, thou wast shown to be a golden-voiced orator to all who attended to thy words with love, and with the power of thy discourse thou didst teach them godly righteousness. Wherefore, O blessed father, accept from us such praises as these:

Rejoice, holy hierarch of God, humble and meek;
Rejoice, good shepherd who lovest thy children!
Rejoice, Chrysostom of the Russian land;
Rejoice, namesake of the revelation of God!
Rejoice, true guide for lost souls;
Rejoice, swift consoler of the grieving!
Rejoice, unshakable confirmation in the faith for the weak;
Rejoice, encouragement for those who despair amid many labors!
Rejoice, O holy hierarch Theophan, all-wise teacher and instructor in the Christian life!

Kontakion X

The way of salvation out of the snares of sin didst thou indicate for the children of God, O favorite of Christ, relating the mysteries of the invisible warfare; and thou didst show the desired crown to those who thirst for salvation, calling upon them to chant in gratitude to God: Alleluia!

Ikos X

Thy divinely wise writings have been shown to be a rampart for the flock of Christ and a wall of defense against the wolves who would destroy it, O holy hierarch of God; and thereby thou protectest the faithful on the path to salvation. And we, illumined by thy teachings, reverently cry out to thee thus:

Rejoice, rule of faith;
Rejoice, all-wise instructor!
Rejoice, teacher of piety;
Rejoice, uprooter of ungodliness!
Rejoice, all-radiant beacon;
Rejoice, bold preacher!
Rejoice, thou who didst cultivate the field of Christ like a good sower;
Rejoice, thou who like a hen givest shelter to thy children!

Rejoice, O holy hierarch Theophan, all-wise teacher and
   instructor in the Christian life!

Kontakion XI

We offer thee most laudatory hymns, O holy hierarch, and bless thee who by thy life and struggles hast glorified the holy name of our Creator and God. By thy supplications vouchsafe that we also may lead a right moral life, that with thee we may chant unto Him: Alleluia!

Ikos XI

Thy splendid life was not hidden from those who sought the righteousness of God, O all-wondrous recluse; and thy good end, untroubled and peaceful, showed thee to be a true vessel of the grace of God. And with one mouth we say to thee with compunction:

Rejoice, blessed vessel of purity of body and soul;
Rejoice, thou who didst serve the Lord until the end!
Rejoice, thou who after thine end wast counted worthy
   of everlasting blessedness;
Rejoice, thou who hast inherited the kingdom of God!
Rejoice, wondrous ornament of the Monastery of
   Vyshensk;
Rejoice, enlightenment of the land of Tambov and
   Shatsk!
Rejoice, boast and joy of the flock of Ryazan';
Rejoice, care for our soul!
Rejoice, O holy hierarch Theophan, all-wise teacher and
   instructor in the Christian life!

Kontakion XII

O wondrous and meek hierarch, supernally illumined by the grace of God, and who didst serve thy flock wisely and most well, never cease to mediate for us before the Lord in heaven, where thou standest in constant glorification, crying out to Him with the angels: Alleluia!

Ikos XII

Hymning thy struggles, we fall down with hope before thy precious relics *[or* icon*]*, O holy hierarch of God; and we beseech thee, our heavenly protector and great intercessor for us before the throne of the Lord of glory, crying out with compunction:

> Rejoice, most excellent favorite of God;
> Rejoice, all-wondrous ascetic of God!
> Rejoice, mighty intercessor for those who trust in thee;
> Rejoice, speedy helper for those who call upon thee!
> Rejoice, friend of Christ, beloved of God;
> Rejoice, fervent mediator of salvation for our souls;
> Rejoice, ardent protector of the chaste;
> Rejoice, comforter amid our tribulations!
> Rejoice, O holy hierarch Theophan, all-wise teacher and instructor in the Christian life!

Kontakion XIII

O divinely wise teacher, boast and preserver of the Russian land, holy hierarch Theophan our father, our meek and fervent helper! Accept from us this meager entreaty and this grateful praise, which we offer unto thee from the depths of our souls. Forget not us sinners in thy supplications, that, trusting in thee, we may unceasingly cry out to the Lord of hosts: Alleluia! Alleluia! Alleluia!

This Kontakion is recited thrice, whereupon Ikos I and Kontakion I are repeated.

Prayer to the Holy Hierarch Theophan

O holy hierarch Theophan our father, all-glorious prelate and all-wondrous recluse, elect of God and minister of the Mysteries of Christ, divinely wise teacher and excellent interpreter of the words of the apostles, recorder of the patristic sayings of the *Philokalia*, eminent proclaimer of Christian piety and skilled guide in the spiritual life, earnest zealot of monastic struggles and mediator of grace for all men! Unto thee, who standest before God in the heavens and prayest for us, do we now fall down and cry out thus: Of the most compassionate God ask: for the Church of Russia and our land, peace and prosperity; for the bishops of Christ, that they may preserve with dignity the truth of God, guide the flock well, and in particular put to shame false teachers and heretics; for those who struggle in asceticism, humility, the fear of God, and purity of body and soul; for teachers, wisdom and the knowledge of God; for those who are taught, zeal and divine help; and for all the Orthodox, that they may be set firmly on the path to salvation: that, together with thee, we may glorify our Lord Jesus Christ, the Wisdom and Power of God, with His unoriginate Father, and His all-holy, good and life-creating Spirit, now and ever, and unto the ages of ages. Amen.

Akathist Hymn
to the Holy Great-Martyr Zlata (Chrysa) of Mglen

The Great-Martyr Zlata (Chrysa) of Mglen

Akathist Hymn
to the Holy Great-Martyr Zlata (Chrysa) of Mglen
*Whose Memory the Holy Church Doth Celebrate
On the 13th of October*

Kontakion I

O chosen servant of the incarnate God and pure preserver of incorrupt virginity, who didst deny thine own parents for the sake of Christ, and didst array thyself in the royal robe dyed purple in the blood of thy confession! All of us who honor thee, having assembled now to form a choir for the forefeast, hymn thee with love, O Zlata, golden ornament of the Church. As the immaculate bride of the Word of God, who hast great boldness before the Lord, pray thou continually for us who are most wretched, that, having navigated the ocean of this world of great suffering, we may be vouchsafed grace from on high on the day of judgment, crying out to thee with thanksgiving and compunction:

> Rejoice, O Great-Martyr Zlata, golden palace of chastity!

Ikos I

Undefiled remained the right-laudable Zlata, the amazement of the angels and all the saints of heaven, who loved Christ with surpassing love and in a pure manner betrothed herself to Him in the preservation of her virginity, and with gladness she presented to her heavenly Bridegroom a dowry of purple raiment and gold. And having received her from God as a fervent advocate, with compunction let us cry out to the divinely wise virgin:

Rejoice, well-spring of heavenly consolations;
Rejoice, all-beauteous glorification of virginity!
Rejoice, betrothed of Christ the King, who wast
    undefiled;
Rejoice, faithful helper of all who love thee!
Rejoice, lustrous censer of the Most Holy;
Rejoice, pure and guileless virgin!
Rejoice, star who shone forth amid the gloom of slavery;
Rejoice, golden moon dispelling the darkness of sin!
Rejoice, O Great-Martyr Zlata, golden palace of
    chastity!

Kontakion II

Perceiving the satanic intent of the infidels, the holy one resolved in her heart to endure tortures bravely; and strengthening herself with prayer, she said: "I believe in Christ, and Him alone do I serve. For He is my Bridegroom, Whom I shall not betray even if I must now endure ten thousand sufferings." And praising this love of the divinely wise virgin, we chant with compunction unto Christ: Alleluia!

Ikos II

Those who could not comprehend the heavenly understanding of the virgin, the vile ones who desired to corrupt Zlata by sin, gave her over to their wives, that, by deceit and persuasion, they might sully the virgin's heart with love of pleasure and gold. Yet the holy one was neither troubled nor moved; but, made all the more courageous in love through grace, she stood steadfastly on the rock of faith, putting the infidel women to shame. Wherefore, we hymn the golden Zlata thus:

Rejoice, chosen one of Christ, who hast received a
    crown;
Rejoice, most laudable guardian of Bulgaria!
Rejoice, glorification of the divine Faith;
Rejoice, thou who didst abase the prating words of the
    Moslems!

Rejoice, thou who lovest God and dost cast the infidels
    into confusion;
Rejoice, loving friend of the Theotokos!
Rejoice, most melodious hymn of the martyrs;
Rejoice, preservation from heresy, greatly desired!
Rejoice, O Great-Martyr Zlata, golden palace of
    chastity!

Kontakion III

Unable to break the guileless Zlata with the power of delusion, the unbelievers summoned her father, mother and sisters, that by their tears they might dissuade the virgin from the pure Faith, that she might no longer be able to chant unto God with praises: Alleluia!

Ikos III

Possessed of a pure love for her parents, the virgin was troubled and almost moved by their persuasion; yet the machinations of the enemies came to nought, and with heavenly wisdom Zlata rejected her parents, saying: "Henceforth I know you not, who tell me to deny the true God! Christ is my Father, the All-Pure Mistress is henceforth my Mother, and all the armies of the martyrs are my brethren and sisters!" Wherefore, we marvel at the celestial wisdom of the pure Zlata, and with untiring voices we cry out to her thus:

Rejoice, nightingale of the Holy Church with voice
    divine;
Rejoice, splendid and all-beauteous vessel of virginity!
Rejoice, blossom attaining the all-eternal spring;
Rejoice, golden-rayed light illumining us!
Rejoice, eternal blessedness of those who hymn thee;
Rejoice, endless joy of all who honor thee!
Rejoice, treasury of good things and healings;
Rejoice, all-wondrous lamp of enlightenment for the
    faithful!
Rejoice, O Great-Martyr Zlata, golden palace of
    chastity!

Kontakion IV

Unable to drive Zlata into the ungodliness of the infidels with the storm of passionate attachment to her parents, the devil was enraged, and he enflamed the bestial character of the infidels, so that they beat her pitilessly. Then the Moslems began to cut away the flesh of the pure virgin and to hang it before her very eyes; yet even more than before Zlata burned with the flame of love for God, and, enduring all, chanted unto Christ: Alleluia!

Ikos IV

To her spiritual father, the Priest Timothy, who was in a place not far from the place of her sufferings, Zlata sent word, asking that by his holy prayers he help her to finish the course of martyrdom. Then, shamed by Zlata, the malefactors grew yet more bestial, and suspended the blameless virgin from a tree, and cut her flesh until it fell away from her body. Wherefore, in spirit she now hearkeneth unto those who hymn her thus:

> Rejoice, golden virgin of Macedonia;
> Rejoice, eagle who giveth us shelter under its wings!
> Rejoice, preserver of honorable marriage;
> Rejoice, golden ornament of monastics!
> Rejoice, right-believing princess of all the faithful;
> Rejoice, faithful friend of all virgins!
> Rejoice, melodious golden harp of the Holy Faith;
> Rejoice, morning-star all-beauteous in chastity!
> Rejoice, O Great-Martyr Zlata, golden palace of
>   chastity!

Kontakion V

Unceasingly praising Zlata, the divinely guided star who by faith lighteth for us the narrow path of salvation in his age of corruption, and who drained to the dregs the cup of bitterness, let us cry out to God: Alleluia!

Ikos V

Having beheld the grievous suffering of his spiritual daughter, Timothy related it all to the holy Nicodemus; and the glorious Nicodemus described the victory of the most golden Zlata to the pious, for their edification. But taking up the most precious relics of the virgin, the devout buried them with reverence and hymnody, and with pure incense, the smoke whereof rose to the heavens, they offered such hymns to the most wondrous one:

>Rejoice, white swallow of the gardens of heaven;
>Rejoice, bold virgin who trampled the enemy underfoot!
>Rejoice, thou who hast shown us the impotence of the devil;
>Rejoice, thou who hast disclosed to all the power of chastity!
>Rejoice, thou who dost exude spiritual milk for us;
>Rejoice, thou who dost reprove the morals of modern man!
>Rejoice, joy of salvation for all who love thee;
>Rejoice, preservation of the faithful from the defilement of the world!
>Rejoice, O Great-Martyr Zlata, golden palace of chastity!

Kontakion VI

In the age of heresies the enslaver of men doth ever strive to set at nought the preaching of the Gospel through falsehood and an increase of the passions, that no one may chant unto the Saviour: Alleluia!

Ikos VI

Shining forth amid the gloom of many long years of enslavement, Zlata hath shown herself to us as a sun of golden radiance, whereby the darkness of Moslem delusion hath been dispelled, and which warmly illumineth our suffering people. Yet today, the noetic sultan reigneth anew, deluding the people through betrayers of Orthodoxy, and the preaching of the Gospel is again by gloom enshrouded. Wherefore, out of the night we cry out to Zlata with tears:

Rejoice, summons to the light of Truth for the deluded;
Rejoice, sure restoration of all who repent!
Rejoice, most golden image of Orthodoxy;
Rejoice, glorious repelling of unclean spirits!
Rejoice, grape pure and sweet for the Slavic peoples;
Rejoice, golden-streamed and all-sweet torrent!
Rejoice, virgin more pure than a dove;
Rejoice, river which maketh the Church golden in its streams!
Rejoice, O Great-Martyr Zlata, golden palace of chastity!

Kontakion VII

O virgin pure in morals, deliver from the mire those who wish to pass from this present age of errors and many heresies to the light of Truth, that we may dwell together in the all-splendid temple of purity, chanting unto Him Who hath freed us forever from corruption: Alleluia!

Ikos VII

We bless thee, the new bride of the King of all, honoring thee, our fervent advocate, O Zlata, as the golden-stalked wheat which grew in the meadow of slavery, watered by the blood of unknown martyrs. With them make thou entreaty, O glorious virgin, in behalf of us who hymn thee thus:

Rejoice, truly faithful handmaid of the Lord;
Rejoice, pure and undefiled bride of Christ!
Rejoice, all-beauteous lily of the field of chastity;
Rejoice, all-sweet honey comb of the meadow of divine knowledge!
Rejoice, heaven-bedewed reflection of love;
Rejoice, blessed lake of the Holy Spirit!
Rejoice, golden effulgence of the virtues;
Rejoice, all-beauteous image of the Creator!
Rejoice, O Great-Martyr Zlata, golden palace of chastity!

Kontakion VIII

Strange and awesome endurance did the passionbearer Zlata, the protectress of Bulgaria, show; for she hath been revealed to us as a consolation in these latter days, and a place of concealment from the malice of all our enemies. Wherefore, concerning her we offer up resounding hymnody unto God: Alleluia!

Ikos VIII

The whole Orthodox Church keepeth festival today with splendor; in the highest the glorification of all the angels resoundeth, and with the denizens of heaven those born on earth join chorus. All earthly creation keepeth the radiant memorial of Zlata. Come, all ye who languish in darkness, and draw forth forgiveness of sins from the wellspring of all-pure waters! Come, all ye who are burdened with griefs, that we may hymn the radiant sun of Orthodoxy, chanting:

>Rejoice, dove of Eden, white as snow;
>Rejoice, all-radiant height of the love of Christ!
>Rejoice, garden rich and laden with fruit;
>Rejoice, golden-rayed cross which rendeth darkness apart!
>Rejoice, all-beauteous chosen one of the King of the ages;
>Rejoice, melodious harp of the Holy Faith!
>Rejoice, precious amethyst of guilelessness;
>Rejoice, all-pure crystal of piety!
>Rejoice, O Great-Martyr Zlata, golden palace of chastity!

Kontakion IX

Every created being and the company of angels marveled at the sight of thee; because, though thou wast a young woman, thou hadst ineffably mastered the mysteries of theology, and in the face of the enemy wast able to chant to the Eternal One: Alleluia!

Ikos IX

Though she had not studied the art of rhetoric, the holy one all-wisely refuted the insanity of the Moslems; and trusting God with the preservation of her virginity, she received ineffable blessedness forever. By her supplications do we sinners hope to be vouchsafed this also, and we hymn Zlata, saying:

> Rejoice, protection of the preachers of the Gospel;
> Rejoice, all-wondrous angel of the holy monasteries!
> Rejoice, help of humble theologians;
> Rejoice, reprover of hypocritical orators!
> Rejoice, bright lamp of these latter times;
> Rejoice, rudder for the ships of the souls of the faithful!
> Rejoice, heavenly beam of the Holy Church;
> Rejoice, thou who didst cast down all the wiles of the most crafty!
> Rejoice, O Great-Martyr Zlata, golden palace of chastity!

Kontakion X

Zlata is a wondrous intercessor for all who desire to be saved, a mighty advocate for all the lowly, the universal comfort of all amid sufferings, and even after her death is protection and grace for those who hymn her and who because of her magnify God, crying: Alleluia!

Ikos X

Thou art a bulwark for those who keep themselves apart from the hell-bent world and dost preserve from falls those who love thee ardently, by thy supplications delivering from everlasting torment all the choirs of the Orthodox who honor thee, O martyr, weaving wreaths of words for thee who art glorified, saying:

> Rejoice, unassailable island for us amid an ocean of misfortunes;
> Rejoice, helper accessible to us in prayer!
> Rejoice, all-pure firmament for us amid the adulterous world;

Rejoice, lustrous font of the forgiveness of sins!
Rejoice, curing balm for ailing souls;
Rejoice, healing rest for wounded hearts!
Rejoice, kindly spiritual mother of true monks;
Rejoice, fervent help for those who live in the world!
Rejoice, O Great-Martyr Zlata, golden palace of chastity!

Kontakion XI

O Master of all, unto those who would praise Thee with hymnody grant words which they may sweetly use to describe Thy mercies, and impart grace unto those who pray to Thee, that with thanksgiving we may cry out: Alleluia!

Ikos XI

As a beacon of golden light shining amid the gloom of the suffering of slavery do we see Zlata, who guideth all to the light of salvation. She hath been revealed to us as a model of the scriptural virtues, wherein the love of God is the crown of all the commandments. And hoping that we also may be vouchsafed this crown, come, let us bow down before Zlata, chanting thus:

Rejoice, unutterable sea of love;
Rejoice, healing of divisions among all the Churches!
Rejoice, cavern of concealment in the face of perils;
Rejoice, one whose hunger for righteousness was satisfied!
Rejoice, phial of divine fragrance;
Rejoice, golden bough of reverence for God!
Rejoice, undefiled daughter of holy Bulgaria;
Rejoice, right-believing commander for those who honor thee!
Rejoice, O Great-Martyr Zlata, golden palace of chastity!

Kontakion XII

Crowned with glory, Zlata hath in her suffering shown us the wonder of grace, that we also may have steadfast trust in God amid tribulations, undaunted by the savagery of the son of iniquity who striveth to deceive all in the world. By her supplications deliver us from the evil-doer, O compassionate God, that we may ever chant unto Thee: Alleluia!

Ikos XII

Hymning thee, O glorious virgin and martyr, we offer thee twofold tearful entreaty in behalf of all who are sick and in evil circumstances:

> Rejoice, abundant help for those who labor;
> Rejoice, all-sweet comfort of the grieving!
> Rejoice, almighty defender of the oppressed;
> Rejoice, meek healer of the wounded!
> Rejoice, good helper of all who weep;
> Rejoice, golden counselor of the despairing!
> Rejoice, abode for us in light, far from the darkness of the world;
> Rejoice, habitation for the faithful in the bridal-chamber of heaven!
> Rejoice, plea to God for us who are greatly sinful;
> Rejoice, wondrous adornment of those corrupted by the passions!
> Rejoice, most golden and all-beauteous virgin;
> Rejoice, divinely voiced lark of the Orthodox Church!
> Rejoice, O Great-Martyr Zlata, golden palace of chastity!

Kontakion XIII

O right wondrous Zlata, boast of Bulgaria! Having now in kindness of heart accepted the hymnody of those who love thee, by thy kindly supplications save us from all perils and enslavement to sin, that in heaven we also may be vouchsafed to magnify Christ God with thee unceasingly, chanting: Alleluia! Alleluia! Alleluia!

This Kontakion is recited thrice, whereupon Ikos I and Kontakion I are repeated.

Prayer to the Holy Great-Martyr Zlata of Bulgaria

O all-glorious scion of the Bulgarian race, virgin resplendent as the sun, arrayed in a purple robe dyed in thine own blood, our all-beauteous mother, Great-Martyr Zlata! Hearken to thy children, who have recourse unto thee with love; accept this our meager entreaty, and render it well-pleasing to the Lord our God. For we have sinned and dealt iniquitously, and are not worthy to look upon the heights of heaven because of the magnitude of our unrighteousness. We are bound with the bonds of sin, and have in nowise done the will of our Saviour, neither kept His commandments. Wherefore, with contrition and humility we bend the knees of our heart before our Creator and Saviour, and ask that in thy mercy thou help us. Lift up thy hands, O beauteous virgin-martyr, all-golden vessel of the love of Christ, and with the All-Pure Theotokos and all the saints of our race beseech the Creator, that He send down His mercy upon our much-suffering land, that He put down the arrogance of the people, that He ease the bitter temptations of the Church, that with the light of His Truth He illumine those who have fallen away from the Orthodox Faith, that He impart wisdom to the elderly and guidance to the young, preserving them well from the corruption of morals and the snares of the heretics, that He nurture the children with the milk of piety, and renew us in the laver of repentance. O mother of golden mien, comely blossom of virginity and adornment of the martyrs, entreat our Lord and Saviour, that He grant us the spirit of humility and meekness, the spirit of chastity and obedience, the spirit of love unfeigned, that He direct our mind and strengthen our heart in the right Faith, that, guided by the Truth and overshadowed with love, we may live here a calm and peaceful life in all piety and purity. O glorious Great-Martyr Zlata, our mother most sweet, pray to the all-blessed Trinity, that we be delivered from every evil circumstance and be preserved undaunted by every assault of enemy, that unafraid of wounding or threats, we may remain faithful to Christ our Bridegroom until the end, calling upon thy God-pleasing aid and continually praising and blessing the All-Blessed Trinity—the Father, the Son and the Holy Spirit—now and ever, and unto the ages of ages. Amen.

Further titles from Holy Trinity Publications:

Season of Repentance
Lenten Homilies
of Saint John of Kronstadt

This selection of St John's Lenten sermons follows the thematic structure of the Lenten season in the Orthodox Church, from the Sunday of the Publican and the Pharisee through to Great and Holy Friday. A sermon for St Thomas Sunday, that follows Holy Pascha, is offered as an Epilogue.

ISBN: 9780884653844

Conversations With My Heart
Contemplations on God and the World

By Metropolitan Anastasy (Gribanovsky)

Metropolitan Anastasy, a leading figure of the Russian emigration, formed a bridge between two worlds—the Imperial Court of the last Tsar and the 20th century Russian diaspora. These reflections from his diary draw upon wisdom from sources as diverse as writers of classical antiquity, authors, composers and inventors of the age of enlightenment, offering unique perspectives on these.

ISBN: 9780884654728

Harbor for Our Hope
On Acquiring Peace Amidst Suffering

By St Ignatius (Brianchaninov)

St Ignatius, a renowned writer on the spiritual life, struggled with chronic illness and disability. His own life experience disposed him to reflect on the meaning of suffering for human existence. He reveals how the love of God may be experienced by all who suffer. His letters, expcerpted and organized thematically provide a source of consolation and encouragement.

ISBN: 9780884654223

From the series:
The Collected Works of St Ignatius (Brianchaninov)

Volume I
The Field: Cultivating Salvation

The field is a place of cultivation and of battle. The author instructs his readers in the cultivation of the field of their hearts, with the aim of producing a harvest of virtues both pleasing to God and of benefit to all humankind. *The Field* draws deeply on the teachings of the ascetic fathers of the Church, from the desert dwellers of Scetis in Egypt to St Ignatius's Russian contemporaries, the Optina Elders.

ISBN: 9780884653769

Volume II
The Refuge: Anchoring the Soul in God

Prayer is a refuge of God's great mercy to the human race. A refuge is a place of inner stillness and peace where the heart is fully opened to the embrace of God's love. This text is an exposition of the concrete actions one needs to take to live with and in God. It weaves together meditations on Scripture (from the Psalms in particular) and amplifies these with the wisdom of early Christian saints.

ISBN: 9780884654292

Volume V
The Arena: Guidelines for Spiritual and Monastic Life

This is one of the most important and accessible texts of Orthodox Christian teaching on the spiritual life, and not unlike the better known *Philokalia*. The author describes this work as his legacy "of soul saving instruction." In an age alienated from spiritual culture and rooted in materialism, his words pose an invitation to all who say to themselves "There must be more to life than this."

ISBN: 9780884652878

Further titles from Holy Trinity Publications:

The Divine Liturgy of Our
Father Among the Saints
John Chrysostom:
Slavonic- English Parallel
ISBN: 9780884653523

All-Night Vigil
Clergy Service Book
Slavonic- English Parallel
ISBN: 9780884654636

The Divine Liturgy
of Our Father Among the
Saints Basil the Great
Slavonic- English Parallel
ISBN: 9780884654346

The Divine Liturgies
of The Holy Apostle James,
Brother of the Lord
Slavonic- English Parallel
ISBN: 9780884654308

The Divine Liturgy
of the Presanctified Gifts
of Our Father Among the Saints
Gregory the Dialogist
ISBN: 9780884654469

The Order
of the Moleben
and the Panikhida
ISBN: 9780884654384

The Rule for Communion
Canons, Order of Preparation
and Prayers After Holy Communion
ISBN: 9780884653301